£37.85

IEE COMPUTING SERIES 12

Series Editors: Dr. B. Carré
               Dr. D. A. H. Jacobs
               Professor I. Sommerville

Speech Recognition BY MACHINE

Other volumes in this series

Speech Recognition BY MACHINE

W.A. Ainsworth

Peter Peregrinus Ltd., on behalf of the Institution of Electrical Engineers

Published by: Peter Peregrinus Ltd., London, United Kingdom
© **1988: Peter Peregrinus Ltd.**

British Library Cataloguing in Publication Data

Ainsworth, William A.
   Speech recognition by machine.—(IEE computing series; 12)
   1. Automatic speech recognition
   I. Title   II. Institution of Electrical
   Engineers   III. Series
   006.4′54   TK7882.S65

ISBN 0 86341 115 0

Printed in England by Billing and Sons Ltd.

Contents

Preface

It was originally intended that this book should be written jointly by Dr. Roger Moore, of the Royal Signals & Radar Establishment, and myself. We drew up a plan of the contents of the book in 1984 and the writing began. Unfortunately events conspired against us and with the expansion of speech research at RSRE, culminating with the amalgamation of JSRU to form the Speech Research Unit, Dr. Moore's extra duties prevented him from completing his part of the book. Consequently I have attempted to finish the book myself keeping as close to the original plan as possible.

I wish to express my gratitude to Dr. Moore for his contribution to the plan, but I must accept full responsibility, including the errors, omissions and inadequacies, for the final text. I must also express my thanks to all those colleagues and friends, too numerous to mention but those names mostly appear in the references, who have contributed to my understanding of the science of speech.

I would like to express my appreciation to all those past and present members of the Department of Communication and Neuroscience of the University of Keele, particularly Professor Donald Mackay and Professor Ted Evans, who have made this Department such a stimulating place in which to carry out multidisciplinary studies.

Finally I must thank my wife Pam and my daughter Lucy for allowing me the time to indulge in the antisocial practice of writing.

W. A. Ainsworth

Chapter 1

Introduction

1.1 What is automatic speech recognition

Automatic speech recognition means many things to many men. At one end of the spectrum is the voice-operated alarm clock which ceases ringing when the word 'stop' is shouted at it, and at the other is the automatic dictating machine which produces a typed manuscript in response to the human voice or the expert system which provides answers to spoken questions. Practical speech recognisers fall somewhere between these two extremes.

It may be argued, with good reason, that a machine should only be regarded as a speech recogniser if it can perform different actions in response to different vocal commands. An alarm clock which ceased ringing in response to the word 'start' as well as the word 'stop' could hardly be termed a speech recogniser, yet its usefulness would not be impaired.

Present-day speech recognisers operate with modest vocabularies of ten to a few hundred words. The words must usually be spoken in isolation in a fairly low-noise environment, though some recognisers are able to cope with connected words such as strings of digits. For good recognition accuracy the machine must be trained with the voice of the person who is going to use it. Such systems seem very limited but they are beginning to find many applications.

Experimental systems are being developed which will deal with much larger vocabularies, of the order of five to ten thousand words. Techniques for dealing with continuous speech are being investigated, and research is being performed to study the multi-user problem. All this is bringing the goal of natural speech communication with machines nearer reality.

1.2 Human communication

Animals employ many modes of communication. They use body postures to convey aggression and submissiveness. They excrete odours and perform elaborate dances to attract mates. They also employ vocalisations to warn other members of the herd or flock of the approach of a predator. Their communicative needs, however, are relatively simple and their use of hearing is no more important than that of other modalities.

Human communication, on the other hand, is dominated by speech and hearing. Sight and the other modalities are used as appropriate, but the immediate transfer of complex information from one person to another is almost always performed by speech. Speech communication is so important that it has been found in every human community that has been discovered.

The other method by which complex information is transferred from one individual to another is, of course, by writing. Writing has the advantage that the reader can receive the information at a later time or at another place at a great distance from the writer. Reading and writing, however, are less universal than speaking. Literacy appears later in the development of both the individual and the civilisation. Indeed many tribes have failed to develop a system of written communication. It has been claimed that the use of the alphabet, the most efficient form of writing, has been invented only once in all history (Gelb, 1963).

The difficulties of communication by speech at a distance have been largely eliminated by the invention of the telephone. No longer need the listener be in the proximity of the speaker in order to converse with him. This has led, in the last half century, to a resurgence of the domination of speech in human communication. And, some would add with regret, to a deterioration in the standard of use of the written word.

1.3 Man–machine communication

Man–machine communication is dominated by typing. This situation has been brought about not by a strong desire to produce words by means of fingers but by the inability of machines to understand speech. It is interesting to consider whether typing would have achieved its present dominant position if automatic speech recognisers had been available when computers began to be widely available.

1.3.1 Typing

The advantage of typing is that the machine can sense which key is pressed with 100% accuracy. Any errors are caused by the typist, or by mechanical or electrical breakdown. There is no inherent inaccuracy.

Typing, however, is a relatively slow form of communication. Whereas a skilled typist can work at 100 to 150 words per minute, an unskilled typist can only manage 10 to 25 words per minute. A great deal of training and practice is required to become a skilled typist.

Another disadvantage of typing is that the number of symbols allowed is decided by the designer of the machine. In order to increase the number of symbols beyond the number of keys, either combinations of keys must be pressed simultaneously or sequences of keys must be employed. Key combinations are difficult to remember, and are therefore error prone. Sequences of key presses slow down the communication process.

1.3.2 Writing

Handwriting is a more universal skill than typing. It is acquired by most people during childhood with a little effort. It is, however, a slow means of communication with a speed of only about 25 words per minute. This is as fast, or faster, than an untrained typist, but considerably slower than a skilled typist.

The main disadvantage of handwriting is the difficulty of machine recognition. A wide variety of shapes is acceptable for most letters, and the machine must somehow be able to recognise that all of these shapes represent the same symbol. Writing has many of the disadvantages associated with speech and yet it is much slower. A busy executive prefers to use a shorthand typist, or a dictating machine and an audio typist, rather than write his own correspondence.

1.3.3 Speaking

Speech is potentially the fastest form of man–machine communication. Speaking rates vary from about 120 to 250 words per minute. This is slightly faster than skilled typing rates.

Speech, however, does not need to be learned, or at least it is learned with little effort in early childhood by every healthy person. Being the most natural form of human communication, it should be seriously considered in the human use of computers.

1.4 Advantages of man–machine communication by voice

1.4.1 Problem solving

One of the advantages of using speech in human communication is that it leads to faster times for the solution of problems. Chapanis (1975) has investigated the effectiveness of various communication channels in aiding problem solving. A typical problem studied was assembling a trolley when one person was given a box of parts and another was given the assembly instructions. Another problem was finding the location of the nearest doctor's surgery to a certain house when one person was provided with a street map and the other a telephone directory of doctors' addresses. In all cases the problem could only be solved by the two participants communicating.

The communication links consisted of a visual channel, a microphone and loudspeaker, a device for transmitting handwriting, and a typewriter and teleprinter. These various communication channels were used both alone and in combination.

It was found that the average time to solve a problem was shorter when the speech channel was used than when it was not. Each of the channels in combination with speech required less than 15 minutes to solve the problem, and speech alone required only 16 minutes. On the other hand, all of the other channels, either alone or in combination, required more than 20 minutes. Handwriting alone or typing alone required over 30 minutes. Surprisingly the solution time for inexperienced typists was only slightly longer than for skilled typists even though their typing speed was only half as great.

Chapanis found that when speech was involved many more messages were sent between the participants. On average 230 messages were sent when all channels were available and 164 with voice alone, yet there were just 16 when only handwriting was permitted and only about 30 by typing. Experienced typists sent 27 messages and unskilled ones 31. Presumably as speech is a more natural form of communication it is possible to think and speak simultaneously, whereas complete sentences need to be composed before they can be written or typed.

1.4.2 Hands and eyes free

Another advantage of speech for man–machine communication is that it leaves the hands and eyes free to perform other tasks. Handwriting requires the use of one hand and typing, at least at speed, needs both hands. The eyes are often used for confirming that the intended words have been entered, and are always used in a dialogue situation to receive messages from the machine.

In certain situations such as flying a plane, driving a vehicle, or controlling machinery, the hands are fully occupied. In such circumstances commands could be given to the machine by voice. The eyes, too, may be busy and so unable to locate switches. Again the instructions could be sent to the machine by speech without the gaze being deflected.

1.4.3 Unconstrained movement

One of the advantages of speech communication is that it is omnidirectional. The speaker and the listener may move about a room performing various tasks and still communicate by voice. Similarly an operator could communicate with a computer by voice from any position in a room without having to walk over to keyboard.

A further potential advantage of speech, possibly in a military situation, is that speech communication can take place in the dark.

1.4.4 Remote access

One of the main advantages of speech communication is that it can take place over large distances via the telephone network. The ubiquitous nature of the telephone means that any computer with speech-recognition facilities could be accessed from anywhere in the world without the necessity for additional equipment such as portable keyboards and acoustic couplers.

This could be a tremendous advantage for distributed organisations employing personnel who travel widely and yet need to be kept informed of various aspects of the total organisation in order to perform their tasks efficiently. The combination of speech recognition and the telephone network makes man–machine interaction at a distance a practical possibility.

1.4.5 *Minimal panel space*

Complex systems, like automated factories and power stations, require large control panels so that their operations can be monitored and controlled. The banks of switches can be so great that an operator cannot reach them all without leaving his seat. If the switches were controlled by a speech recogniser, they could all be operated from a single position.

In other situations, such as in the cockpit of an aircraft, the amount of physical space available for mounting switches may be insufficient. Again the use of a speech recogniser for the man–machine interface would alleviate this problem.

1.5 Outline of the book

Speech-recognition technology is an interdisciplinary subject involving phonetics, acoustics, electronics, linguistics, psychology and computer science. It is expected that scientists and engineers with backgrounds in any of these areas might become interested in speech recognition, so this book attempts to summarise the relevant work and provide references to original research in each of these areas. The subject is relatively new and growing quickly, so it might be expected that the emphasis provided here will change in time.

Chapter 2 provides a review of the relevant background work on speech. Speech can be represented by many levels of description and these are outlined. Speech communication involves both a transmitter and a receiver, either of which may be a man or a machine. It is thus necessary to study speech production by man and speech synthesis by machine in order that a comprehensive understanding of speech communication can be obtained.

The ideal speech-recognition machine is provided by the human listener. Many experiments have been performed to discover how humans process speech. Others have been performed to measure the limits of speech perception. These are discussed together with some observations on language acquisition.

Chapter 3 outlines the problems encountered by speech-recognition machines. These are introduced by means of a historical review, and then each problem is considered in more detail. The variable and ambiguous nature of speech is emphasised.

The next two chapters outline some of the proposed solutions to these problems. Chapter 4 considers the techniques available for processing speech, and Chapter 5 describes some of the algorithms which have been used in speech recognition systems. Each Chapter is divided into three parts. In the first, signal processing is described, especially the techniques which are applicable to speech signals. Speech recognition is essentially the transformation of acoustic patterns into linguistic symbols. In the second parts of Chapters 4 and 5 pattern processing is discussed. In order to effect this transformation sources of knowledge other than acoustic and phonetic are thought to be necessary. The third parts of these Chapters, therefore, deal with knowledge processing, particularly lexical, prosodic, syntactical and semantic knowledge.

Many speech-recognition systems have been implemented on general-purpose digital computers. The amount of computation required, however, may be very great, leading to large time delays in recognition. Because of this, special architectures are being developed which will perform the processing in more efficient ways. Some of these are described in Chapter 6.

Speech recognisers are complex systems, so assessing their performance is not a simple task. A number of performance measures have been proposed and these are dicussed in Chapter 7. Speech recognisers will only be acceptable for practical tasks if they can be shown to be accurate, fast, reliable and convenient.

There is an increasing number of applications of speech recognisers. The types and areas of application are outlined in Chapter 8. Speech recognisers form only parts of systems. In order to integrate them satisfactorily, economic, human and system factors have to be considered.

The last Chapter discusses some of the current lines of research in speech recognition, and outlines some of the problems which have yet to be solved.

Chapter 2

Speech production and perception

2.1 Symbolic representation of speech

It is useful to be able to describe spoken utterances by means of discrete symbols representing the sounds that have been produced. The letter symbols of writing are obviously unsuitable as they are used to represent different sounds in different contexts. The letter 'o', for example, is pronounced differently in the word 'one' and in the word 'bone'.

A convenient unit for representing speech sounds is the 'phoneme'. Whether or not this unit has any physical, or even psychological, reality need not concern us.

2.1.1 Phonemes

Phonemes are used as descriptive tools by phoneticians. The phoneme is a linguistic unit defined such that if one phoneme is substituted for another in a word, the meaning of that word may be changed. The set of phonemes used in each language may thus be different. For example, in English /l/ and /r/ are two distinct phonemes ('lot' has a different meaning from 'rot'), whereas in Japanese they are not. However, as the vocal apparatus used in the production of all languages is universal, there is much overlap of the phoneme sets of different languages, and the total number of phonemes is finite. A consistent set of phonetic symbols for languages is provided by the International Phonetic Alphabet (IPA).

The phonemes of English are shown in Fig. 2.1 and examples of words in which they are used are given in Table 2.1. The phonemes are classified as vowels or consonants. The vowels are then divided into pure vowels and diphthongs. The pure vowels are then subdivided into front, middle or back depending upon the position of the tongue hump when they are produced.

The consonants are subclassified as semivowels, nasals, fricatives and plosives. The semivowels are sometimes called approximants. The fricative category is divided into voiced and voiceless fricatives. The plosive category contains the voiced plosives, the voiceless plosives and the affricates. Plosives are sometimes referred to as stop consonants.

2.1.2 Allophones

Another way of classifying speech sounds is in terms of the way in which they are produced. The units are then known as 'phones'. These are usually represented by symbols enclosed in square brackets, e.g. [l], to distinguish them from phonemes, which are represented by symbols enclosed in oblique lines, i.e. /l/.

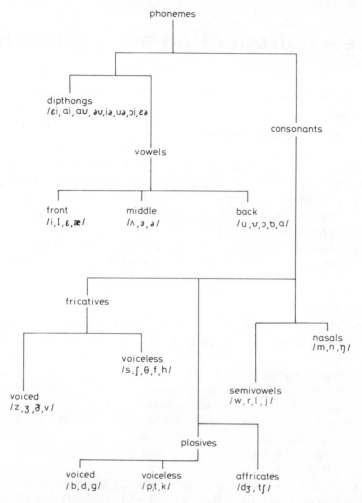

Fig. 2.1   *Classification of the phonemes of British English*

There are many more phones than there are phonemes because certain of them are produced in different ways depending on context, The velarised 'l' represented by [ɫ], for example, occurs before consonants and at the end of utterances. The non-velarised 'l', represented by [l], occurs in other positions in English. As both of these phones are realisations of the same phoneme, they are known as 'allophones'.

It is important for machine recognition to be aware of the existence of allophones, although human speech recognition takes place automatically without the listener normally being aware of their presence.

Table 2.1 *The International Phonetic Alphabet (IPA) symbols of the phonemes of British English and examples of words in which they are used*

Vowels		Diphthongs		Semivowels		Nasals	
/i/	heed	/ɛi/	bay	/w/	was	/m/	am
/I/	hid	/ɑi/	by	/r/	ran	/n/	an
/ɛ/	head	/əʊ/	bow	/l/	lot	/ŋ/	sang
/æ/	had	/ɑʊ/	bough	/j/	yacht		
/ɑ/	hard	/iə/	beer			*Fricatives*	
/o/	hod	/uə/	doer	*Plosives*		/s/	sail
/ɔ/	hoard	/ɔə/	boar	/b/	bat	/ʃ/	ship
/ʊ/	hood	/ɔi/	boy	/d/	disc	/f/	funnel
/u/	who'd	/ɛə/	bear	/g/	goat	/θ/	thick
/ʌ/	hut			/p/	pool	/h/	hull
/3/	heard	*Affricates*		/t/	tap	/z/	zoo
/ə/	the	/dʒ/	jaw	/k/	kite	/ʒ/	azure
		/tʃ/	chore			/ð/	that
						/v/	valve

2.1.3 Transcription

Any utterance can be represented by a string of symbols. This is known as a 'transcription' of the utterance. The transcription may be made at one of two levels: a phonemic (or broad) transcription or a phonetic (or narrow) transcription.

A phonemic transcription consists of a string of phonemes and uses just sufficient symbols in order that transcriptions of utterances having different meanings will be transcribed by different strings. In order to reproduce the utterance, however, the speaker needs to know the phonology of the language; i.e. he needs to know which allophones of each phoneme to employ in which context.

A phonetic transcription, however, consists of a string of phones. The specific allophone to be employed at each instant in the utterance is specified by an appropriate symbol. The IPA system specifies a symbol to represent each phone. The symbols often include modifiers. In the example above, the phoneme /l/ appearing in the phonemic transcription would be replaced by [l] in initial position but by [ɫ] in final position and by [l̥] after a voiceless plosive (as in the words 'play' or 'clay').

2.1.4 Prosodics

A phonetic transcription specifies implicitly the speech organs which are involved in producing an utterance. There are, however, other factors which influence the way in which the utterance is spoken. These are the prosodic features of stress, rhythm, and intonation.

Stress is used in two ways: 'sentence stress' indicates the most important words in a sentence and 'word stress' indicates the prominent syllables in a word. The IPA system allows three levels of stress to be recorded. ' is placed before a syllable with primary stress and   before one with secondary stress. Unstressed syllables are not marked.

Rhythm refers to the timing of an utterance. Some languages, such as English, are claimed to be stress-timed. The durations between stresses are equal. Subjectively this is so, but objective measurements have shown that there is merely a tendency in this direction. The portion of an utterance beginning with one stressed syllable and ending immediately before the next is known as a 'foot'. A foot containing four syllables (one stressed and three unstressed) is longer than a foot containing a single (stressed) syllable, but it is not four times longer. Other languages, such as French, are believed to be syllable-timed.

Intonation, or pitch movement, is very important in indicating the meaning of a sentence. A high pitch is represented in the IPA system by ⁻ and a low level by _ . A high rising pitch is shown by the symbol / and low rising by , . Similarly high falling by \ and low falling by , . Other symbols which may be used are Λ for a rise-fall and V for a fall-rise.

2.2 Speech production

Speech is produced by a set of organs which probably evolved for other functions such as breathing and eating. These limit the range and types of sounds which can be employed for encoding the message to be transmitted.

2.2.1 Vocal apparatus

The organs involved in the production of speech are shown in Fig. 2.2. Speech is produced by inhaling, expanding the rib cage and lowering the diaphragm, so that air is drawn into the lungs. The pressure in the lungs is then increased by the reverse process, contracting the rib cage and raising the diaphragm. This increased pressure forces the air to flow up the trachea (wind pipe). At the top of the trachea it encounters the larynx, a bony structure covered by skin containing a slit-like orifice, the glottis (vocal cords).

The flow of air through the glottis causes a local drop in pressure by the Bernoulli effect. This drop in pressure allows the tension in the laryngeal muscles to close the glottis, thereby interrupting the flow of air. The pressure then builds up again, forcing the vocal cords apart, and enabling the air flow to continue. This cycle then repeats itself, producing a train of pulses. This process is known as phonation. A typical glottal pulse waveform is shown in Fig. 2.3.

The rest of the vocal tract, the oral and nasal passages, then act as a filter, allowing the harmonics of the glottal waveform which lie near the natural

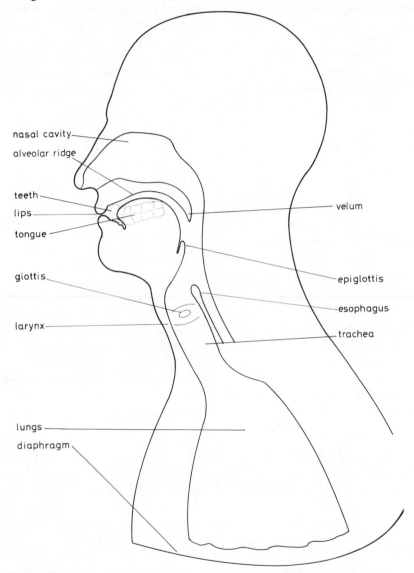

Fig. 2.2 *Articulators used in the production of speech sounds*

resonances of the tract to pass, whilst attenuating the others. The acoustic wave so produced radiates from the lips. A typical speech waveform is shown in Fig. 2.4.

2.2.2 *Vowel production*

The vowel sounds are produced by the process outlined above. The different vowels are produced by changing the shape of the vocal tract, by moving the tongue, jaw and lips so that the natural resonances occur at different frequencies. Lowering the jaw, so that the oral tract becomes wider, causes the frequency of the lowest resonance to increase (as in an /ɑ/ vowel), whilst raising the jaw causes it to fall (as in /i/ and /u/). Similarly moving the tongue hump from the back of the mouth to the front affects the frequency of the next highest resonance.

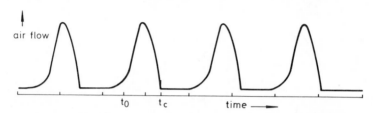

Fig. 2.3 *Glottal waveform during voiced speech*
The glottal opening, t_0, and the glottal closing, t_c, are shown

These resonances are most easily seen in sonagrams, or sound spectrograms (Fig. 2.5). A sonagram shows the distribution of frequencies in a sound. Time is plotted as the abscissa and frequency as the ordinate. The intensity of the sound of a particular frequency at a given point in time is shown as the darkness of the trace. With such a display the resonances of the vowels appear as horizontal lines. These are known as 'formants', and are numbered in terms of increasing frequency. The lowest frequency resonance is known as 'formant one', the next as 'formant two', etc.

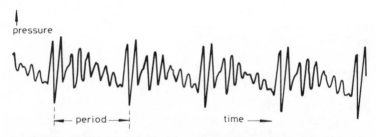

Fig. 2.4 *Pressure waveform of a segment of voiced speech*

Vowel sounds are generated with the vocal cords vibrating. Consequently they have a quasi-periodic structure which appears as vertical striations on wide-band sonagrams (see Section 4.1.2). The spacing of these stripes is proportional to the period of vibration of the vocal cords, so some indication of excitation frequency is apparent from sonagrams.

Sonagrams of some of the vowels are shown in Fig. 2.6. For an /i/ vowel (as in 'heed'), the first formant is low and the second is high. For an /u/ (as in 'who'), the frequency of the first formant is similar to that of an /i/ vowel but that of the second is much lower. For an /ɑ/ vowel (as in 'hard'), the frequency of the first formant is high but that of the second is low, so that they appear on this sonagram as single broad formant. The formants of a /3/ vowel (as in 'heard') are approximately equally spaced.

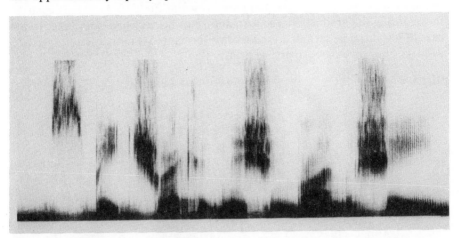

Fig. 2.5 *Sonagram of the phrase 'speech recognition by machine' spoken by a male speaker*
Duration: 2 s
Frequency range: 0–6 kHz

Fig. 2.6 *Sonagrams of the vowels /i/ as in 'heed', /u/ as in 'who'd', /a/ as in 'hard' and /3/ as in 'heard'*
Duration: 2 s
Frequency range: 0–6 kHz

The diphthongs are produced like the vowels except that the articulators are moved during production from a position for one vowel at the start of the gesture towards a position suitable for another. The word 'I', for example, is produced with the jaw initially lowered and the tongue hump at the back of the mouth (suitable for an /ɑ/ vowel). Then the jaw is raised and the tongue hump is moved forward (towards the position for an /i/ vowel).

Sonagrams of the diphthongs /ɛi/ (as in 'bay'), /ɑi/ (as in 'by'), /aʊ/ (as in 'bough'), and /əʊ/ (as in 'bow-(tie)') are shown in Fig. 2.7. As the articulators move during the production, the formant frequencies change with time. In the case of /ɑi/ it can be seen that the first two formants are initially close together, as in /ɑ/, but they move apart, as in /i/.

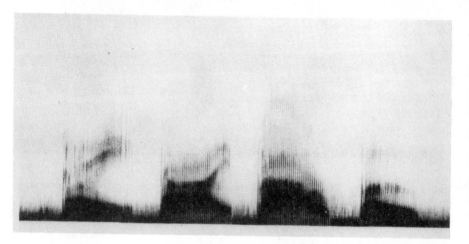

Fig. 2.7 *Sonagrams of the words 'by, boy, bough, bow' illustrating the diphthongs /ɑi/, /ɔi/, /aʊ/ and /əʊ/*
Duration: 2 s
Frequency range: 0–6 kHz

2.2.3 *Consonant production*

Semivowels are produced in a similar way to diphthongs, but the initial articulator configuration is held for a much briefer period, and the final articulator configuration is the vowel which follows the semivowel. The sonagrams shown in Fig. 2.8 reflect this. The duration of the formant transitions in semivowels is less than that of diphthongs, being only 50 – 100 ms.

All initial semivowels have a rising first formant. The second formant of /w/ also rises whilst that of a /j/ falls. The slopes of the second formant transitions of /r/ and /l/ depend upon the following vowel, but the initial frequency of the second formant of /l/ is usually slightly higher than that of /r/ for a given following vowel. The main distinguishing feature for the two phonemes is the third formant transition which starts at a relatively low value for /r/. The shape of the transitions is also somewhat different. It is much more abrupt for /l/, reflecting the greater speed at which the tongue tip can be moved.

The sonagrams of nasals (Fig. 2.9) are dominated by a low-frequency resonance. This occurs because the sound is emitted by the nasal tract, which is longer than the oral tract. The oral tract is closed by the lips for /m/, by the tip of the tongue on the teeth ridge for /n/, and by the velum for /ŋ/. The closed oral tract acts as a resonator producing reflected waves which cause zeros in the spectrum. The structure of the formants above the first is thus different for each nasal.

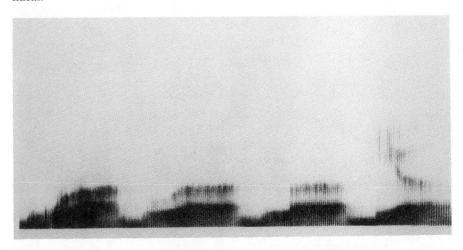

Fig. 2.8 *Sonagrams of the semivowels /w/, /r/, /l/ and /j/ in the syllables 'wer', 'rer', 'ler' and 'yer'*
Duration: 2 s
Frequency range: 0–6 kHz

Fig. 2.9 *Sonagrams of the nasals /m/, /n/ and /ŋ/ in the syllables 'am', 'an' and 'ang'*
Duration: 2 s
Frequency range: 0–6 kHz

Fricatives are produced by a narrow constriction in the vocal tract giving rise to turbulent flow in the air stream, rather than by periodic vibrations of the vocal cords. The vertical striations which appear on sonagrams of voiced sounds are thus absent in voiceless fricatives, and are replaced by a more random pattern (Fig. 2.10). The voiceless fricatives are produced entirely by this process,

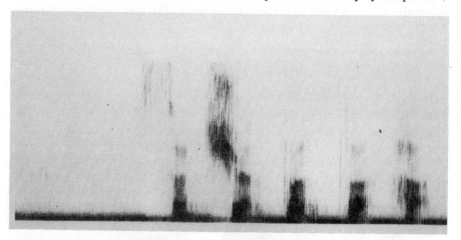

Fig. 2.10　*Sonagrams of the voiceless fricatives in the syllables /sə/, /ʃə/, /fə/, /θə/ and /hə/*
Duration: 1·6 s
Frequency range: 0–6 kHz

Fig. 2.11　*Sonagrams of the voiced fricatives in the syllables /zə/, /ʒə/, /və/ and /ðə/*
Duration: 2 s
Frequency range: 0–6 kHz

whereas the voiced fricatives by a combination of this process and laryngeal vibrations. The main differences between the patterns produced by the voiceless fricatives are the frequency regions where the energy is concentrated and the intensity of that energy.

The voiced fricatives (Fig. 2.11) have complex spectra. The vocal-cord vibrations give rise to striations in the lowest part of the spectrum, whereas turbulent flow gives the upper region a more random appearance. In general, the concentration of fricative energy occurs in about the same frequency region as that of its voiceless counterpart, but with low-frequency periodic energy superimposed. The voiced fricatives have shorter durations than their voiceless counterparts. Final voiced fricatives often contain no periodic energy, and are distinguished from their voiced equivalents on the basis of duration alone.

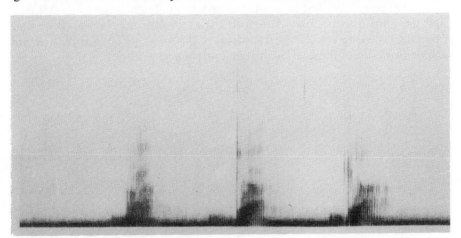

Fig. 2.12 *Sonagrams of the voiced plosives in the syllables /bə/, /də/ and /gə/*
Duration: 1·6 s
Frequency range: 0–6 kHz

The production of plosives is more complex. The vocal tract is closed at some point, so the flow of air ceases. Very little energy may be apparent in any part of the spectrum. Then the pressure is released, giving rise to impulsive excitation. Whilst the articulators which caused the closure are close together turbulent flow may occur, giving rise to fricative excitation. The vocal cords may be held close together giving rise to aspirant energy, or they may be allowed to vibrate producing periodic energy. At the same time the articulators will be moving to a configuration appropriate to the following phoneme, so the formant frequencies will be changing. The resulting sonagrams are shown in Fig. 2.12 for the voiced plosives and in Fig. 2.13 for the voiceless ones.

All plosives are produced by closing the vocal tract. This gives rise to a silent period followed by a burst of energy with a rising first formant as the vocal tract is opened. With voiced plosives the vocal cords are allowed to vibrate at, or before, the instant of release. (In some languages voicing is forced to begin before the release, giving rise to the category of prevoiced plosives, which are not distinguished from voiced plosives by English listeners). When the vocal cords begin to vibrate before the release this is sometimes seen as stripes in the very-low-frequency region of the 'silent' interval (or stop gap) of sonagrams. These stripes are known as the voice bar, and may continue through a stop gap.

A /b/ is produced by closing the vocal tract with the lips. After the release the second and third formants rise as well as the first. The formant transitions are rapid, being complete in less than 50 ms. A /d/ is produced with the tip of the tongue on the tooth ridge. After release the first formant rises and the third formant falls. The second formant begins at about 1800 Hz (for a typical male speaker), then rises or falls depending upon whether the second formant of the following vowel is above or below this value. A /g/ is produced by closure at the velum. On release the first formant rises and generally the second formant falls and the third formant rises. However, the exact formant transitions depend upon the following vowel. The transitions of the formants of velar plosives are a little slower than those of bilabial and alveolar plosives.

Fig. 2.13 *Sonagrams of the voiceless plosives in the syllables /pə/, tə/ and /kə/*
Duration: 1·5 s
Frequency range: 0–6 kHz

The voiceless plosives are produced in a similar manner to their voiced counterparts, except that the vocal cords are not allowed to vibrate until some 50 ms after the instant of release. The time interval between the release and the start of vocal-cord vibration is known as voice onset time, or VOT. The formant transitions are not so obvious and, because the fricative excitation has less low-frequency energy than periodic excitation, the first formant transition is often missing. The main difference between /p/, /t/ and /k/ is the concentration of energy in the burst following release. In /p/ this is generally diffuse but with more energy in the low-frequency region of the spectrum than the others. In /t/ the energy reaches into the highest regions with a concentration at about 4 kHz. In /k/ the spectrum is very variable with the greatest concentration of energy at, or a little above, the frequency of the second formant of the following vowel. There is, however, another lesser peak near the frequency of the third formant of the following vowel.

An affricate is produced by a sequence of a plosive followed by a fricative.

This can be seen from the sonagrams shown in Fig. 2.14. The voiced affricate /ʤ/ (as in 'jaw') has most of the attributes of a voiced plosive except that there is some mixed excitation for a while. Similarly /ʧ/ (as in 'chore') has the properties of a voiced plosive, but the fricative excitation continues for longer than in a normal plosive. The durations of the affricates are generally less than the sum of the plosives and fricatives of which they are composed.

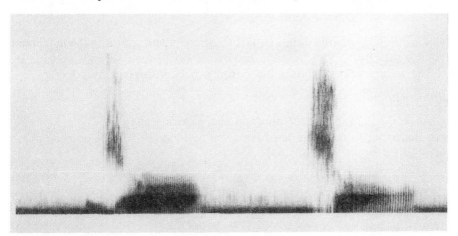

Fig. 2.14 *Sonagrams of the affricates /dʒ/ and /tʃ/ in the words 'jaw' and 'chore'*
Duration: 2 s
Frequency range: 0–6 kHz

Although the mechanisms involved in the production of each speech sound are distinct, the articulators move continuously from the production of one phone to the next, so that there is, in general, no acoustic boundary between phones. In fact, an articulator which is not essential for the production of the current phone may move into a position suitable for the production of the subsequent phone. This phenomenon is known as co-articulation. Consequently the acoustic manifestation of each speech sound is not a distinct segment, like a letter in a printed word, but is highly dependent upon its context, that is upon the sounds which precede and follow it.

2.2.4 Acoustic model
An acoustic model of speech production was developed by Fant (1960). This is known as the source-filter model, and consists of an excitation source driving a series of filters. An important simplification is that the source and filters are considered to be independent of each other.

The excitation source, $e(t)$, excites the column of air in the vocal tract, represented by a filter having a transfer function $v(f)$, and the resulting signal is radiated from the lips. The lip radiation may be represented by a filter $l(f)$. The speech signal, $s(t)$, is then modelled by

$$s(t) = v(f)^*l(f)^*e(t) \tag{2.1}$$

The excitation source has the shape shown in Fig. 2.3. It consists of three phases: a gradual opening phase where the flow of air builds up, a rapid closing phase where the glottis closes cutting off the flow of air, and a closed period in which the subglottal pressure builds up again.

Glottal pulse shapes have been modelled by Rosenberg (1971). The volume velocity during the opening phase, u_1, is given by

$$u_1 = 3u_0a^2 - 2u_0a^3 \qquad (2.2)$$

where $a = t/t_1$, t_1 is the duration of the opening phase, and u_0 is the maximum volume velocity.

The volume velocity during the closing phase, u_2, is given by

$$u_2 = u_0 - u_0b^2 \qquad (2.3)$$

where $b = t/t_2$, and t_2 is the duration of the closing phase.

An alternative formulation has been given by Fant (1979). The opening phase is modelled by

$$u_1 = 1/2u_0(1 - \cos w_0 t) \qquad (2.4)$$

where $w_0 = 2\pi F_0$, F_0 is the fundamental frequency, and the closing phase by

$$u_2 = u_0(k \cos (w_0(t - t_2)) - k + 1) \qquad (2.5)$$

where k specifies the steepness of the curve in the closing phase.

The oral tract may be considered to be a tube, about 17 cm long, closed at the source end (the glottis) and open at the other end (the lips). Its cross-sectional area is small compared with its length, so plane acoustic waves propagate in the tract. The waves may described by the pressure, P, and the volume velocity, u, as a function of the distance along the tract from the glottis.

In a real physical system there are losses through the walls of the vocal tract. The transfer function is then given by

$$v(w) = \frac{s_1 s_1^*}{(jw - s_1)(jw - s_1^*)} \qquad (2.6)$$

where $w = 2\pi f$, $s_1 = \sigma_1 + jw_1$, $s_1^* = \sigma_1 - jw_1$, $w_1 = 2\pi F_1$, and σ_1 is a constant which depends on the amount of dissipation. The complex numbers s_1 and s_1^* are the poles of the transfer function.

A vocal tract, however, is not a simple resonator. It is more like a transmission line. The wave is reflected back from the opening of the mouth, interfering with the wave from the source. Such a system has an infinite number of resonances with the transfer function given by

$$v(w) = \prod_{i=1}^{\infty} \frac{s_i s_i^*}{(jw - s_i)(jw - s_i^*)} \qquad (2.7)$$

where $s_i = \sigma_i + jw_i$ are the poles of the function (Fant, 1960).

The source signal from the glottis is thus modified by the resonances of the vocal tract, and then radiates from the lips.

During the production of nasals, the velum is opened so that the wave propagates along the nasal tract to the nostrils. The oral tract is closed at the lips for /m/, by the tongue against the alveolar ridge for /n/, and near the velum for /ŋ/. The tract thus consists of a tube closed at one end (the glottis), and open at the other end (the nostrils), but with a closed side branch (the mouth). The point of closure of the oral tract determines the length of the side tube, and hence the frequency at which the oral tract will resonate. The wave in the oral tract may interfere with that in the nasal tract producing zeros as well as poles in the transfer function. The acoustics of nasal production are thus somewhat more complex than vowel production.

Yet another vocal tract configuration is employed in the production of fricatives. These are characterised by a rather narrow constriction, the position of which depends upon the particular consonant being produced. Air is forced through this constriction, and turbulent flow occurs. Noise is generated as a result of this turbulence, which excites the resonances of the vocal tract.

The constriction can occur at a number of places in the vocal tract. The configuration consists of a source with one (closed) acoustic tube behind it and another (open) tube in front. The noise source will excite the resonances of both of these tubes. Depending upon its size, the posterior cavity will absorb the energy of the source at certain frequencies, so the spectrum of the signal at the lips will contain zeros as well as poles. The transfer function of the vocal tract during the production of fricatives is thus proportional to

$$\prod_{i=1}^{\infty} \frac{s_i s_i^*}{(jw - s_i)(jw - s_i^*)} \prod_{j=1}^{\infty} \frac{(jw - s_j)(jw - s_j^*)}{s_j s_j^*} \tag{2.8}$$

where s^* is the complex conjugate of s, s_i are the poles and s_j are the zeros of the transfer function (Heinz and Stevens, 1961).

The acoustic model of voiced fricatives is even more complex. It consists of a periodic source, a closed acoustic tube, a noise source, and then another acoustic tube closed at one end and open at the other, all arranged in series.

For the /h/ sound, the constriction is at the glottis. The acoustic model for the production of this sound is thus similar to that of a vowel except that the source is aperiodic rather than periodic. The vocal tract tends to assume a shape appropriate for the vowel following, and the formant frequencies of this vowel are apparent in the spectrum of the /h/.

2.3 Speech synthesis

There are a number of ways in which speech may be synthesised. These differ in two ways. Firstly there are different units which may act as input to the system. These may be phonemes (Holmes, Mattingly and Shearme, 1964), orthographic text (Ainsworth, 1973; Carlson *et al.*, 1982) or even concepts (Fallside and Young, 1978). Secondly they differ in the aspects of the speech-production process which they attempt to match. Articulatory speech synthesisers attempt to model the motions of the articulators, whilst terminal analogue speech synthesisers attempt to generate signals whose acoustic patterns are identical to speech signals.

2.3.1 Articulatory synthesis

Articulatory synthesisers are based on a representation of the vocal tract. The original synthesisers employed a series of dynamically controlled, analogue filters for this purpose (Rosen, 1958; Dennis, 1962), but modern systems are simulated on digital computers (Ladefoged *et al.*, 1978; Scully and Clark, 1986).

The input to the system is a number of parameters representing the positions of the articulators. These might be the amount of lip opening, the amount of jaw lowering, and the positions of the tongue tip and tongue hump. Not all of these parameters are independent. The body of the tongue, for example, is incompressible; so if it is lowered at one point it will be raised at another.

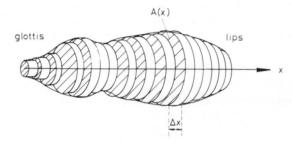

Fig. 2.15 *Modelling of the vocal tract as a series of uniform cylinders of cross-sectional area A(x) and thickness Δx*

These parameters are used to specify the vocal tract shape. This is sampled at uniform intervals, usually 0·5 cm apart, and the tract is modelled as a series of tubes (Fig. 2.15). In order to synthesise a speech sound this compound tube is excited by glottal pulses of the shape given by Rosenberg (1970) or Fant (1960). The signal at the lips can be computed by solving Webster's horn equation (Webster, 1919; Chiba and Kajiyama, 1941; Fant, 1960; Linggard, 1985)

$$d^2 P/dt^2 \ = \ c^2/A(x).d/dx[A(x)dP/dx] \tag{2.9}$$

where P is the pressure, $A(x)$ is the cross-sectional area, c is the velocity of sound, x is the distance from the larynx, and t is time.

In order to synthesise syllables the articulatory parameters must change with time. These changes usually follow an S-shaped curve; beginning slowly, then speeding up, and finally slowing down as the target is reached. Physiological data suggests that it takes about the same time to complete a gesture independently of the distance between the initial and target positions.

Thus it is possible to synthesise speech from a set of articulatory targets. This method of synthesis has the advantage that co-ordination between the articulators is achieved naturally, and the acoustic consequences are similar to those observed in natural speech. The disadvantage of this method is the complexity and the consequent amount of computation involved.

2.3.2 Formant synthesis

Another way of synthesising speech is by formant synthesis. In this method the input parameters are acoustic data such as the frequencies and intensities of the formants. This method was first developed by Lawrence (1953) and by Fant (Fant and Martony, 1962). The input data for a formant synthesiser are much easier to obtain than for an articulatory synthesiser. They can be derived from sonagrams.

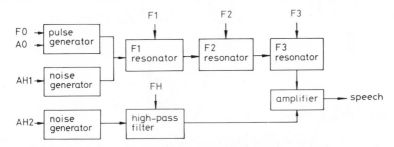

Fig. 2.16 *Schematic diagram of a typical serial formant speech synthesiser*

There are two configurations of formant synthesisers: serial and parallel. A typical serial configuration is shown in Fig. 2.16. A periodic pulse generator (for the production of voiced sounds) excites a number of resonators connected in series. The frequencies (and sometimes the bandwidths) of the resonators are dynamically controlled, as are the frequency and intensity of the pulse generator. A switch allows the resonators to be excited by a noise generator (for the production of fricative sounds). In some systems the excitation signals may be mixed (for the production of voiced fricatives). A high-pass filter, also excited by the noise generator, is connected in parallel with the resonators for the synthesis of certain consonants such as /s/ sounds. An extra resonator may also be connected in parallel with the series of resonators for the synthesis of nasalised sounds.

A typical parallel formant synthesiser is shown in Fig. 2.17. The principle of operation is similar to the serial formant synthesiser except that intensity controls are required for each individual formant resonator. Although more control signals are required for parallel synthesisers, this additional flexibility is useful for the synthesis of certain consonants. Holmes (1982) has made a detailed comparison of the serial and parallel configurations.

The original formant synthesisers were constructed from analogue electronic components. They contained second-order resonators. These can be simulated digitally by the recurrence relation

$$y(n) = a_1 y(n-1) - a_2 y(n-2) + a_0 x(n) \tag{2.10}$$

where $y(n)$ is the output signal at the nth sampled interval and $x(n)$ is the input signal.

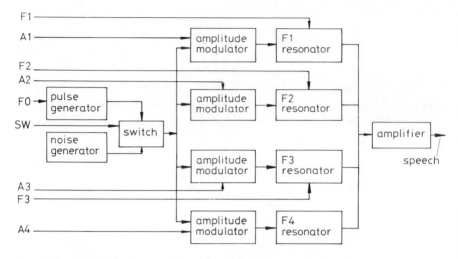

Fig. 2.17 *Schematic diagram of a typical parallel formant speech synthesiser*

It can be shown that the transfer function of such a system is as shown in Fig. 2.18, where

$$a_2 = \exp\left(-2\pi B_i T\right) \tag{2.11}$$

$$a_1 = 2 \exp\left(-2\pi B_i T\right) \cos\left(2\pi F_i T\right) \tag{2.12}$$

and

$$a_0 = 1 - a_1 + a_2 \tag{2.13}$$

where F_i is the formant frequency, B_i is the formant bandwidth, and T is the sampling interval (Section 4.1.1).

It is possible to store the formant parameters for each of the phonemes (or phones) of a language in a look-up table. The control signals for a formant synthesiser can then be derived automatically from a phonemic (or phonetic) transcription. Such a system is known as synthesis by rule. The first such systems were developed by Kelly and Gerstman (1961) and by Holmes, Mattingly and Shearme (1964).

2.3.3 Diphone synthesis

One method of speech synthesis which was not found to be successful was to make a recording of each phoneme, and then string these together in the order specified by the input phonemic transcription. This method does not work because the formant transitions from one phoneme to the next will not be correct, because of the context and allophonic variation.

One way of circumventing this problem is by means of diphone synthesis. Instead of taking the phonemic segments of speech as the units, the segments are taken from the centre of one phone to the centre of the next. As the acoustic parameters are relatively steady in the middle of a phone it is then possible to concatenate these new units, the diphones, in order to synthesise utterances.

This technique has been investigated by Dixon and Maxey (1968). They extracted and then stored the parameter transitions between many of the allowable sequences of pairs of phones. Then they tested them by synthesising new utterances with a formant synthesiser. They found that they required about 1000 diphones in order to synthesise speech of a reasonable quality, but they suggest that many more diphones will be required for high-quality speech.

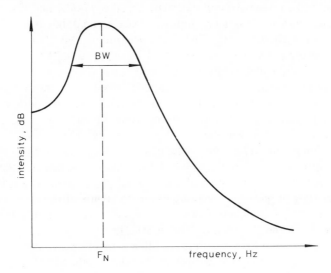

Fig. 2.18 *Transfer function of a digital resonator*
F_N is the resonance frequency and *BW* is its bandwidth

A similar approach to synthesis has been proposed by Fujimura (1976). He suggested that the units to use for speech synthesis (and recognition) are demisyllables and affixes. Co-articulation effects are much stronger within syllables than between syllables, so it is possible to concatenate segments spanning half a syllable, i.e. from the beginning to the middle or from the middle to the end of a syllable. Certain sounds, such as /s/, can be added to syllables to form new syllables. These are referred to as affixes.

2.4 Speech perception

One way of approaching the problem of speech recognition is to study the perception of speech by humans. This will not necessarily guarantee a solution but it may offer useful clues. After all the only completely adequate speech recogniser which we have at present is the human auditory system and brain.

2.4.1 Auditory representation

Speech waves, like any other sounds, enter the ear via the *pinna* and are transmitted to the eardrum via the *meatus*, or external canal. Attached to the eardrum is the *malleus*, or hammer, one of the ossicles of the middle ear. The *malleus* makes contact with the *incus*, or anvil, causing it to rotate. This is in turn connected to the *stapes*, or stirrup, which is attached to the oval window. The purpose of this system is to transduce the acoustic vibrations of the sound waves into mechanical vibrations in the inner ear.

The inner ear consists of a coil-like structure, the *cochlea*. This transforms the mechanical vibrations into nerve impulses, the electrical signals which transmit the information to the brain. The *cochlea* contains two channels, the *scala vestibuli* and the *scala tympani*, separated by a partition. These channels are filled with a liquid called perilymph.

The cochlear partition is itself a channel filled with another liquid, endolymph. It is bounded by the basilar membrane and Reissner's membrane. These membranes terminate about 1 mm from the ends of the *scalae* so the perilymph can flow between them at the *helicotrema* (Fig. 2.19).

The motion of the *stapes* pumps the oval window, causing a travelling wave to be set up in the perilymph, which is turn causes the basilar membrane to vibrate. The basilar membrane is about 35 mm long. It tapers towards its apex, so its resonating properties vary along its length. Tones of 100 Hz cause maximum vibration at about 30 mm from the *stapes* end, those of 1000 Hz at about 23 mm from this end, and those of 10 000 Hz at only 10 mm. The basilar membrane acts like a broad band-pass filter with successive points having an approximately constant-Q characteristic, the width of the filter being approximately proportional to its resonance frequency.

Attached to the basilar membrane is the organ of *Corti*. This contains the hair cells which perform the mechanical to neural transduction. There are three rows of outer hair cells and one row of inner hair cells, comprising some 30 000 cells in all. The motion of the basilar membrane causes the the hair cells to bend, creating a potential. The dendrites of the neurones of the auditory nerve are in contact with the hair cells. A current flows which is sufficient to produce nerve impulses in these cells.

The ear thus acts as an acoustic to neural transducer, and also performs a broad-band frequency analysis. A display of the neural activity in the auditory nerve might show some similarities to a sonagram.

There is, however, much more processing in the auditory system. The auditory nerve leads to the ventral and dorsal cochlear nuclei, which in turn connect to the left and right superior olives. These connect via the lateral *lemnisci* to the inferior *colliculi*, and thence via the medial geniculate bodies to the left and right auditory cortices. The details of the functions performed by these organs are not yet understood, but it is known that, although neurones at the lowest levels always respond to certain frequencies, some of the neurones in the auditory cortex only respond to more complex sounds.

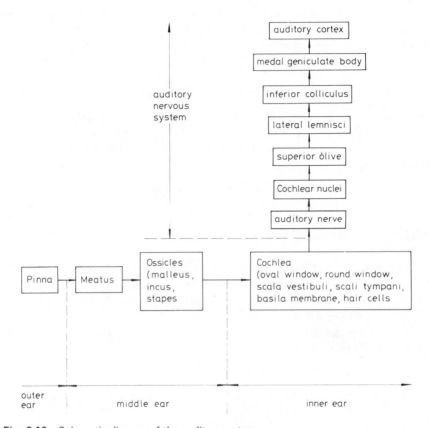

Fig. 2.19 *Schematic diagram of the auditory system*

A good deal about the functioning of the human auditory system has been discovered by psychophysical investigations. It was found by Fletcher and Munson (1937) that the threshold for hearing a weak tone is raised in the presence of an adjacent tone. This only occurs if the tones are close to each other in frequency. These experiments have led to the concept of the 'critical band'. Signals within the critical band influence the perception of those in the band, but not those outside.

Critical bands have been measured throughout the range of hearing (Zwicker and Fastl, 1972). The critical bandwidth for a centre frequency of 200 Hz is about 100 Hz, whereas for 5000 Hz it is about 1000 Hz. These measurements have led to a psychophysical scale of frequency known as the 'bark' scale (one bark is a critical band). This is related to the usual physical scale approximately by

$$f = 650 \sinh (x/7) \tag{2.14}$$

where f is the frequency in herz and x is the frequency in barks.

In order to compute the auditory representation of a sound, the signal must first be modified by the transfer function of the middle ear. This can be approximated by a function due to Schroeder (Fourcin *et al.*, 1977)

$$M(f) = 1 + 6/(1 + [1·07(f - 3·5)]^4)$$
$$\div (1 + \exp[0·144|f - 8|(f - 8)] \tag{2.15}$$

Next the frequency scale is transformed into barks by the expression given above. Then the masking effects of the critical bands can be taken into account by convolving the resulting power spectral density with a function $F(x)$, also due to Schroeder (Fourcin *et al.*, 1977)

$$10 \log_{10} F(x) = 15·8 + 7·5 (x + 0·5)$$
$$- 17·5 (1 + (x + 0·5)^2)^{1/2} \tag{2.16}$$

which corresponds to a filter with a $+25\,dB/bark$ slope below the centre frequency and a $-10\,dB/bark$ slope above it.

This yields the excitation function $E(x)$, which may be thought of as the mean-square amplitude of the basilar membrane motion, although the function for $F(x)$ was obtained from psychophysical measurements and may contain components due to other organs.

The loudness density is then obtained by raising $E(x)$ to the fourth power (Stevens and Davis, 1938):

$$L(x) = L_0(E(x) - \theta(x))^{0·25} \tag{2.17}$$

where $\theta(x)$ is the threshold of hearing and L_0 is a scale factor chosen to make the loudness of a 1 kHz tone at 40 dB equal to one.

2.4.2 Difference limens

The frequency difference limen is a measure of the ability of a listener to detect a change in the frequency of a tone. Shower and Biddulph (1931) showed that over the range 500–8000 Hz frequency discrimination follows Weber's law:

$$df/f = \text{a constant} \tag{2.18}$$

where f is the frequency and df is the smallest difference that can be detected at that frequency. They found that Weber's law did not hold at lower frequencies; df was about 3 Hz in the range 125–2000 Hz, 12 Hz at 5 kHz, and 30 Hz at 10 kHz. More recent experiments by Nordmark (1968) gave smaller values. He obtained a difference limen of 0·2 Hz at 100 Hz, rising to 1·5 Hz at 2 kHz and to about 30 Hz at 12 kHz.

Flanagan and Saslow (1958) have measured the difference limen for the fundamental frequency of vowels generated with a formant synthesiser. They obtained a value of 0·3 to 0·5% of the fundamental frequency. For a male speaker, the fundamental is about 120 Hz, so the difference limen is about 0·5 Hz, which is similar to that found by Nordmark for pure tones.

Flanagan (1955) has also measured the difference limen of the formant frequencies of synthesised vowels. He found that this depends on the proximity of the other formants, but is of the order of 3–5% of the formant frequency for both the first an the second formants.

The difference limen for the intensity of the second formant of a synthesised /æ/ vowel has also been measured by Flanagan (1957). He found that a difference of about 3 dB could just be detected. This is the same order of magnitude as found by Riesz (1928) for pure tones. He showed that the intensity difference limen is about 15 dB for a 1000 Hz tone of 10 dB intensity, but this falls to 1 dB for a tone of 60 dB intensity.

2.4.3 Vowel perception
One of the most important tools for the study of speech perception is a speech synthesiser. Speech signals contain many features which may, or may not, be used in speech perception. Sometimes the utility of these features can be established by filtering natural speech, but in general the importance of these features in the recognition process can only be ascertained by listening to sounds synthesised with and without these features.

The most important features for vowel perception were found by Delattre *et al.* (1952) to be the frequencies of the two lowest formants. They synthesised vowels containing one, two and more formants, and found that two formants were necessary in order to produce a complete set of American English vowels. With three or more formants more natural sounding vowels could be generated, but the full set could be produced with just two formants.

As the formant frequencies are the resonances of the vocal tract, it might be thought that formants have nothing to do with perception. Pols *et al.* (1969), however, devised an ingenious method for determining the dimensions of vowel perception without imposing any preconceived ideas about formants being involved. They recorded a set of vowels produced by a Dutch speaker, and then measured the similarities between them by the method of triadic comparisons. Listeners were played three vowels sounds and asked to judge which two were the most similar. All combinations of vowels were tested, and a similarity matrix was constructed. A multidimensional analysis of this was performed in order to determine how many orthogonal dimensions were necessary to explain the differences between the vowels. They found that two dimensions explained 70% of the variance, three dimensions 80%, and four dimensions 90%. Pols *et al.* then analysed the same vowel sounds by passing them through a bank of third-octave filters, whose bandwidths correspond approximately to critical bands, and performed a multidimensional analysis on the outputs in order to determine the principal components. When the vowels were plotted in a two-dimensional space determined by the two most important components, similar plots resulted with the data from both the perceptual and physical analyses. Furthermore, a similar plot was obtained when the first two formant frequencies were used as the two dimensions. The first principal component corresponded to the second formant frequency and the second principal component corresponded to the first formant frequency.

It has sometimes been suggested that vowels are reduced to two-formant equivalents by the processing of the auditory system. Carlson *et al.* (1975) asked listeners to match two-formant synthesised vowels against four-formant vowels by adjusting the frequency of the second formant of the two-formant vowel until it sounded like the four-formant vowel. They found that the second formant frequencies of the resulting two-formant vowels lay between the frequencies of the second and third formants of the four-formant vowels. They suggested a spectral prominence model which explained their results for nine Swedish vowels. Bladon and Fant (1978) repeated this matching experiment for the full set of 18 IPA cardinal vowels but found that the performance of the model of Carlson *et al.* was unsatisfactory. They introduced a new model based on the acoustic theory of speech production (Fant, 1960) which gave better results for their data. A vowel identification experiment involving two-formant synthesised vowels was performed by Paliwal *et al.* (1983), however, which produced data which was incompatible with this model, and this led in turn to a further model. The perceptual viability of all of these models has been questioned by Bladon (1983), who has demonstrated that the models predict that certain vowels sound the same when in fact they sound different.

Although the foregoing experiments suggest that formant frequencies are the main factors in the perception of isolated vowels, the situation is more complex in continuous speech. The speed at which some of the articulators can move is limited by their inertia, and so there is sometimes not sufficient time for a steady vowel configuration to be reached before the shape of the tract must be changed for the next consonant. The acoustic consequence is that the formants do not reach their target values. This is known as 'vowel reduction' (Lindblom, 1963). Listeners, however, do not appear to confuse the identity of the intended vowel (Lindblom and Studdert-Kennedy, 1967), so it is possible that they use the direction and rate of change of formant frequencies in order to make allowance for the sluggishness of the articulators.

Another factor which influences the perception of vowels is duration. Vowel duration is affected by the consonantal environment as well as by the tempo and stress pattern of the utterance, so it is difficult to ascertain by analysis alone the importance of vowel duration in recognition. However, Peterson and Lehiste (1960) showed that, when these factors are subtracted or neutralised, the resulting vowel nuclei fall into two classes: the vowels /i,æ,a,ɔ,u/ may be classed as 'long' and /I,ɛ,ʊ,ə/ may be classed as 'short'.

Cohen *et al.* (1967) found that three factors, first and second formant frequency and duration, have to be combined in an optimal way for maximal recognition of synthetic vowels, and other investigators have suggested that duration may be an important factor. Bennett (1968) showed that duration could be an important factor in distinguishing certain vowels that have a similar spectral form; Stevens (1959) found that although duration affects the discrimination of some vowels, it does not affect the discrimination of others; and Ainsworth (1972) reported that, as the duration of a set of synthesised vowels is increased, the proportion of 'long' vowels increases and the proportion of 'short' vowels decreases.

The duration of vowels varies considerably in fast and slow speech. It is thus possible that if duration is one of the factors in speech recognition it is relative, rather than absolute, duration which is important.

Ainsworth (1974) performed an experiment in which a test vowel was preceded by a sequence of sounds whose tempo could be varied. He found a contrast effect. With a fast-tempo precursor more 'long' test vowels were heard, and for a slow tempo more 'short' test vowels.

It will be seen in Section 3.2.2 that the formant frequencies of the vowels produced by men are lower than those produced by women and children because of their different vocal-tract sizes. This causes difficulties for machine recognition of vowels, but not for human recognition. It has been suggested that some kind of vocal-tract normalisation takes place but the mechanism by which it acts is not known. Miller (1953), however, found that when the fundamental frequency of synthetic vowels was doubled there was a shift in the categorisation of some vowels near perceptual boundaries. One possibility, therefore, is that the perceptual mechanism exploits the correlation between vocal-tract size and the fundamental frequency of voices. This hypothesis was explored by Fujisaki and Kawashima (1968) who found a perceptual boundary shift for Japanese vowels which was large enough for normalisation provided that fundamental frequency and third formant frequency were varied together. Similar experiments by Ainsworth (1976) with English listeners, however, showed great individual variation.

Another factor which might be used in vocal-tract normalisation is the frequency of the formants in the part of the utterance preceding the vowel being recognised. Ladefoged and Broadbent (1960) synthesised the phrase 'Please say what this word is' followed by the test word 'bet'. They then lowered the frequency of the second formant of the carrier phrase (so that it sounded like the same words spoken by someone else), but kept the formant frequencies of the test word constant. When they played the new carrier phrase the test word sounded like 'bit'. In order to discover whether the fundamental frequency or the preceding formant frequencies had the greatest effect Ainsworth (1975) presented listeners with test vowels preceded by the vowels /i,u,ɑ/. The fundamental frequency and the formant frequencies of the precursor vowels were systematically varied. It was found that the precursor vowels had the greater effect.

These experiments suggest some ways in which the human perceptual mechanism might cope with vowels produced by different speakers. The situation is rather complex, however, as Fant (1975) has shown that there is a non-linear relationship between the formant frequencies of vowels produced by male and female speakers.

2.4.4 Consonant perception

The features involved in the perception of consonants have been determined by the same methods as those used for vowels. Consonants have been synthesised with and without the features and their utility for perception has been assessed by listening tests.

The feature which enables the glides /w, r, l, j/ to be discriminated from the other speech sounds was shown by Liberman *et al.* (1956) to be the duration of the formant transitions. They synthesised a series of syllables in which the first and second formant frequencies were initially low but which rose linearly to values appropriate for an /ɛ/ vowel. With the durations of the formant transitions greater than about 150 ms the syllable appeared to begin with a /u/ vowel. Between 50 and 150 ms the syllable appeared as /wɛ/, and with the transitions less than 50 ms /bɛ/ was heard. A similar series with an initially high second formant frequency produced the series /iɛ/, /jɛ/, /gɛ/. Further experimentation showed that it was the transition duration rather than the rate of change which was the significant factor.

The features which serve to distinguish between the glides have been investigated for initial position by O'Connor *et al.* (1957) and for intervocalic position by Lisker (1957b). The same features were found in both cases. A high initial second formant frequency indicates the presence of /j/ and a low one /w/. Intermediate values are perceived as /r/ or /l/. The feature that determines which one is perceived is the third formant frequency. If this is low and rising an /r/ is heard, otherwise /l/ is perceived. O'Connor *et al.* were not able to produce an /l/ before /ɛ/ which was perceived correctly by all their subjects. Later Ainsworth (1968a) demonstrated that a step-function was required for the first formant in this case.

Voiced plosives are distinguished from semivowels by the duration of the formant transitions, and also by the silent interval which precedes the release. Liberman *et al.* (1954) were the first to investigate the effects of formant transitions on the perception of voiced plosives. They synthesised a series of syllables with a rising first formant frequency and various shapes for second formant frequency. They found that a rising second formant was generally perceived as /b/, and a falling one as /d/ or /g/. Harris *et al.* (1958) later showed that it is the third formant transition which is required in order for /d/ to be reliably discriminated from /g/. A high initial third formant frequency is used as a cue for /d/ and a low one for /g/ and /b/.

Another cue which is used to distinguish between voiced plosives is the frequency of the burst which occurs immediately after the silent interval (Hoffman, 1958), and in certain syllables where the formant transitions are minimal the frequency of the burst becomes the main cue (Ainsworth, 1968b). Most of the experiments with voiced plosives have been performed with prevocalic stops, but Wang (1959) has studied final plosives. His results suggest that the features for discriminating final plosives are in the vowel transitions prior to the silent interval.

There are several features which have been shown to be involved in distinguishing voiced from voiceless plosives. The main feature is the voice onset time (Liberman *et al.*, 1958). In voiceless plosives voicing begins some 50 ms after the release burst, but in voiced stops it is coincident with it. Other cues which are used are the duration of of the silent interval (Lisker, 1957a), and the fundamental-frequency change which is low and rising in a voiced plosive and falling in a voiceless one (Haggard *et al.*, 1970).

The most important feature which enables voicelesss plosives to be distinguished from one another is the frequency of the noise burst at the moment of release (Liberman *et al.*, 1952). If the centre frequency is above 3 kHz, /t/ is perceived. If the centre frequency is near the centre frequency of the following vowel, /k/ is heard. With the burst frequency below the first formant frequency /p/ is usually heard.

Fricatives are also distinguished perceptually on the basis of the centre frequency of the noise (Hughes and Halle, 1956; Strevens, 1960). Another feature is the formant transitions into and out of the noise region. Harris (1958), using a tape-splicing technique, separated the fricative part from the voiced part of syllables consisting of /s,ʃ,f,θ/ combined with the vowels /i, ɛ,a,u/, and then recombined with them all in possible ways. It was found that the identification of /s/ and /ʃ/ was based mainly on the fricative part, whilst the identification of /f/ and /θ/ depended more on the voiced transitions. Similar experiments were performed with the voiced fricatives.

Nasals are probably identified by the presence of a strong low-frequency formant and relatively weak formants in the rest of the spectrum. Liberman *et al.* (1954) showed that formant transitions into and out of the nasal are important features for distinguishing between /m,n,ŋ/. In vowel-nasal syllables a falling second formant produces an /m/, and a rising one an /n/. Hecker (1962) has studied the time course of nasal—vowel syllables using an articulatory synthesiser.

2.4.5 Categorical perception

In many experiments it has been observed that, when a series of synthetic syllables which differ systematically in a certain parameter are presented to listeners, the listeners hear mainly one consonant until a certain point in the series is reached, and then they hear another. The sounds are heard as belonging to one phoneme category or the other and never partly to both. This phenomenon is known as 'categorical perception' and the point at which the stimuli change categories is called the 'perceptual boundary'.

This phenomenon was demonstrated for the plosives /b,d,g/ by Liberman *et al.* (1957). They presented a number of synthesised syllables which differed only in their second formant-freqyency transitions to a group of listeners for identification. Below 1500 Hz mostly /b/, between 1500 and 2000 Hz /d/ responses, and above 2000 Hz /g/ responses were obtained.

The listeners were then presented with the same set of stimuli using an ABX paradigm. A was one of the stimuli, B was another, and X was identical to either A or B. The listeners' task was to say whether X was more like A or B. If the correct response was obtained A could be discriminated from B, but if random responses were obtained A and B were not discriminable.

Liberman *et al.* hypothesised that A and B would only be discriminable if they belonged to different phonemic categories. Hence the discrimination function should have peaks at the perceptual boundaries between the phonemes. The peaks obtained did indeed fall near to the boundaries obtained from the identification experiment. Moreover, they were able to predict the shape of the discrimination function from the identification results, and found a correlation between the obtained and predicted discrimination functions.

Similar experiments were performed for vowels by Fry *et al.* (1962) but these did not yield results that supported the categorical perception hypothesis. This may have been because vowels are easier to discriminate than to identify. Fujisaki and Kawashima (1971) repeated these experiments with /i/ and /ɛ/ using stimuli which differed only by 10 Hz in the first formant and 20 Hz in the second formant, and obtained clear peaks in the discrimination function. Similar results were obtained by Stevens (1968) using /b/-vowel-/l/ stimuli.

Fujisaki and Kawashima (1971) proposed a model to account for the results of their experiments. A sound entering the auditory system is stored in a short-term auditory memory. An identification is made and the result is placed in phonetic memory. When a new sound is received judgments are made in terms of both their auditory images and their phonetic categorisations. The auditory images of vowels last longer than those of plosives, so vowels belonging to the same phonetic category are easier to discriminate by means of their auditory images.

Pisoni (1973) has obtained evidence which supports the notion of two memories. He measured the discrimination functions for both plosives and vowels using an AX paradigm. (The listener has to judge whether X is the same or different from A). He varied the interval between A and X. For vowels the accuracy of discrimination decreased, suggesting that auditory memory was involved, whereas for plosives the discrimination remained relatively stable.

2.4.6 Speech streaming

When a number of conversations are being carried on simultaneously it is usually possible to follow one, even though the total loudness of the others seems greater. This is known as the 'cocktail party effect'. Cherry (1953) has shown that if two recorded messages, spoken by the same speaker, are played to the same ear of a listener he has great difficulty in separating the messages.

Yet if they are presented from different directions, or to different ears, it is easy to follow one at the expense of the other. Also if the messages are spoken by different speakers they are easy to separate.

This suggests that there is some auditory process which groups together frequency components of the incoming sounds which share certain properties. Bregman (1978) has called this process 'streaming' and has shown that the properties which influence the grouping include rate, fundamental frequency and onset time. The suggestion is that speech from different voices will have different fundamental frequencies and different onset times, and so will be grouped separately.

Darwin and Bethell-Fox (1977) have shown that, if the fundamental frequency of synthetic speech is made to alternate rapidly between two values, two different voices are heard, whereas only one is heard when the fundamental frequency is steady or changes smoothly and slowly. Continuity of fundamental frequency groups events occurring at different times into the speech of a single speaker.

Fundamental frequency also groups the harmonics of speech sounds together. Broadbent and Ladefoged (1957) played separate formants of a synthetic sentence into the two ears of a listener. They reported that when the formants in the two ears had different fundamentals the listeners heard two voices, but when the formants had the same fundamental the listeners heard only one voice.

From the above experiments it appears that a common fundamental is a necessary condition for sounds to be grouped together as a stream. The question remains as to whether it is a sufficient condition. Darwin (1981) synthesised a number of vowels whose formants were excited at different fundamental frequencies. He found that they could be identified with just about the same accuracy as vowels having the same fundamental exciting all formants. He also found the same to be true for vowels whose formants had differing onset times. He also found no tendency for the formants of diphthongs synthesised with the same fundamental frequency to be grouped together with either binaural or dichotic modes of presentation. He did find, however, that using four widely spaced formants, a configuration of three of which produced /ru/ and another configuration of three of which produced /li/, listeners were more likely to hear the syllable corresponding to the common fundamental than the other one. A common fundamental, therefore, does not seem to be a sufficient condition for grouping frequency components into a stream.

2.4. Rhythm and intonation

The perceived rhythm of an utterance depends on the intervals between stressed syllables. Fry (1955) has investigated the features which give rise to stress. He measured the duration and intensity of the vowels in a number of words such as 'object' and 'permit' which may be used as a noun (with the stress on the first syllable) or as a verb (with the stress on the second). He found, as expected, that the syllable with the greatest intensity and the longest duration was perceived as stressed. He also produced synthesised versions of these words, and found that duration appeared to be a more important feature than intensity. Fry (1958) later repeated these experiments but included fundamental frequency. He found that the syllable with the higher fundamental was perceived as stressed.

It was mentioned in Section 2.1.4 that English is claimed to be a stress-timed language, i.e. the intervals between the onsets of successive stressed syllables are equal. These intervals are known as 'feet' by analogy with poetry. The notion of the 'isochronous foot' as a description of the rhythm of English was introduced by Classe (1939) and developed by Abercrombie (1965). Measurements by Uldall (1971) did not support this description completely, but did suggest a tendency towards isochrony. Darwin and Donovan (1980) have shown that, within a tone group, the perceived rhythm of speech is more regular than physical measurements of the speech would suggest. Between tone groups this perceived tendency towards isochrony is not found.

A tone group consists of one or more feet, and is the region of an utterance spanned by an intonation contour. It may be up to seven syllables long. Halliday (1963) calls the most prominent syllable in the tone group the 'tonic syllable'. The syllables preceding the tonic syllable are known as the 'pretonic' and the remainder as the 'tonic'. The pretonic is sometimes divided into the 'head', the region beginning with the first stressed syllable, and the 'prehead'. The tonic may also be subdivided into the 'nucleus'. the most prominent syllable, and the 'tail'. For a review see Crystal (1969).

According to Halliday (1963) the pitch movement on the tonic, in British English, can take one of five courses. These are known as the primary tones and are shown in Fig. 2.20. If the tone group contains two prominent syllables the pitch movement can take one of two complex primary tones.

A falling fundamental frequency (tone 1) is used for a statement, and a rising one (tone 2) for a question. A fall–rise may also be used for a question. A slight rise (tone 3) is used for a non-committal reply, and a rise-fall-rise (tone 4) for a hesitant or reserved reply. A rise-fall is used for an emphatic statement.

Ainsworth and Lindsay (1984, 1986) have synthesised the word 'yes' with a range of intonation contours including the ones described above. They found that the tones described by Halliday were selected in a semantic labelling experiment. They also performed a discrimination experiment with the tones, and obtained results which showed category boundary effects with intonation perception.

2.4.8 Theories of perception

Liberman *et al.* (1967) have argued for a 'motor theory' of speech perception. Speech sounds are identified by selecting the gesture needed to produce them oneself. This theory explains many of the experimental results which have been obtained in perception experiments. For example, with the human vocal apparatus it is possible to produce /b/ and /d/, but not any intermediary sounds because /b/ is produced with the lips and /d/ with the tongue. Any synthetic sound will be perceived as /b/ or /d/ depending on whether it could be most readily imitated by the lips or tongue. Hence categorical perception.

One factor with which the motor theory does not explicitly deal is normalisation. This could be introduced by some mechanism which normalised the input signal or by normalising the internal representation of the vocal tract to which the production rules are applied. In either case problems are posed for the motor theory (Fourcin, 1975). In order for a baby to imitate his mother's speech he must begin with a knowledge of the scaling factors involved. This is not impossible, but it does increase the complexity of the motor theory.

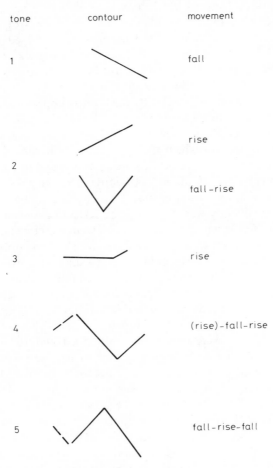

Fig. 2.20 *A five-tone system of intonation*

An alternative theory of speech perception is one based primarily on audition. Speech sounds, like any other sounds, enter the auditory system and are compared with other sounds which have been heard previously. The more frequently heard sounds are remembered and are associated with other sensations which occur at about the same time. Later sounds which are produced by one's own vocal apparatus are found to be similar to sounds which have previously been heard.

The motor theory would predict that those unable to speak would have difficulties in comprehending speech, but persons have been found without speech-production ability who have excellent comprehension (Fourcin and Lennenberg, 1973).

2.4.9 Spectrogram reading

Many of the acoustic features which have been shown to be relevant for the perception of vowels and consonants can be seen in spectrograms. It seems reasonable to suppose, therefore, that the message conveyed by the speech waveform could be obtained by visual inspection of the waveform. The first attempt to test this hypothesis was made at the Bell Laboratories (Potter, Kopp and Green, 1947). The intention was to provide a means of making speech visible so that it could be understood by the hearing impaired. It was reported that after some 90 hours of training the subjects could converse among themselves with a device for producing running spectrograms by speaking slowly and using the small vocabulary which they had learned. It took 15 – 20 min of practice to learn a new word. A deaf engineer who joined the group managed to acquire a vocabulary of about 800 words. Despite these achievements spectrograms are still not used a means of communicating with the deaf.

A more analytical study was performed by Klatt and Stevens (1973). They were interested in seeing whether spectrograms were a useful starting point for the automatic recognition of continuous speech. They attempted to produce phonetic transcriptions of utterances by making a single pass over each spectrogram, viewing it through a window which allowed only 300 ms to be visible at a time. They themselves were very experienced spectrogram users and acted as subjects. They found that they were only able to transcribe 33% of the phonetic segments correctly, but a further 40% were given a partially correct transcription. Of the rest, 17% were incorrectly transcribed and 10% were missed. Despite this relatively low score they were able to achieve a word recognition rate of 96% by means of a computerised search of a 200-word lexicon.

The ability to transcribe spectrograms has, however, been achieved by at least one person (Cole *et al.*, 1980). Victor Zue began studying spectrograms in 1971 and was tested in 1977 after about 2500 hours of spectrogram reading. At this time he was able to identify the existence of about 97% of the segments in both normal and anomalous (e.g. 'good tar hand zaim to come by') sentences. His labels agreed with a panel of phoneticians who listened to the sentences, between 81 and 86% depending on the scoring method employed.

The technique used by Zue was to segment the continuous speech into units corresponding approximately to phones. This is most easily done at the spectral discontinuities, for example between voiced and voiceless or nasal and non-nasal sounds. Placing boundaries between sequences of voiced sounds is difficult, but can be done approximately by looking for dips in first formant frequency or by knowing that a voiced portion of a spectrogram is too long for a single segment.

Once the segmentation was complete, the most easily identifiable segments, such as strong fricatives, were labelled. Other, less distinct segments were then identified making use of his knowledge of how co-articulation effects distort the patterns. He also made use of the constraints imposed by English phonology.

2.5 Language acquisition

Certain motor skills, such as walking, are acquired by almost everyone without any specific training, whereas others, such as piano playing, require many hours of learning and practice. Speech production, and presumably speech understanding, is acquired by all normal children merely by being exposed to the speech sounds produced by other human beings, though adults do tend to modify their speech when they talk to young children.

2.5.1 Child development

The development of speech skills by children has been summarised by Lennenberg (1967). At 12 weeks the child cries less than at 8 weeks and produces 'cooing' sounds which have a vowel-like character. At 20 weeks the 'cooing' sounds begin to be interspersed with more consonant-like sounds such as bilabial fricatives and nasals. By 6 months the coooing changes to a babbling resembling one syllable utterances such as /ma/, /mu/, /dɑ/, or /di/. In the next few months intonation patterns become distinct and the utterances appear to signal emphasis and emotions.

At the end of the first year, when walking is beginning, certain sound sequences, such as /mama/ or /dada/, occur more frequently. There are also signs that some words and simple commands are understood. By 18 months a definite vocabulary of between 3 and 50 words has developed. The words may include 'thank you' and 'come here' but there is no attempt to join lexical items into phrases such as 'come here dadda'. Understanding appears to be progressing rapidly. At two years the vocabulary is greater than 50 words and two-word phrases are produced. By 30 months these phrases consist of three- to five-word phrases and have a characteristic child grammar. The child appears to understand everything that is said to him.

After three years the vocabulary will have reached about 1000 words and most of the utterances are intelligible, even to strangers. The grammatical complexity is similar to colloquial adult language but mistakes still occur. By the age of four language is well established.

There is some evidence, however, that language devlopment, even at a phonetic level, continues until about 12 years of age. Simon and Fourcin (1978) showed that English-speaking adults use at least two cues, rising first formant frequency and first formant cut-back, in discriminating /g/ from /k/. Three-year old children use only the rising first formant, but with increase in age the other cue is progressively also used.

2.5.2 Second-language acquisition

Learning a second language, at least for adults and teenagers, appears to be more like learning to play a piano. One possible reason for this according to Lennenberg (1967) is that the brain undergoes a continuous process of maturation and is only in a state during which language may be acquired naturally during a 'critical period'. This period lasts from about the age of two until the onset of puberty.

The critical period is thought to be related to lateralisation in the brain. The left side of the brain, in normal right-handed subjects, is specialised for speech and language. Brain damage in the left side of the brain often interferes with these functions. In children language-related skills usually recover because they can be re-established in the right side of the brain, but this is not so for adults.

Seliger (1978) agrees about the critical period of Lennenberg for acquiring a perfect phonology of a second language, but he argues that there may be other critical periods for acquiring other aspects of a language such as syntax and semantics.

It was found in modern-language teaching that drill consisting of imitation and repetition of semantically discrete parts language was successful in making an adult learner do things which he could not do naturally. However, it was also found that the learner was unable to integrate these parts into the language he was learning. It seems that this process unwittingly makes use of the wrong side of the brain (Seliger, 1978).

The normal practice in second-language teaching is to teach pronunciation as well as comprehension at the same time. Studies by Postovsky (1974), Asher (1972) and Gary (1975) indicate that second-language skills are acquired more rapidly if oral practice is delayed by up to seven weeks at the start of an intensive course. The notion behind this is that speaking is difficult before a knowledge of the structure of the language has been acquired. The system is overloaded if speaking and comprehending are learned simultaneously, and mistakes occur. The experiments suggest that even speaking accuracy is better at the end of a course of instruction for a group receiving delayed oral practice compared with a conventionally taught control group.

In Section 2.5.1 it was seen that infants tend to understand many more words than they can utter in the early stages of language acquisition. This, together with these recent findings in second-language learning, tends to support an auditory rather than a motor theory of speech perception.

Chapter 3

Problems of automatic speech recognition

3.1 History of automatic speech recognition

The history of automatic speech recognition is a catalogue of the realisation of the problems involved in ASR. The first attempts to build machines which could recognise speech were made about 50 years ago. In those days when one telephone subscriber wished to call another, the caller spoke to the operator at the exchange and gave the number of the person he wished to contact. The operator then established the connection. Engineers realised that, if a machine could be built which could recognise spoken digits, the operator could be dispensed with, and a more efficient and less expensive system could be introduced. However, attempts to build machines which could cope with a wide variety of different voices failed, and an alternative solution was sought. The telephone dialling system was subsequently introduced, and this has changed very little, in principle, until the present day.

Later, in the 1950s, digital computers began to be employed in a variety of tasks. The data they processed was entered via a keyboard and the results of the computations were obtained via a printer or VDU. It was argued that speech, being the natural mode of communication between humans, should also be used in man–machine communication. This gave a new impetus to research in automatic speech recognition.

3.1.1 Pre-1960: The acoustic approach

Experience with the sound spectrograph had shown that different spoken words gave rise to different acoustic patterns. It was therefore believed that all the information required for recognising speech resided in the acoustic signal. This view was reinforced by contemporary work on speech synthesis, which was demonstrating that it was the patterns of formant movements which were utilised in the human perception of speech.

One of the first attempts to build a recogniser based on acoustic patterns was by Davis *et al.* (1952). They devised an apparatus for recognising spoken digits (Fig. 3.1). The speech signal was first split into two bands by passing it through a 1000 Hz high-pass filter and an 800 Hz low-pass filter. The number of zero crossings in each band was then counted, giving an approximate measure of the first and second formant frequencies. The first-formant range (200 – 800 Hz) was quantised into six 100 Hz steps, and the second formant range (500 – 2500 Hz) into five 500 Hz steps. A matrix with 30 elements representing the F1–F2 plane was thus established. For a given spoken digit the time during which the F1–F2 trajectory occupied each element was determined.

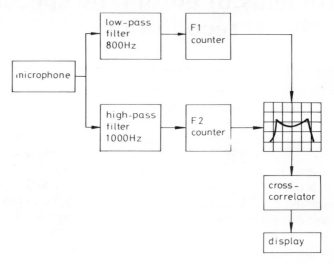

Fig. 3.1 *Schematic diagram of the speech recogniser of Davis, Biddulph and Balashek (1952)*

A reference pattern was formed for each digit. When a new digit was spoken, the pattern produced was cross-correlated with each of the stored reference patterns. This gave an approximate measure of the probability that a particular digit had been spoken, and so enabled the most likely digit to be chosen.

Provided that the reference patterns were adjusted for a particular speaker, it was reported that the digit spoken was correctly recognised about 98% of the time. With a new speaker, however, with no adjustments, the recognition score was often as low as 50%.

In a later development of a similar system, Dudley and Balashek (1958) built a machine which performed a spectral analysis of the speech signal with a bank of ten band-pass filters each 300 Hz wide. The output of the filter bank (see Section 4.1.4) was cross-correlated with stored patterns of spoken digits, and the best match was selected. This system also produced good results with the speaker who generated the patterns, but was less successful with other speakers. The problem with this system, and that of Davis *et al.*, was not that the acoustic analysis was inadequate, though it probably was too crude for a larger vocabulary than the ten digits, but that no attempt was made to deal with the inherent variability of speech produced by different speakers.

Another early attempt at automatic speech recognition was the so-called 'phonetic typewriter' of Olson and Belar (1956). This system also used a bank of filters, eight in this case, but also employed a 'compressor' which attempted to adjust the mean level of the signal to about the same intensity for both quiet and loud speakers. This reduced some of the variability. The outputs from the filter bank set relays every 40 ms if a threshold current had been exceeded. The output was thus a crude spectrogram, which was decoded as one of the ten syllables and thence into individual letters which actuated typewriter keys.

The machine was tested with sentences consisting of syllables of the set 'are,see,a,I,can,you,read,it,so,sir' in various permutations. With careful pronunciation it was claimed that an accuracy of 99% was again obtained. A later development of the system (Olson *et al.*, 1962) worked with isolated words and attempted to translate English and French into English, French, Spanish or German.

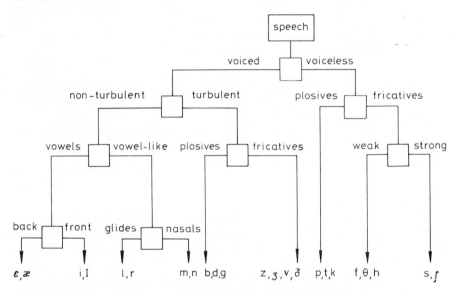

Fig. 3.2 *Principle of the speech recogniser of Wiren and Stubbs (1956)*

It is still a matter of debate as to whether words, syllables, phonemes or some other quantity should be used as the basic unit in speech recognition. There are tens of thousands of words in English and over a thousand syllables, but only about 50 phonemes. Phonemes can be represented by an even more efficient unit, the distinctive feature (Jacobson *et al.*, 1952). About 12 features are required for each phoneme, but each feature can take only one of two values. For example, /p/ which is a bilabial, voiceless plosive will be presented by the features [+labial, −vocalic, +consonantal, −continuant etc.], whereas /ɑ/ which is a back vowel will be represented by [+vocalic, −consonantal, +continuant, etc.].

A system based on distinctive-feature theory was developed by Wiren and Stubbs (1956). The principle of their recogniser is shown in Fig. 3.2. First the 'voiced' sounds were separated from the 'voiceless'. Then the 'voiceless' sounds were divided into fricatives and voiceless plosives. This principle of binary classification was repeated until a single phoneme was isolated. The decisions were based on the acoustic features present in the signal.

Fairly good results were again reported. For vowels in short words spoken by 21 speakers, an accuracy of 94% was claimed. One of the problems with this type of system, however, is that a classification error made at an early stage will propagate through the system.

3.1.2 1960–1968: The pattern-recognition approach

It was gradually realised that the simple matching of acoustic patterns was of limited utility. The acoustic patterns of a word spoken on different occasions differed in duration and intensity, and the same word spoken by different persons produced acoustic patterns which differed in frequency content as well. It was suggested that the recognition of spoken words might be analogous to the recognition of objects in optical patterns. Objects produce different patterns on the retina depending upon the distance and perspective from which they are viewed. The patterns produced by the same object, however, can be matched against each other if appropriate geometrical transformations are applied.

One of the first speech-recognition systems to deal successfully with a number of different speakers was that of Forgie and Forgie (1959). They noted that there is an inverse relationship between the pitch of the voice and the size of the vocal tract, so the fundamental frequency can be used to normalise formant frequencies. Their speech recogniser consisted of a 35-channel filter bank connected to a computer. The formant frequencies of an incoming speech signal were determined from the spectrum, and then normalised. From these measurements the vowels in /b/-vowel-/t/ words were recognised. Forgie and Forgie reported an accuracy of 93% for ten vowels spoken by each of 21 male and female speakers with no adjustment for speaker.

A similar speech recogniser was built by Denes and Mathews (1960), but this attempted to normalise other dimensions. In this case a 17-channel spectrum analyser formed the input to a computer. Spectrum patterns were formed from the spoken digits, and a number of utterances of each word were averaged and stored as reference patterns. Unknown utterances were recognised by comparing with the stored patterns by a cross-correlation process. The novel feature of this system was that provision was made for the duration of the patterns to be normalised before classification.

The system was tested with one female and six male speakers. An error rate of 6% was obtained with time normalisation, and 12% without it.

At about this time some interest was being taken in the recognition of periods of speech longer than isolated vowels and digits. This involves segmenting the speech stream into small units such as phonemes. This process is very difficult to perform satisfactorily because many speech sounds merge into their neighbours without an apparent physical boundary.

Hughes (1961) attempted to solve this problem by tracking the acoustic features using a scheme similar to that of Wiren and Stubbs (1956). Similar work was undertaken by Sakai and Doshita (1963) and Gold (1966). Sakai and Doshita used special-purpose electronic equipment rather than a general-purpose computer. They claimed that for Japanese monosyllables they obtained a recognition rate of 70% for consonants and 90% for vowels. Some adjustments had to be made for individual speakers.

Another method that was being investigated during this period was to attempt to recognise patterns by artificial neurones or adaptive threshold elements. The idea was to simulate the pattern-recognition abilities of humans by means of networks of elements which possessed similar properties to the neural elements of the brain. This technique was applied to speech recognition by Talbert *et al.* (1963) and Nelson *et al.* (1967).

3.1.3 1969–1976: The linguistic approach

Although the speech signal contains all the information necessary for a listener to understand a spoken message, the message will not be understood unless the speaker and the listener use the same language. The listener uses his knowledge of the language in order to decode the message. The early attempts at speech recognition mostly neglected this linguistic knowledge.

One of the exceptions was a system built and evaluated by Fry and Denes (1958). They tried to take advantage of the fact that the probability of one phoneme following another depends upon the identity of the first phoneme. Their system consisted of a spectrum analyser, a pattern matcher, and a store of the digram probabilities of some of the phonemes of English. The recognition set comprised four vowels and nine consonants. The overall performance of the system was not particularly good, but the use of the digram probabilities improved the word-recognition accuracy from 24% to 44%.

There are many sources of linguistic knowledge which may be used in speech recognisers in order to improve their performance. In the early 1970s it was felt that the use of such knowledge could be applied to solve the problem of recognising spoken sentences and longer periods of speech. In the USA a major effort, funded by the Advanced Research Projects Agency, was begun to tackle the problems encountered in continuous speech, as opposed to isolated word, recognition.

All speech recognisers obviously use acoustic knowledge, but in the systems that were developed at this time acoustic knowledge ceased to be of prime importance. In some top–down systems, for example the vocal data-management system (Barnett, 1973), the use of acoustic knowledge was heavily constrained.

The use of lexical knowledge is almost mandatory. It is necessary to know the structure of each word in the vocabulary. This may be expressed as a sequence of phones. In a system developed by Green and Ainsworth (1972) a 1000-word dictionary of the words of Basic English (Ogden, 1930) was included. This knowledge, together with an indication of the errors which were likely to occur in phoneme recognition, was used to decode the noisy phonetic string (i.e. a sequence of phonemes containing errors of insertion, deletion and substitution) from the acoustic processor into an acceptable word sequence.

The pronunciation of words and phonemes changes with their environment. For example, 'did' is normally pronounced /dɪd/ and 'you' is pronounced /ju/, but 'did you' is often pronounced /dɪdzə/. These systematic changes are known as phonological rules, and may be used to improve the performance of speech recognisers (Oshika *et al.*, 1974). Lea (1973) investigated how prosodic features can be extracted from fundamental-frequency contours, and energy and voicing parameters. He also made proposals as to how these quantities could be used in speech-recognition systems.

Tappert *et al.* (1974) developed a speech recogniser which made use of syntactic knowledge. The acoustic processor produced a noisy phonetic transcription. From this a tree structure was formed which represented possible matches of sequences of words with this string. Syntactic constraints were then used to choose the most likely path through the tree. In experiments reported by Tappert (1974), using a 250-word vocabulary and a finite-state grammar, a sentence-recognition accuracy of 54% was achieved, corresponding to a word-recognition rate of 91%. These results were obtained with a single speaker after training.

Other speech understanding systems used semantic knowledge. SPEECHLIS (Woods, 1975), for example, contained a network representing associations between words and concepts. In this system, if the word 'chemical' was recognised, the semantic processor would suggest that words such as 'analysis' and 'element' should be searched for in the speech data.

Finally the use of pragmatic knowledge was incorporated into a system called HEARSAY (Reddy *et al.*, 1973). In one application this system was connected to a chess-playing program. In this situation the state of the board could be used to determine the likely moves. From this knowledge the likely set of utterances could be deduced.

Most of the systems developed at this time used a different module for each source of linguistic knowledge. One of the problems encountered was how to integrate these different knowledge sources. Various organisations of the modules were investigated (see Section 4.3.3). The most successful, at least in terms of meeting the goals of the ARPA projects (Klatt, 1977), was found to be to integrate the different sources of knowledge into a network. This organisation was adopted in the Dragon system (Baker, 1975) and in HARPY (Lowerre, 1976).

Whilst the main thrust of research during this period was in the utilisation of linguistic knowledge, important developments were taking place in other areas. A speaker-independent digit recogniser (Sambur and Rabiner, 1975) was developed which self-normalised its acoustic parameters. With 25 male and 30 female speakers it was claimed that this system operated with an error rate of 2·7% in good acoustic conditions and 5·6% in a noisy computer room.

Perhaps even more important, a speech recogniser reached the market place. This was known as the Threshold Technology VIP-100 (Ackroyd, 1974), and was based on the analogue threshold logic system developed by Nelson *et al.* (1967). It had a vocabulary of 32 words or phrases and it was claimed that a recognition rate of 100% was attainable for 'phonetically dissimilar' words. The system had to be trained for each individual user.

3.1.4 1977–1980s: The pragmatic approach

During the last decade the work on automatic speech recognition has increased enormously. Not only has the activity in research laboratories accelerated, but also the number of speech recognisers that are commercially available has increased considerably. No particular theoretical approach underlies this work, although a number of more mathematically sophisticated algorithms have been applied.

The major advance that has taken place in isolated word recognisers is the use of dynamic-programming algorithms. This has enabled optimum non-linear timescale distortions to be introduced in the matching process (see Section 5.2.1). A dynamic-programming algorithm was used by Velichko and Zalgoruyko (1970) in a system which recognised 200 Russian words with a 5% error rate. The power of the method, however, was demonstrated by Sakoe and Chiba (1978) who optimised a number of dynamic-programming algorithms and achieved a 0·2% error rate for the Japanese digits with their best system.

A two-level dynamic-programming algorithm was investigated later by Sakoe (1979) as a means of recognising sequences of connected digits. The recognition accuracy was found to be 99·6%, and this algorithm was used as the basis of the NEC DP200 system. A more efficient algorithm for this purpose was developed by Bridle and Brown (1979). This was used in the LOGOS system (Section 6.2.1).

Other algorithms based on stochastic models were developed which gave encouraging results (Jelinek, 1976). A system based on hidden Markov modelling was developed by Levinson *et al.* (1983). This is described in Section 4.2.9. When this was trained on 1000 digits, spoken by 50 men and 50 women, it performed with a recognition accuracy of 96%. Several systems based on hidden Markov models have appeared on the market, including the Verbex 1800 and the Dragon System.

During this period work on linguistically based recognisers has continued. Klatt (1979) has proposed a system based on phonetic units in which all possible utterances are represented as paths through a network. De Mori and Laface (1980) have applied fuzzy-set algorithms to problems of phonetic labelling of continuous speech. The KEAL speech-understanding system has been developed for the French language (Mercier *et al.*, 1980), and Niemann *et al.* (1982) are developing a system for recognising continuous German speech.

3.2 Nature of the problem

This progress has been achieved by an increasing awareness of the problems of speech recognition and the application of various techniques to attempt to solve these problems. The basic problem is the paradox that speech consists of a continuous stream of sound with no obvious discontinuities at the boundaries between words, and yet speech is perceived as a sequence of words. The problem is to segment this stream of sounds into linguistic units such as words, or into sub-word units such as syllables or phonemes, and to identify these units. This problem is compounded by the wide variation of the acoustic signals which are accepted by human listeners as being examples of the same linguistic unit.

3.2.1 Recognition units
The first step in solving the recognition problem is to decide which units to recognise. Possible candidates are words, syllables, diphones, phonemes and distinctive features.

The word is a basic unit in speech recognition. The meaning of an utterance can only be deduced after the words of which it is composed have been recognised. The word is so basic that a whole class of speech recognisers, discrete utterance or isolated word recognisers, have been designed for the sole purpose of identifying spoken words. However, these devices require each word to be spoken in isolation. This is not the way in which sentences are normally produced.

One of the problems of employing the word as the recognition unit is the number of words in the language. This is of the order of 100 000. For recognition to take place some representation of each word needs to be stored. This implies that a large, though not impossible, amount of storage is required.

Another problem emerges as a result of the large number of words in the language. The representation of each word must be obtained from somewhere, and these representations are usually generated from speech produced by a human. The sheer amount of effort required to pronounce all of the words in the language is enormous.

Nevertherless there are a number of domains of man–machine interaction where the vocabulary can be restricted to a much smaller number of words. In these situations the word is often employed as the recognition unit.

Another problem encountered in using words as the recognition units is in determining where one word ends and the next begins. There is often no acoustic evidence of word boundaries. In fact, in the pronunciation of continuous speech co-articulation effects take place across word boundaries, altering the acoustic manifestation of each word, and obscuring the boundaries.

Instead of using words as the recognition units, smaller units such as the syllable may be considered. The syllable is attractive as it has a fixed structure. It consists of an initial consonant or consonant cluster, a medial vowel or diphthong, and a final consonant or consonant cluster, $C_i V C_f$. The vowel is obligatory but the consonants are optional. The intensity of every consonant is less than that of the vowels, so an algorithm can be devised for segmenting the speech stream into syllables. Problems arise, however, with strings of consonants as it is often difficult to decide whether a consonant is part of the final consonant cluster of the last syllable or part of the initial consonant cluster of the next syllable.

Table 3.1 *Syllable initial and syllable final consonant clusters occurring in British English*

Initial consonant clusters

/b/ /bl/ /br/ /d/ /dj/ /dw/ /g/ /gl/ /gr/ /gj/ /gw/
/p/ /pl/ /pr/ /pj/ /t/ /tr/ /tw/ /tj/ /kr/ /kw/ /kj/
/m/ /mj/ /n/ /nj/ /w/ /r/ /l/ /j/
/f/ /fr/ /fj/ /fl/ /θ/ /θj/ /θr/ /θw/
/s/ /sp/ /st/ /sk/ /sf/ /sm/ /sn/ /sl/ /sw/ /sj/
/spl/ /spr/ /spj/ /str/ /stj/ /skr/ /skj/ /skw/
/ʃ/ /ʃr/ /h/ /hj/
/v/ /vj/ /z/ /ʒ/ /ʧ/ /ʧj/ /ʤ/ /ð/

Final consonant clusters

/b/ /bd/ /bz/ /d/ /dθ/ /dz/ /dst/ /g/ /gz/
/p/ /pt/ /pθ/ /ps/ /t/ /tθ/ /k/ /kt/ /ks/ /kst/ /ksθ/ /ksθs/
/m/ /mp/ /mf/ /mθ/ /mz/ /md/ /mpts/
/n/ /nt/ /nʃ/ /ns/ /nθ/ /nd/ /nz/ /ndθ/ /nd/ /nst/ ndθs/ /ndz/
/ŋ/ /ŋk/ /ŋd/ /ŋz/ /ŋkθ/ /ŋks/ /ŋkt/
/l/ /lp/ /lt/ /lk/ /lf/ /lʃ/ /lm/ /ls/ /lθ/ /lb/ /ld/ /lv/ /lz/
/lpt/ /lkt/ /lks/ /lst/ /lfθ/ /lfθs/
/f/ /ft/ /fs/ /fθ/ /θ/ /θt/ /θs/
/s/ /sp/ /st/ /sk/ /ʃ/ /ʃt/
/v/ /vd/ /vz/ /z/ /zd/ /ð/ /ðd/ /ðz/ /ʧ/ /ʧt/ /ʤ/ /ʤd/ /ʒd/

Another advantage of employing the syllable as the recognition unit is that the numbers of initial and final consonant clusters are restricted in a given language. Those found in English are shown in Table 3.1. There are about 70 initial consonant clusters and about 100 final ones. If there are 12 vowels and 9 diphthongs (see Section 2.1.1), then there will be a maximum of 154 000 syllables. As not every consonant cluster is found in combination with every vowel and diphthong (clusters such as /lfθs/ in 'twelfths' are very rare and clusters such as /dst/ in 'hadst' are archaic), the actual number of syllables is very much less than this. It has been estimated that the number of syllables in English is about 10 000 (Moser, 1969).

A very significant reduction in the number of units can be achieved by employing demisyllables instead of syllables. A demisyllable consists of half a syllable, from the beginning of the syllable to the middle of the vowel, $C_i V$, or from the middle of the vowel to the end of the syllable, VC_f. A syllable can be segmented into demisyllables by splitting it at the point of maximum intensity. If there are 70 initial consonant clusters and 12 vowels, there will be 840 initial demisyllables, and if there are 100 final consonant clusters and 12 vowels, there will be 1200 final demisyllables. The total number of demisyllables is thus of the order of 2000.

A large number of consonant clusters are formed by preceding an initial cluster by an affix, usually a fricative, or by adding an affix to a final cluster. The most common way of forming the plural of a noun in English is to add /s/. Fricatives can easily be segmented from the rest of the cluster as they have a random structure as opposed to the periodic structure of voiced sounds. It has been suggested by Fujimura (1976) that useful units for recognition are de-misyllables and affixes.

If such affixes are removed from the consonant clusters shown in Table 3.1, the number of initial clusters decreases to about 50 and the number of final clusters to about 80, making about 600 initial demisyllables and about 960 final ones. The number of recognition units is thus reduced to about 1600. The number of demisyllables in other languages may be similar as Dettweiler and Hess (1985) found that 1630 demisyllables were needed for synthesising German.

Another possible recognition unit is the diphone. These have been found useful as the unit for speech synthesis (Dixon and Maxey, 1968) but the number required, 1000 – 2000, is similar to that of demisyllables. The problem of segmentation, deciding where one ends and the next begins, however, is much more difficult with diphones than demisyllables.

The other possible recognition unit is the phoneme. The advantage of the phoneme is the small number. There are only 40 – 60 phonemes. However, phonemes have a number of contextual variations known as allophones, and there are some 100 – 200 of these. Even so the small numbers involved make the phoneme, or phone (Section 2.1.2), an attractive recognition unit.

The problem with phoneme recognition units is segmentation. The acoustic manifestation of each phoneme is modified by co-articulation effects. Except in certain cases where a voiced phoneme is followed by a voiceless one, or vice versa, it is impossible to tell where one phoneme ends and the next begins.

3.2.2 Variability
There are a great number of factors which cause variability in speech. These include the speaker, the context, the environment (extraneous sound and vibration) and the transducer employed.

The speech signal is very dependent on the physical characteristics of the speaker. The size of the vocal tract increases during childhood, and this gives rise to different formant frequencies for the productions of the same vowel at different ages. The vocal tracts of men are, on average, about 30% longer than those of women. This again gives rise to different formant frequencies.

The fundamental frequencies of speech sounds uttered by women are about an octave higher than those of men, and those of childen are even higher. Speech waveforms thus show great variability with both the age and sex of the speaker.

People from different parts of the country and different social and economic backgrounds speak with different dialects. This involves the substitution of one phoneme for another in certain words (e.g. 'bath' is pronounced /bɑθ/ in the south and /bæθ/ in the north), and changes in the rhythm and intonation of the utterance.

This variability is even greater with people speaking a second language. The competence with which it is spoken depends on the motivation, intelligence, and perceptual and motor skills of the speaker, and also on the age at which the second language was learned. Often the prosody and phoneme set of the first language are transferred to the second language, giving rise to a foreign accent. This introduces a great deal of extra variability.

Even the same speaker uttering the same words on different occasions shows some variability. Generally people tend to speak more precisely on more formal occasions and less precisely in familiar surroundings amongst acquaintances of long standing. This poses a problem for machine recognition of speech. When a person first encounters a speech recogniser he will be in an unfamiliar situation and so will speak to it in a formal manner. However, it is on this occasion that the machine will be trained to recognise his voice. At subsequent meetings he will be more relaxed, so he will address the machine in a less formal manner. This may cause the recognition accuracy to decline.

The production of each word still exhibits variability, even when the familiar situation has been reached. Co-articulation effects cause each word to be pronounced differently depending upon context. The articulators anticipate the beginning of the next word whilst the end of the present word is still being produced. Words are also pronounced differently depending on their position in the sentence and their degree of stress.

Another source of variability is speaking rate. The tempo of speech varies widely depending upon the situation, the topic being discussed, and the emotional state of the speaker. Unfortunately the durations of all sounds in fast speech are not reduced proportionally compared with their durations in slow speech. In fast speech pauses are eliminated and steady sounds, such as vowels, are compressed whilst the durations of some consonants remain almost constant.

The amplitude of speech signals depends on the amount of vocal effort employed and the distance of the microphone from the mouth. The vocal effort affects the shape of the glottal pulse, and thus the intensity and frequency of the speech signal. The distance beteen the microphone and the mouth can vary with a hand-held microphone, but can be kept approximately constant by means of a microphone on a boom attached to a headset.

There are three main factors which cause distortion of the speech signal. Firstly, there is the background sound, which is many circumstances is an uncontrollable variable. If this sound is constant and always present, such as the hum from the cooling fan in a computer, the level can be measured and its effect subtracted from the speech signals. If the background noise level is variable it is important that the signal/noise should be made as high as possible. This is usually achieved by holding the microphone close to the mouth, and using a directional, noise-cancelling microphone.

Secondly, the speech signal may be distorted by reverberation. As well as the direct path from the mouth to the microphone, there will be other acoustic paths due to reflections from objects such as walls and furniture. These paths will be longer than the direct path, and so will add delayed and distorted versions of the signal to the original. Reverberation could be eliminated by working in an anechoic chamber, but this is not usually practical. It should be noted that the introduction of extra items of equipment or the presence of other bodies may distort the signal.

Thirdly, the transducer used for converting the acoustic signal into an electrical signal may introduce distortion. If the same microphone is always used this will not cause variability. If different microphones are used, however, as will be the case when a speech recogniser is used via the telephone system, the characteristics of the different microphones and their associated transmission channels, will introduce variability.

Finally, the parametrisation of the speech signal (see Section 4.1.1) will introduce variability. The signal will be sampled at discrete time intervals, so the values obtained will depend upon the synchronisation between the start of the signal and the sampling clock. These values, upon which all subsequent processing is performed, will thus exhibit some variation even if the same speech signals are reprocessed (Smith *et al.*, 1986)

3.3 Ambiguity

A further problem for a speech recogniser is that of ambiguity. This becomes important when the system is required to perform some action as a result of the signals which it has received.

3.3.1 Homophones
There are a number of words which have different spellings, and meanings, but which, nevertheless, sound alike. For example, consider the words 'to', 'too' and 'two'. In applications such as a speech-driven word processor homophones present problems. These problems cannot be resolved at the acoustic or phonetic levels. Recourse must be had to higher levels of linguistic analysis.

3.3.2 Overlapping classes
Most vowels can be identified from the frequencies of their first and second formant frequencies. However, if a plot is made of F1 versus F2 for a large

number of vowels spoken by a variety of speakers, the points plotted do not form separate areas (Peterson and Barney, 1952). For example, the vowel /ɑ/ spoken by one person may have identical formant frequencies to a vowel /ɔ/ spoken by another. This poses a problem for a speaker-independent speech recogniser which is required to determine the meaning of a sentence such as 'The ship left the part/port'.

It has been demonstrated that people resolve this ambiguity by taking note of the formant frequency range in the rest of the sentence. Ladefoged and Broadbent (1960) showed that the perception of a word could be changed from /bɪt/ to /bet/ by shifting the second formant frequency in the precursor sentence 'Please say what the next word is'.

3.3.3 Word boundaries

Another problem of ambiguity concerns the location of word boundaries. Occasionally a sequence of phonemes occurs which has one interpretation with the word boundary inserted at one location, and another meaning with it inserted at another location. This may involve shifting the boundary by a single phoneme, such as /greɪteɪp/ which may be interpreted as 'grey tape' or 'great ape', or it may mean moving the word boundary by a whole syllable, for example /lɑɪthɑuskipə/ may mean 'light housekeeper' or 'lighthouse keeper'.

3.3.4 Syntactic ambiguity

Even if the phoneme sequence can be recognised and correctly segmented into words, there may still be ambiguity of meaning until all the words are grouped into appropriate syntactic units. For example, the sentence 'The boy jumped over the stream with the fish' could mean that the boy with the fish jumped over the stream, or it could mean that the stream in which the fish was swimming was jumped over by the boy. Correct interpretation of sentences of this type is often only possible if the context of the sentence is available.

3.3.5 Semantic ambiguity

Consider the sentence 'The council decided to subsidise the port'. This sentence has been unambiguously segmented into words, and there is only one possible syntactic interpretation. Yet the sentence could either mean that the council had decided to reduce the harbour dues, or it could mean that the council was going to provide inexpensive after-dinner beverages! It is impossible for the correct meaning of sentences of this type to be determined by humans unless the context of the sentence is known. Machines that deal with only one utterance at a time will not be able to cope with this problem.

Chapter 4

Techniques for processing speech

4.1 Signal processing

A number of techniques have been developed for analysing signals. Detailed treatments are given by Rabiner and Gold (1975) and Oppenheim and Schafer (1975). Some of those techniques which have been found useful for processing speech signals are described below.

4.1.1 Analogue-to-digital conversion

The process of analogue-to-digital conversion is the production of a set of discrete data points which represent a continuous waveform with sufficient accuracy for the original waveform to be reproduced (Fig. 4.1). The reverse process of producing a continuous waveform from discrete data points is known as digital-to-analogue conversion.

There are two parameters in this conversion process: the frequency at which the waveform should be sampled, and the accuracy (number of bits) with which the samples should be represented. The sampling theorem, due to Nyquist, states that in order not to lose information a waveform should be sampled at a frequency of at least twice the highest frequency in the waveform. The usual way to guarantee that a waveform contains no energy above a given frequency is to pass the waveform through a low-pass filter which has a cut-off at that frequency. Such a filter used for this purpose prior to A–D conversion is known as an anti-aliasing filter.

In automatic speech recognition the only frequencies of interest are those in the range of human hearing. This range is usually stated to be 20 Hz to 20 kHz, although the upper limit reduces progressively with the age of the listener. Thus an anti-aliasing filter of 20 kHz followed by an A–D convertor sampling at 40 kHz is more than adequate. In fact most of the energy of speech sounds lies below 5 kHz, although some fricative sounds, such as /s/, have energies up to 10 kHz. For this reason a low-pass filter with a cut-off frequency of 5 kHz followed by an A–D convertor sampling at 10 kHz is often used to obtain a digital representation of speech sounds. The second parameter which should be considered in A–D conversion is the accuracy with which the waveform should be sampled. The intensity range of human hearing, from the threshold of hearing to the threshold of pain, is about 120 dB. If this range is represented by n bits:

$$\text{Range in dB} = 20 \log_{10} 2^n = 120 \tag{4.1}$$

Hence,

$$n = 120/20 \log_{10} 2 = 20 \text{ bits} \tag{4.2}$$

So the accuracy required to cover the whole range of human hearing is about 20 bits.

Speech signals, however, span a range of about 70 dB. Hence,

$$n = 70/20 \log_{10} 2 = 12 \text{ bits} \tag{4.3}$$

Thus in order to obtain a digital representation of a waveform which covers the whole range of human hearing a sampling frequency of 40 kHz with an accuracy of 20 bits should be employed. For speech signals, a sampling frequency of 10 kHz and an accuracy of 12 bits is usually adequate.

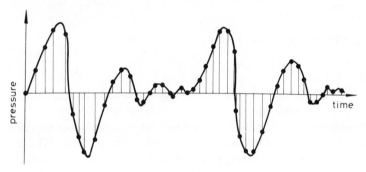

Fig. 4.1   *Digitisation of a speech waveform*

It is interesting to note that a frequency range of 3·4 kHz has been found to be sufficient for telephone communication. Digital telephone systems use a sampling frequency of 8 kHz and an accuracy of 8 bits. This accuracy is sufficient if a logarithmic convertor is employed before sampling in order to restrict the intensity range.

4.1.2 Short-term frequency analysis
It was seen in Chapter 2 that the information conveyed by speech sounds is encoded in the frequencies of vibration of the resulting waveforms. The standard method of analysing the frequency content of a waveform is by Fourier analysis. Fourier's theorem states that any periodic signal can be synthesised by adding together an infinite series of harmonics:

$$f(t) = a_0 + \sum_{n=1}^{\infty} a_n \sin(nwt + \phi_n) \tag{4.4}$$

where a_n are the coefficients and ϕ_n are the phase angles. The angular frequency is $w = 2\pi/T$, where T is the period of the signal. This can be rewritten in terms of the sum of two infinite series:

$$f(t) = a_0 + \sum_{n=1}^{\infty} (a_n \cos nwt + b_n \sin nwt) \tag{4.5}$$

It can then be shown that the coefficients can be calculated from

$$a_0 = 1/2\pi \int_{-T/2}^{T/2} f(t)\,dt \tag{4.6}$$

$$a_n = 1/\pi \int_{-T/2}^{T/2} f(t) \cos(nwt)\,dt \tag{4.7}$$

$$b_n = 1/\pi \int_{-T/2}^{T/2} f(t) \sin(nwt)\,dt \tag{4.8}$$

These equations can be rewritten in terms of complex numbers. They then have the form

$$f(t) = \sum_{n=-\infty}^{\infty} c_n e^{inwt} \quad \text{where} \quad c_n = \int_{-T/2}^{T/2} f(t)e^{-inwt}\,dt \tag{4.9}$$

If the period of the signal covers an infinite range, these become

$$f(t) = \int_{-\infty}^{\infty} F(w)e^{iwt}\,dw \quad \text{and} \quad F(w) = \int_{-\infty}^{\infty} f(t)e^{-iwt}\,dt \tag{4.10}$$

where $F(w)$ is known as the Fourier transform of $f(t)$. Alternatively, if $f(t)$ is a signal $F(w)$ is its spectrum.

With speech signals $f(t)$ is not known for all time, and because of the changing nature of speech signals it would not help very much if it was. What is required in speech analysis is a running spectrum, with time as an independent variable, where the calculation is performed on weighted past values of the signal.

It can be shown that this can be achieved by viewing the waveform through a window, or weighing function $h(t)$. A Fourier transformable signal results if $h(t)$ is taken as the response of a low-pass filter (Fig. 4.2). The operation is:

$$F(w, t) = \int_{-\infty}^{t} f(k)h(t - k)e^{-iwk}\,dk \tag{4.11}$$

where k is a dummy integration variable.

It can be shown that this can be implemented in practice by a band-pass filter followed by a rectifier and a low-pass filter (Flanagan, 1965). Sweeping the centre of the band pass filter through the frequency range of the signal causes the spectrum of the signal to appear at the output of the low-pass filter (Fig. 4.3). This method of signal analysis is employed in the sound spectrograph, or sonagraph; the instrument used to obtain the sonagrams shown in Chapter 2.

The bandwidth of the band-pass filter determines the type of analysis obtained. A narrow-band filter (often 45 Hz) produces good frequency resolution, whereas a wide-band filter (300 Hz) produces good time resolution.

4.1.3 Discrete Fourier transform

If a waveform has been digitised a frequency analysis can be performed by means of a technique known as the discrete Fourier transform or DFT. Suppose that the waveform is represented by $x(n)$ where $n = 0, 1, \ldots, N - 1$. The relationship is then

$$x(n) = 1/N \sum_{n=1}^{N-1} X(r)e^{2\pi irn/N} \qquad (4.12)$$

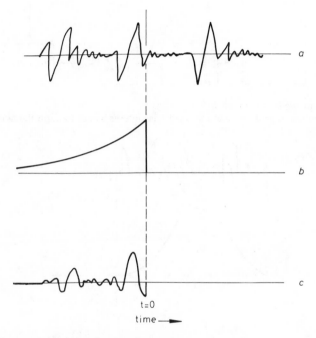

Fig. 4.2 *Short-term analysis of a speech waveform*
  a Speech signal
  b Weighting function
  c Fourier transformable signal which is assumed to be zero in the future and which decays to zero in the past

where

$$X(r) = \sum_{n=1}^{N-1} x(n)e^{-2\pi irn/N} \qquad (4.13)$$

is the discrete Fourier transform.

These equations can be simplified by writing $W = e^{-2\pi i/N}$, so that

$$x(n) = 1/N \sum_{n=1}^{N-1} X(r)W^{-rn}; \qquad X(r) = \sum_{n=1}^{N-1} x(n)W^{rn} \qquad (4.14)$$

A speech signal is not exactly periodic, but it does not change much from period to period. If the start of each period could be determined, it would be possible to take N equal to the number of points in a glottal period and perform pitch-synchronous DFT. This is sometimes done, but it is difficult to locate the beginning of each period in practice.

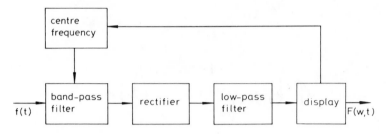

Fig. 4.3 *Principle of the sonagraph*
The centre frequency of the band-pass filter is swept through the audio range

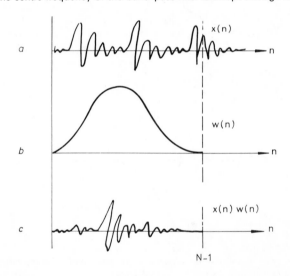

Fig. 4.4 *Windowing of a speech waveform by means of a raised cosine function*
a Speech waveform
b Raised cosine
c Windowed waveform

Normally an arbitrary sequence of N points is taken. This is equivalent to multiplying the signal by a rectangular window which is zero everywhere except during the period to be analysed. This introduces discontinuities at the edges which distort the spectrum by adding spurious high frequency components.

A better technique is to multiply the signal by a smooth window function. Triangular, Gaussian and cosine-shaped windows have been used, but the effects are much the same. A common technique is to use a raised cosine or

Hanning window. The equation is

$$w(n) = 1/2(1 - \cos(2\pi n/N - 1))), \quad n = 0, 1, \ldots, N - 1 \quad (4.15)$$

The effect of this is shown in Fig. 4.4

The equations given above express the DFT in terms of complex numbers. Usually in speech analysis it is the energy at each harmonic number (or frequency) which is required. This is given by the power spectrum

$$p_r = 10 \log_{10}(a_r^2 + b_r^2) \, \text{decibels} \quad (4.16)$$

where a_r and b_r are the real and imaginary components of the complex spectrum.

The human ear is relatively insensitive to the phase of the incoming signal. Consequently the phase spectrum

$$\phi_r = \tan^{-1}(b_r/a_r) \quad (4.17)$$

is not usually required.

It will be seen that in order to compute an N-point DFT approximately N^2 operations are required where each operation consists of a complex multiplication and add. With speech signals it has been found that an analysis period of about 20–30 ms is required. With a sampling frequency of 10 kHz this corresponds to about 250 points. In order to obtain a single spectrum over 60 000 operations must be performed. As speech is a time-varying signal it is necessary to compute the DFT every 10 ms. Hence more than six million operations must be performed in order to analyse one second of speech.

A more computationally efficient algorithm for computing the DTF has been discovered by Cooley and Tukey (1965). In this algorithm the operations are divided into two sets, then each set is itself subdivided. This process is repeated until each set contains only one term. This technique required only $N \log N$ operations; a considerable saving for $N = 250$. In order to utilise this technique, however, it is necessary for N to be a power of 2. In the above example a value of 256 would be appropriate.

This algorithm is known as the fast Fourier transform or FFT.

4.1.4 Filter bank

In the past the amount of computation involved in calculating the DFT was too great for processing useful quantities of speech in a reasonable time, so an alternative method of estimating the power spectrum was employed. The speech signal was passed through a set of band-pass filters and the amount of energy in each channel was measured. Waveforms representing the energy in each passband as a function of time were then digitised and stored in the computer for further processing.

This method of analysis is derived from a technique developed for transmitting speech at reduced bandwidth. The equipment for performing this task is known as a channel vocoder (Dudley, 1939).

A vocoder consists of two parts: an analyser and a synthesiser. The analyser contains a set of overlapping band-pass filters. The speech signal is passed through these filters and the energy in each is measured. An estimate of the fundamental frequency is also obtained together with a signal indicating at each instant whether the input speech signal is voiced or voiceless.

The synthesiser consists of an identical bank of filters. These are excited by periodic pulses of fundamental frequency obtained from the analyser. If the original speech was voiceless the pulses are replaced by a random-noice signal. A set of amplitude modulators, controlled by signals from the analysing filters, shapes the spectrum of the output of the synthesiser.

It has been found in practice that between 10 and 20 band-pass filters are required for intelligible speech to be reproduced. The values of the centre frequencies and bandwidths of a 19-channel vocoder described by Holmes (1980) are shown in Table 4.1. With such a vocoder speech can be transmitted through a channel with a capacity of 2·4 kbits/s.

Table 4.1   *Filter specifications for a 19-channel vocoder (Holmes, 1980)*

Channel number	Centre frequency, Hz	Bandwidth, Hz
1	240	120
2	360	120
3	480	120
4	600	120
5	720	120
6	840	120
7	1000	150
8	1150	150
9	1300	150
10	1450	150
11	1600	150
12	1800	200
13	2000	200
14	2200	200
15	2400	200
16	2700	200
17	3000	300
18	3300	300
19	3700	500

The analyser of a vocoder has often been used as a fast and convenient method of obtaining power spectra of speech signals for subsequent analysis in a speech recogniser.

4.1.5 Autocorrelation analysis

Speech waveforms repeat approximately, but not exactly, during each glottal cycle. One way of estimating the repetition rate, or fundamental frequency, is by examining the autocorrelation function. This function is obtained by multiplying a signal $x(n)$ by a delayed version of itself:

$$\phi(k) = \sum_{n=1}^{N} x(n)x(n + k) \qquad (4.18)$$

where k is the delay.

In practice with samples waveforms it is necessary to restrict the range of summation to N points. This is especially necessary for speech signals because of their non-stationary nature. This does not matter, however, if the waveform is windowed as explained in Section 4.1.3.

For a periodic function, $\phi(k)$ will exhibit a number of peaks corresponding to the periodicity and multiples of it. For a speech signal the peaks will occur at the excitation frequency and its harmonics.

The autocorrelation function can be used for estimating the fundamental frequency of a waveform of voiced speech. It can also be used to determine whether a speech signal is voiced or voiceless. A periodic waveform will exhibit peaks in the autocorrelation function, whereas a random waveform will produce a flat autocorrelation function.

4.1.6 Cepstral processing

The technique of cepstral processing is used for separating the excitation signal of a speech wave from the filter part. This makes it easier to estimate both the frequency of the excitation and the frequencies of the formants.

The speech waveform $s(t)$ is the convolution of the excitation signal $e(t)$ and the transfer function of the vocal tract and lip radiation (eqn. 2.1). First the DFT of the speech waveform is computed:

$$F[s(f)] = F(e(f)]F(h(f) \quad \text{where} \quad h(f) = v(f)*1(f) \qquad (4.19)$$

or

$$S = E \times H \qquad (4.20)$$

Then the logarithm of the transform is obtained:

$$\log S = \log E + \log H \qquad (4.21)$$

Finally the inverse DFT of the transform is computed:

$$F^{-1}(\log S) = F^{-1}(\log E) + F^{-1}(\log H) \qquad (4.22)$$

The result, the spectrum of the log of the frequency spectrum, is called the 'cepstrum' (an anagram of spectrum). The horizontal axis of a cepstrum, which has the dimension of time, is called 'quefrency' (an anagram of frequency) (Noll, 1964).

The result of this complex transformation is to increase the effects of the fundamental relative to other frequencies present in the original waveform.

Consequently the cepstrum will contain a large peak corresponding to the fundamental. The position of this peak can be used to obtain an estimate of the fundamental frequency.

If this peak is removed by cutting off the cepstrum from below this quefrency, the ripple on a spectrum caused by the effects of the fundamental can be reduced. Taking a DFT of the cepstrum with the fundamental removed results in a smoothed spectrum. The formants are usually easier to identify in such a smoothed spectrum.

4.1.7 Linear prediction analysis

All of the foregoing techniques for analysing speech signals, make no assumptions about how the speech was produced. Linear prediction analysis, however, assumes that the signal being analysed was produced by passing an excitation signal through a suitable filter. As this is a good model of the production of many speech sounds (see Section 2.2.3), linear prediction analysis is a particularly appropriate technique for speech signal analysis.

Suppose that a waveform $x(t)$ has been digitised. If $x(t)$ was continuous, then the current sample $x(n)$ can be predicted from the previous sample:

$$x(n) = a_1 x(n - 1) + e(n) \tag{4.23}$$

where the coefficient a_1 is chosen such that the error signal $e(n)$ is small. If the waveform is only changing slowly a_1 will be constant for a few samples.

This idea can obviously be extended by predicting $x(n)$ from the last p samples:

$$x(n) = a_1 x(n - 1) + a_2 x(n - 2) + \cdots$$
$$+ a_p x(n - p) + e(n) \tag{4.24}$$

or

$$x(n) = e(n) + \sum_{k=1}^{p} a_k x(n - k) \tag{4.25}$$

The waveform can thus be predicted from the coefficients a_k and the signal $e(n)$. The problem is how to estimate the values of the coefficients. This can be achieved by minimising the mean square error

$$M = e(n)^2 = \left[x(n) - \sum_{k=1}^{p} a_k x(n - k) \right]^2 \tag{4.26}$$

In order to minimise this, differentiate with respect to each of the coefficients and set the result equal to zero:

$$dM/da_j = -2 \sum_{n} x(n - j) \left[x(n) - \sum_{k=1}^{p} a_k x(n - k) \right] = 0, \tag{4.27}$$

or

$$\sum_{k=1}^{p} a_k \sum_{n} x(n-j)x(n-k) = \sum_{n} x(n)x(n-j) \qquad (4.28)$$

where $j = 1, 2, \ldots, p$.

This is a set of p simultaneous linear equations for p unknowns, $a_1 \ldots a_p$. This set of equations can be solved by standard methods. However, these involve matrix inversion and require a good deal of computation. More efficient methods have been devised (Markel and Gray, 1976). The main techniques are the autocorrelation and covariance methods.

The different methods exist because the range of summation has not been defined. In the autocorrelation method the range is assumed to be infinite. Of course, the signal cannot be known over an infinite range, so as usual it is windowed as discussed in Section 4.1.3. The result is a signal which is known within the window and zero everywhere else.

With these assumptions it is possible to simplify the above equation in terms of the autocorrelation function:

$$R(m) = \sum_{n} x(n)x(n+m) \qquad (4.29)$$

This leads to a set of simultaneous equations which can be solved by the Durbin–Levinson algorithm (Levinson, 1947).

In the covariance method the range of summation is taken as finite, from $n = h$ to $n = h + n$. The above equations then become

$$\sum_{k=1}^{p} a_k \sum_{n=h}^{h+N-1} x(n-j)x(n-k) = \sum_{n=h}^{h+N-1} x(n)x(n-j), \qquad (4.30)$$

$$j = 1, \ldots, p$$

These equations can be solved by the Cholesky decomposition algorithm. Details are given by Witten (1982) which includes both this and the autocorrelation algorithm as Pascal procedures. Fortran subroutines are given by Markel and Gray (1976).

Other methods for computing linear prediction coefficients based on lattice structures have been devised. These are particularly suitable for synthesis applications (Linggard, 1985).

It can be shown that linear prediction analysis is equivalent to decomposing the speech signal into source and filter components which are equivalent, for non-nasalised voiced sounds, to the source-filter model of speech production described in Section 2.2.4. Moreover, the error signal can be related to the source and the coefficients can be used to determine the poles of the complex filter.

The linear prediction equation can be used to synthesise the speech signal from the linear prediction coefficients. It has been found that about ten coefficients are required in order to reproduce acceptable quality speech.

4.2 Pattern processing

The result of a signal-processing operation is usually to produce the values of a set of features. These features may be spectral or linear prediction coefficients, or they may be acoustic or other parameters such as formant frequencies or amplitudes. If there are n such features, each set of values may be represented by a point, or vector, in an n-dimensional space. Each vector may be regarded as a pattern.

The purpose of this Section is to explore the techniques available for processing these patterns. The object of this processing is usually to determine the category of each pattern.

4.2.1 Pattern classifiers

A pattern classifier is a system for estimating the class to which a pattern belongs. If the patterns are thought of as points in an n-dimensional space, there are three methods by which the patterns may be classified. These have been described by Levinson (1985) as geometric, topological and probabalistic. These methods are illustrated for a 2-dimensional space in Fig. 4.5.

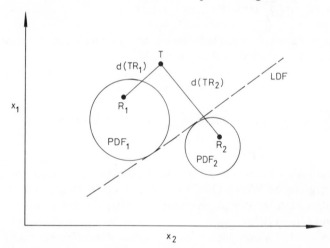

Fig. 4.5 *Geometric, topological and probabilistic classification of patterns in a two-dimensional space*
R_1 and R_2 are the reference patterns and T is a test pattern. In a geometric classification T belongs to the same class as R_1 because it lies on the same side of the linear discriminant function LDF. In a topological classification T belongs to the same class as R_1 if the distance $d(TR_1)$ is less than the distance $d(TR_2)$. In a probabilistic classification T belongs to the same class as R_1 if the probability density function PDF_1 at T is greater than PDF_2

In the geometric methods the space is divided into regions by means of boundaries. The positions of these boundaries are chosen so that the patterns of one class fall one side of the boundary and those of other classes fall on the other side. In an n-dimensional space the boundaries of the regions will be surfaces. Often, for ease of computation, hyperplanes are employed as the decision surfaces.

In the topological methods each class is represented by one, or more, points in the hyperspace. An unknown pattern is classified by measuring the distance between the point representing this unknown pattern and the points representing the classes. The point having the least distance is taken to represent the class of the unknown pattern.

Both of these methods depend only on the co-ordinates and the local topology of the pattern space. Methods which depend only on distance methods are often called non-parametric classifiers (Patrick, 1972).

In the probabalistic methods a probability density function (PDF) is defined for each pattern in the space. The probability that an unknown pattern belongs to a certain class is estimated from the PDFs by choosing the class for which the value of its PDF is greatest at the point in space occupied by the pattern. As the PDFs are usually characterised by parameters such as the positions and spreads of the peaks of these functions, probabalistic methods are sometimes called parametric classifiers (Patrick, 1972).

4.2.2 Correlation

One of the earliest techniques to be used for pattern recognition was correlation. Each class, k, of patterns is represented by a vector

$$Y_k = (y_{1k}, y_{2k}, \ldots, y_{nk})$$

These patterns are sometimes known as templates.

An unknown pattern is represented by the feature vector

$$X = (x_1, x_2, \ldots, x_n)$$

The correlation between the unknown pattern and each of the templates is computed by evaluating

$$C(X, Y_k) = \sum_{i=1}^{N} x_i y_{ik} \tag{4.31}$$

The class to which the unknown pattern belongs is estimated by computing $C(X, Y_k)$ for each k and then choosing k for which this function is maximum.

The correlation technique suffers from certain disadvantages. For example, in letter recognition a pattern which actually represents an 'O' may correlate as highly with the 'Q' template as with the 'O' template.

4.2.3 Discriminant analysis

Another pattern-recognition technique is discriminant analysis. The patterns are represented as points in an n-dimensional space. Hypersurfaces are then constructed in this hyperspace in such a way that they separate the patterns into classes. These hypersurfaces are known as discriminant functions.

In certain instances, especially when the classes are well separated, the discriminant functions may be represented by hyperplanes, the equations of which take the form

$$\sum_{i=1}^{N} w_{ik}x_i + w_0 = 0 \qquad (4.32)$$

where the x_i are the variables and the w_{ik} are coefficients.

The determination of the coefficients, w_{ik}, is known as discriminant analysis, and the hyperplanes represented by eqn. 4.32 are called linear discriminant functions. Note that the form of these equations is similar to those in correlation analysis.

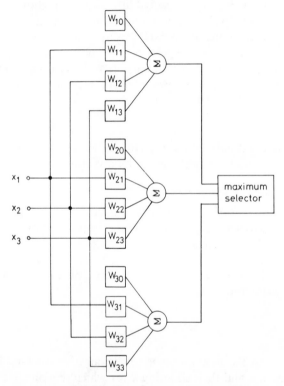

Fig. 4.6 *Pattern classifying machine based on linear discriminant analysis*

The structure of a pattern-classifying machine based on linear discriminant analysis is shown in Fig. 4.6. The coefficients or weights, w_{ik}, are often determined iteratively by training the machine on a set of patterns whose classes are known. The weights are adjusted after each pattern in the training set is recognised in such a way that the probability of a correct response is increased. Machines of this type are known as perceptrons (Rosenblatt, 1961) or learning machines (Nilsson, 1965).

Often it may not be possible to separate two classes of patterns by means of a hyperplane. However, it may be possible to separate them by means of two or more hyperplanes. An example is shown in Fig. 4.7. The surfaces which separate the classes are then known as piece-wise linear discriminants. A learning machine based on piece-wise linear discrimination is shown in Fig. 4.8.

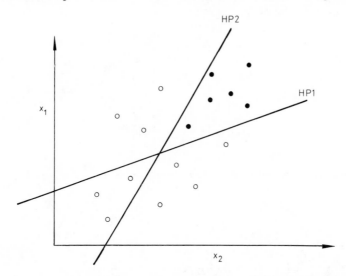

Fig. 4.7 *The two classes of patterns (O and ●) cannot be separated by a single hyperplane, but they can by the two hyperplanes HP1 and HP2*

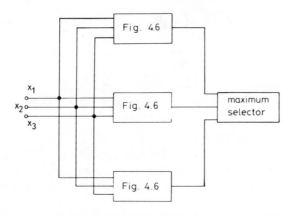

Fig. 4.8 *A piecewise linear pattern classifying machine*

Alternatively it may be possible to separate the classes by means of non-linear discriminants such as quadratic hypersurfaces. A machine based on quadratic discriminants is shown in Fig. 4.9.

By using the outputs of one learning machine as the inputs of another (Fig. 4.10), a multilayered learning machine is produced. The recognition capabilities of these machines are interesting, as such a system is, in theory, able to generalise classes of patterns. However, until recently no satisfactory method had been devised of automatically adjusting the weights in order to train the machine to exhibit specific types of behaviour. Current research on multi-layered perceptrons (Rumelhart *et al.*, 1986), however, shows that weight-adjustment algorithms can be devised.

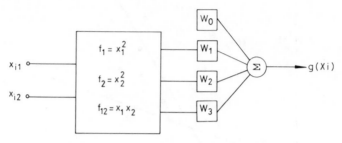

Fig. 4.9 *A quadratic discriminator for the patterns $X_i(x_{1i}, x_{2i})$*

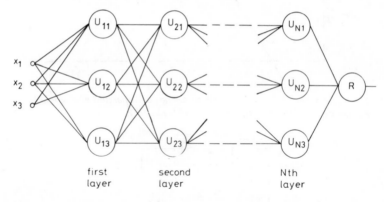

first
layer

second
layer

Nth
layer

Fig. 4.10 *Multilayered learning machine*
Each unit U_{ij} consists of a set of adjustable weights and a threshold element.

4.2.4 Nearest-neighbour classifiers

Instead of classifying a pattern by determining the region in pattern space in which it falls, a pattern may be classified by measuring its distance from known members of each class. The theory of such classifiers is discussed by Cover and Hart (1967).

In order to determine the relative proximity of patterns some distance measure is required. In general the distance between two points, X and Y, in an n-dimensional space is given by

$$D_r(X, Y) = \left(\sum_{i=1}^{N} |x_i - y_i|^r \right)^{1/r} \tag{4.33}$$

In the case where $r = 2$, this defines the familiar Euclidean distance

$$D_2(X,\ Y)\left(\sum_{i=1}^{N}(x_i - y_i)^2\right)^{1/2} \tag{4.34}$$

The case where $r = 1$ is known as the 'city block' distance

$$D_1(X,\ Y)\ =\ \sum_{i=1}^{N}|x_i - y_i| \tag{4.35}$$

This is the sum of the distances between the two points projected onto the axes.

In a nearest-neighbour, or minimum-distance, classifier the system is trained by means of a representative pattern from each class. These are known as the pattern templates. An unknown pattern is classified by calculating the distance from each of the templates and then choosing the class of the template nearest to it.

As the square root of a number increases monotonically with its value the distance measure given in eqn. 4.34 is often simplified to

$$D(X,\ Y)\ =\ \sum_{i=1}^{N}(x_i - y_i)^2 \tag{4.36}$$

thus saving computation. This is known as the 'square' distance between the patterns. Moore (1986) has shown that this distance measure can be derived as a consequence of assuming Gaussian statistics.

If eqn. 4.36 is expanded it becomes

$$D(X,\ Y)\ =\ \sum_{i=1}^{N}x_i^2 + \sum_{i=1}^{N}y_i^2 - 2\sum_{i=1}^{N}x_i y_i \tag{4.37}$$

The term $\sum x_i^2$ is common to all of the templates and so may be neglected in a nearest neighbour classifier. The term $\sum y_i^2$ is constant for each template, and so may be replaced by $-2w_k$. Hence a new distance measure between the unknown pattern and the template k may be defined as:

$$D'(X,\ Y_k)\ =\ w_k + \sum_{i=1}^{N}x_i y_{ik} \tag{4.38}$$

Note that as the sign has been changed it is the maximum value of this function which is required. Note also that this has a similar form to the linear discriminant eqn. 4.32, and the correlation eqn. 4.31.

When the features of a pattern have a physical interpretation, geometric distance measures are probably appropriate, but when the features are mathematical constructs, such as linear prediction coefficients, more sophisticated distance measures need to be employed. Itakura (1975) suggests that for linear-prediction-coefficient representations of signals an estimate of the distortion introduced by the model is a suitable distance measure. He shows that the logarithm of the prediction residuals (the mean-square values of the prediction errors) is an appropriate estimate.

4.2.5 Probabilistic classifiers

The probability that a pattern belongs to a class k given the observation O_i may be written as $Pr(H_k/O_i)$. It is not possible to measure this directly but Bayes' theorem states that

$$Pr(H_k/O_i) \ = \ Pr(O_i/H_k) \cdot Pr(H_k)/Pr(O_i) \tag{4.39}$$

where $Pr(O_i/H_k)$ is the probability of the observation given that the pattern belongs to class k, $Pr(H_k)$ is the *a priori* probability of class k, and $Pr(O_i)$ is the *a priori* probability of the observation.

$Pr(O_i/H_k)$ may be estimated from a large number of patterns belonging to class k. It is the probability density function in the n-space for class k. If all of the patterns are equally likely to occur $Pr(H_k)$ will be a constant.

If there are several observations suggesting that the pattern belongs to class k, and these observations are independent, eqn. 4.39 may be written:

$$Pr(H_k/O_i) \ = \ \text{const.} \ (Pr(O_1/k) \cdot Pr(O_2/k) \ldots /(Pr(O_1) \cdot Pr(O_2) \ldots)) \tag{4.40}$$

The observations will consist of the values of the features which define the pattern space. It is thus possible to define a function such as

$$g(k) \ = \ \text{const.} \ (Pr(x_1/k) \cdot Pr(x_2/k) \ldots) \tag{4.41}$$

which is proportional to the probability that a pattern belongs to class k given that it consists of the feature vector $(x_1, x_2, \ldots, x_n)$. By taking logarithms this can be written as

$$g'(k) \ = \ \sum_{i=1}^{N} \log \ (Pr(x_i/k)) + \text{const.} \tag{4.42}$$

In other words the likelihood of a pattern belonging to class k given the feature vector X can be interpreted as the sum of the logarithms of the probabilities of the features.

4.2.6 Multidimensional scaling

The extension of Bayes' theorem only applies if the different observations are independent of each other. This is certainly not the case when spectral coefficients, for example, are used as the features of the patterns.

One technique for reducing the dimensions of a set of patterns to a lesser number of underlying orthogonal dimensions is multidimensional scaling (Kruskal, 1964). Related techniques are principal component analysis and factor analysis (Harmon, 1967).

The points representing the patterns in an n-dimensional hyperspace are mapped into a hyperspace of lower dimensionality in such a way that correlations between the dimensions are eliminated. For example, if there is no variation among the patterns in one dimension (the value of one feature is the same for all patterns), this dimension may be eliminated without the separations between the patterns being affected. Similarly if the patterns are perfectly correlated in two of the dimensions, one of these may be eliminated without any loss of discrimination.

Multidimensional scaling works by mapping of all the points into a new dimension constructed so that it accounts for the maximum amount of variance between the patterns. A new dimension is then added, orthogonal to this, which accounts for the maximum amount of the remaining variance. This process is repeated until the remaining variance is negligible.

Similar techniques can be used to construct a hyperspace when all that is known is the distances between the patterns (Kruskal, 1964). These techniques have been applied to vowel sounds by Pols *et al.* (1969), who found interesting similarities between the physical space, constructed from dimensions represented by an 18-channel third-octave filter bank, and the perceptual space, derived from subjective judgments of the differences between vowels. They found that the dimensions obtained in both cases were related to the first and second formant frequencies.

4.2.7 Dynamic programming

The patterns considered so far have consisted of a set of features which could be represented by a point or vector in an n-dimensional space. Certain patterns, including speech, are better represented by a sequence of such vectors. Such patterns, however, can be classified by similar methods to those described in the foregoing Sections. For example, a nearest-neighbour classifier could calculate the distance between corresponding pairs of vectors in the input pattern and the templates:

$$D_k = \sum_{j=1}^{m} \sum_{i=1}^{n} (x_{ij} - y_{ijk})^2 \qquad (4.43)$$

where both pattern and templates consist of a sequence of m vectors each of which contains n features. The class to which the pattern belongs is determined by choosing the template having the minimum distance from the pattern.

A difficulty arises, however, when the patterns and templates consist of sequences with different numbers of vectors. Linear time normalisation may be applied if this is appropriate, but a technique for dealing with non-linear normalisation known as dynamic programming (Bellman, 1957), has been developed.

The first step in a dynamic programming algorithm is to compute the distance matrix between each vector of the input pattern and each vector of the templates. This is done using one of the distance measures described in Section 4.2.4, such as

$$d_k(i, j) = \sum_{q=1}^{p} [x_i(q) - y_{jk}(q)]^2 \qquad (4.44)$$

where $x_i(q)$ are the features of the unknown pattern consisting of n p-dimensional vectors and $y_{jk}(q)$ are the elements of the kth template which consists of m p-dimensional vectors.

The next step is to compute the cumulative distance matrix. This is calculated from the local distance matrix by means of the recurrence relation

$$g(i, j) = \min [g(i - 1, j) + d(i, j), g(i - 1, j - 1)$$

$$+ kd(i, j), g(i, j - 1) + d(i, j)] \tag{4.45}$$

This is an example of a Viterbi algorithm (Viterbi, 1967).

In other words, the cumulative distance is the sum of the distance between two vectors and the minimum of the cumulative distances of the neighbouring elements in the matrix. The optimum value of the weight k is not known (Moore, 1981), but it is usually taken as 1 or 2.

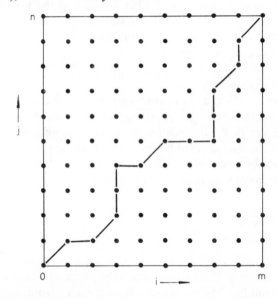

Fig. 4.11   *Time-registration path*
Dynamic programming enables the optimum mapping of the sequence of n vectors along the ordinate onto the m vectors along the abscissa by tracking backwards from the point (m, n) of the cumulative distance matrix to the origin

The total cumulative distance, $G(m, n)$, is usually normalised to compensate for the advantage of short sequence patterns:

$$G(m, n) = g(m, n)/(m + n) \tag{4.46}$$

where m is the number of vectors in the template and n is the number of vectors in the unknown pattern.

Dynamic programming, as well as providing a method for computing the minimum distance between two patterns of different sizes, also provides a method for optimally mapping one pattern on to another. This mapping is formed by tracing through the cumulative distance matrix from the point (*m, n*) to the origin, selecting at each point the neighbouring cell having the smallest distance (Fig. 4.11).

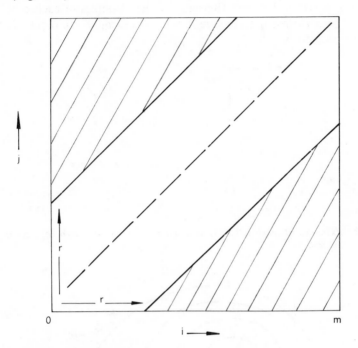

Fig. 4.12 *Warping window length r*
The time registration path is constrained to lie within this window

If the sequence of vectors occurs along the dimension of time, this mapping is known as the time-registration path. In order to optimally match one pattern against the other, time must be expanded or compressed according to the shape of this curve. This is often known as dynamic time warping.

In practice the amount of computation allowed must usually be limited. This limitation may be introduced into the algorithm by means of a warping window as shown in Fig. 4.12.

A number of dynamic programming algorithms have been investigated by Sakoe and Chiba (1978). The one described above is a symmetric algorithm, but asymmetric algorithms are also possible. Some of the possibilities are shown diagrammatically in Fig. 4.13.

4.2.8 Cluster analysis
Dynamic programming enables the similarity between an unknown pattern and each of a number of templates to be measured. The technique works well if each template is a good representation of its class. However, this is unlikely to be the

case if just one example of a pattern from each class is obtained. The method can be improved by having several examples of each class, but only at the expense of increased computation, and dynamic programming is a computationally expensive technique. Alternatively the examples of each class can be combined by a clustering technique, but many examples are required for clustering methods to be reliable.

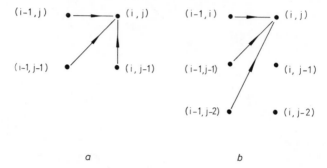

Fig. 4.13   *Examples of local paths (a) symmetric DP algorithms, and (b) asymmetric DP algorithms*

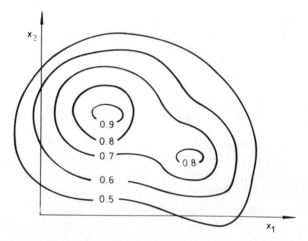

Fig. 4.14   *Contour map of a probability density function PDF (x₁, x₂) which has two peaks*

The patterns in a cluster can either be combined to form an average pattern or a representative pattern can be chosen from the centre of each cluster. It is not known whether an average pattern is typical, so the latter method is preferred.

One way of finding a typical pattern to represent each cluster is to estimate the probability density function for each class of pattern. A typical probability density function for a 2-dimensional space is shown in Fig. 4.14. It often happens, as shown here, that there are a number of peaks in this function. In order to recognise any pattern in this class, a number of template patterns are required for each cluster.

In a practical system the number of templates for each class is limited by the amount of computation that can be performed. In this case it is important to choose patterns near the most important peaks in the probability density function. One way of doing this is by means of the 'maximindist' technique (Bachelor and Wilkins, 1969; Patrick, 1972).

First the set of probability density functions is estimated from a set of sample patterns (Sebestyen, 1962; Sebestyen and Edie, 1966; Mucciardi and Gose, 1971; Fukunaga, 1972). The point with the highest PDF estimate is taken as the first template of the class.

Next the function:

$$H(Y) = \text{PDF}(Y)[D_2(B_1, Y)] \tag{4.47}$$

is computed for each point, where $\text{PDF}(Y)$ is the PDF estimate at the point Y and $D_2(B_1, y)$ is the Euclidean distance between the first template, B_1, and the point Y. The point having the greatest value of $H(Y)$ is taken as the second template.

If further templates are required for that class, the function

$$H(Y) = \text{PDF}(Y) \min_{i=1,2} [D_2(B_i, Y)] \tag{4.48}$$

is computed, where $D_2(B_i, Y)$ is the smallest distance between the point Y and the nearest template. Again the point having the greatest value of $H(Y)$ is chosen as the next template.

This process is repeated until a sufficient number of templates have been found.

With patterns consisting of sequences of feature vectors of varying lengths it is useful to employ a dynamic programming algorithm to compute the distances between the patterns (Rabiner *et al.*, 1979).

4.2.9 Hidden Markov models

Instead of using cluster analysis to obtain a number of examples of each class of pattern, an alternative approach is to build a generative model of each class. One way of doing this is by means of a Markov model. A Markov model is one in which the next state depends only on the present state and the transition probabilities, a_{ij}, to the next possible states (Fig. 4.15).

In a hidden Markov model (HMM) the states of the model cannot be observed directly. Only the output symbols of the state can be observed, and these are determined by another probability function. The probability that the output of the state q_j is the pattern represented by the symbol s_k is given by b_{jk}. To complete the model the initial state distribution is given by the vector $V = (v_1, v_2, \ldots, v_N)$ where v_1 is the probability that the model is initially in state 1, etc. The model is thus defined by $M(V, A, B)$ where $A = [a_{ij}]$ is the matrix of transition probabilities and $B = [b_{jk}]$ is the matrix of output probabilities.

Given a set of models $M_i(V_i, A_i, B_i)$, i.e. the hypotheses of Section 4.2.5, and a sequence of observations $O = (O_1 O_2 O_3 \ldots O_T)$ of an unknown pattern, the problem of recognition becomes that of estimating which model is most likely to produce this sequence of observations. This can be done by means of dynamic programming algorithms (Moore, 1986). One way is by means of the 'forward–backward' algorithm of Baum (1972). A function $\alpha_t(i)$ is defined as $\text{prob}(O_1 O_2 \ldots O_t$ and q_i at $T/M)$, that is as the probability of the observations $(O_1, O_2 \ldots O_t)$ and that the model is in state q_i at time t. Then at time $t = 1$, $\alpha_1(i) = V_i b_i(O_1)$ where $b_i(O_1)$ means b_{ik} if O_1 is equivalent to symbol s_k. There is then a recursive formula for the forward probabilities

$$\alpha_{T+1}(J) = \left[\sum_{i=1}^{N} \alpha_t(i) a_{ij} \right] b_j(O_{t+1}), \qquad 1 < t < T - 1 \qquad (4.49)$$

Similarly another function $\beta_t(j) = \text{prob}(O_{t+1} O_{t+2} \ldots O_T$ at t and $M)$ can be defined leading to another recursion for the backward probabilities:

$$\beta_t(i) = \sum_{j=1}^{N} a_{ij} b_j(O_{t+1}) \beta_{t+1}(j), \qquad T - 1 > t > 1. \qquad (4.50)$$

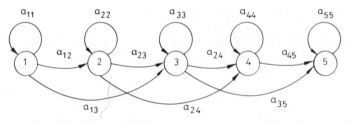

Fig. 4.15   *One form of a Markov model*
The possible transitions from one state to another are shown. Each state has a vector of patterns associated with it. At each instant in time the vector may change to the next state, to the next but one state, or it may remain in the same state. The transition probabilities a_{ij} can thus model timescale variability

The two functions can be combined to compute the probability of the observations, given the model according to

$$P = \text{prob}(O/M) = \sum_{i=1}^{N} \sum_{j=1}^{N} \alpha_t(i) a_{ij} b_j(O_{t+1}) \beta_{t+1}(j) \qquad (4.51)$$

for any t such that $1 < t < T - 1$ (Baum 1972).

In order to compute this function the parameters of the model, V, A and B, must be estimated. These may be found by starting with randomly selected values, then using re-estimation formulas in conjunction with observations of patterns whose classes are known. The re-estimation formulas are:

$$\bar{a}_{ij} = \left[\sum_{t=1}^{T-1} \alpha_t(i) a_{ij} b_j(O_{t+1}(j)) \right] \bigg/ \sum_{t=1}^{T-1} \alpha_t(i) \beta_{t+1}(i) \qquad (4.52)$$

and

$$\bar{b}_{jk} = \left[\sum_{t=w_k} \alpha_t(j)\beta_t(j) \right] \bigg/ \sum_{t=1}^{T-1} \alpha_t(j)\beta_t(j) \qquad (4.53)$$

Finally the new values of the initial state probabilities may be obtained from

$$V_i = \alpha_i(i)\beta_1(i)P \qquad (4.54)$$

These formulas are based on a theorem of Baum and Sell (1968) and are usually referred to as the Baum–Welch algorithm.

There are other ways of estimating the parameters of the models. These are discussed, together with the above method, by Levinson *et al.* (1983). In particular they show that the estimation problem is an instance of constrained optimisation, and so may be solved, at least formally, by the classical method of Lagrange multipliers. Levinson *et al.* also discuss the practical problems of computer implementation.

4.2.10 Adaptive networks

When using HMMs it is necessary to choose *a priori* the number of states of each model. An alternative approach is to build an adaptive network of processors and allow the structure of the models to develop during training.

One form of such a network is known as a Boltzmann machine (Hinton *et al.*, 1984). It consists of a distributed network of processors which are connected to their neighbours. Each processor is a 2-state unit which may be either on or off. The state of each unit at a given time depends on the signals it receives from its neighbours. These signals also depend upon the strengths of the connections between the units.

Some of the units are connected to the external world, whereas others only have internal connections to other units. The 'knowledge' embodied in the system resides in the strengths of the connections.

The external units are connectd to an analyser. A particular input then sets these units into a pattern of on and off states. This will cause the states of the other units to change, but the configuration of states that ensues will depend not only on the current input but also on the previous states of the units and the strengths of the connections. In order for such a network to function as a pattern classifier the strengths of the connections need to be adjusted so that patterns belonging to the same class tend to induce the same configuration of states in the network.

A crucial problem which must be solved in such a machine is how to develop a suitable algorithm for adjusting the strengths of the connections. Hinton *et al.* (1984) have discovered a way of doing this which depends only on the states of the local units.

The energy of such a system can be defined as

$$E = -\sum w_{ij}s_is_j + \sum \theta_is_i \qquad (4.55)$$

where w_{ij} is the weight, or strength, of the connection between units i and j, s_i is 1 if the unit is on and 0 otherwise, and θ_i is a threshold.

If each unit switches to its local minimum energy state, the system as a whole will settle into a local energy minimum (Hopfield, 1982). This may not be the global minimum. One way of ensuring that the system reaches the global minimum is to allow occasional jumps to higher energy levels. The parameter controlling the frequency of these jumps can be thought of as analogous to temperature in physical systems. The Boltzmann machine then becomes mathematically equivalent to a thermodynamic system. It can be shown that, if P_a is the probability of the system having energy E_a and P_b is the probability of the system having energy E_b, the relative probability of these global states follows a Boltzmann distribution

$$P_a/P_b = e^{-(E_a - E_b)/T} \tag{4.56}$$

where T is the temperature.

The weight adjustment problem can be solved in the Boltzmann machine formulation (Hinton *et al.*, 1984). It can be shown that the weights should be adjusted by

$$dw_{ij} = a(p_{ij} - p'_{ij}) \tag{4.57}$$

where p_{ij} is the probability of two units being on when the states of the external units are set by a stimulus and p'_{ij} is the probability when the external units are running freely. The adjustments of the weights in a learning situation thus only depend upon the local states in the network.

4.2.11 Syntactic pattern recognition

The pattern classifiers discussed so far are based on a decision-theoretic approach. A set of measurements is made and this is used to estimate the probability that a given pattern occurred. In the syntactic approach each pattern is expressed as a sequence of sub-patterns which are represented by symbols. The pattern is recognised by means of the relationships between these symbols analogously to the way that sequences of words are recognised as sentences by applying the syntax of language. The recognition of each pattern is made by parsing the string of symbols according to a set of syntax rules.

In order to parse the symbols a formal grammar is defined. Grammars of various degrees of complexity are outlined in Section 4.3.2.5. A grammar usually takes the form

$$G = (V_N, V_T, P, S) \tag{4.58}$$

where V_N are non-terminal symbols, V_T are terminal symbols, P are the production rules, and S is the start symbol.

Each non-terminal symbol represents one of the sub-patterns. Syntactic pattern recognition can only be performed if the pattern can be segmented into sub-patterns, but at present no general technique for performing this segmentation has been discovered.

The terminal symbols represent the sub-patterns which occur at the end of the strings.

Sequences of sub-patterns which are legal in the grammar are known as productions. These are specified by strings of symbols. For example

$$A \longrightarrow (B, C)D$$

means that A may be the string BD or the string CD.

The strings may be recursive. If another production rule is

$$B \longrightarrow B(D, E)$$

then the strings BD and BE are legal. So also are BDD, BED, BEE, and BDE etc.

A pattern is recognised by segmenting it into sub-patterns and then replacing the sub-patterns by symbols. The string of symbols is then parsed in order to determine whether it could be generated by the production rules. Algorithms for performing this operation are discussed by Fu (1982).

4.3 Knowledge processing

In recent years the use of knowledge sources in computer-based problem solving has become explicit. Programs of this type are known as expert systems. They are currently being investigated as a means of solving problems in automatic speech recognition. The usefulness of linguistic knowledge in speech recognisers, however, has been acknowledged for many years and other, less explicit, ways of processing this knowledge were developed before the advent of expert systems.

4.3.1 Intelligent knowledge-based systems
Classical computer systems consist of two parts: the data and the program. Expert systems, on the other hand, have a three-part structure: data, knowledge base, and control. This is illustrated in Fig. 4.16.

The knowledge base contains rules for manipulating the data. These rules can be obtained from human experts via the man–machine interface. The control structure decides how to use the knowledge available in the base. It produces interferences from this knowledge.

There are many ways in which knowledge can be represented in a computer: sets, lists, networks, frames, and production rules have been used.

A set is simply a collection of items. If a system is required to identify nouns at some stage in the analysis of a sentence, a set of articles would obviously be useful. Likewise a set of prepositions would be helpful for identifying phrases.

In a list the order in which the items are stored is important. The vocabulary of a recognition system is often stored as a list of words arranged in alphabetical order. This facilitates searches, and enables questions such as 'Are there any words in the vocabulary beginning with /b/ and ending with /t/?' to be answered efficiently.

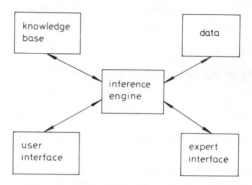

Fig. 4.16 *Structure of an expert system*

A network consists of nodes and branches. It can be useful for storing syntactical knowledge as it can be used to show which part of speech can follow which. Paths through the network can be used to check allowable word orders.

A frame is a more complex data structure. It was introduced by Minsky (1975) and has been used in many artificial intelligence (AI) systems. It is composed of nodes and the relationships between nodes. There are two kinds of nodes: one type contains fixed information about a situation, and another type (terminal node) contains information which may be altered to fit a particular case. Each terminal node contains an estimate of the value of the feature it concerns together with admissible limits for this value, and a 'slot' into which a real value may be stored if found. If sufficient slots are successfully filled, a match is deemed to have occurred and the situation described by the frame is assumed to exist in the real world. The frame may contain information about what to do if this occurs. Alternatively, or in addition, the frame may contain information about what to do if the frame is not matched.

Knowledge may also be represented by a set of production rules (Davis and King, 1977). A production rule has the form:

IF ⟨condition⟩ THEN ⟨action⟩

where ⟨condition⟩ can represent a logical relation (such as energy in the 100–200 Hz region is greater than 30 dB and the second formant frequency is rising). ⟨Action⟩ means a change in the current state of the problem (such as the last phoneme is nasalised) which constitutes a step towards the solution of the problem.

Expert systems make it possible to decompose complex expertise into a large number of relatively simple rules. Each rule represents only a small portion of knowledge, yet the total can approach that of a human expert. In fact, it is possible that human experts use a production-rule scheme when they are solving a problem by reasoning. Some verbatim accounts confirm this view. Expert systems have been built for medical diagnosis, mineral prospecting and computer vision as well as for automatic speech recognition.

4.3.2 Knowledge sources
There are a number of sources of linguistic knowledge which may be used in speech-recognition systems. These may be specified as acoustic–phonetic, lexical, phonological, prosodic, syntactic, semantic and pragmatic.

4.3.2.1 Acoustic–phonetic knowledge
Acoustic–phonetic knowledge expresses the relationship between the acoustic data and a phonetic transcription of the spoken utterance. In a typical system the speech waveform is first transformed by one of the signal-processing techniques into a set of acoustic features. The most common techniques are the filter bank and the FFT, which give a representation of the power spectrum as a function of time. From the spectrum the formant parameters may be estimated. The formant parameters may also be estimated by linear prediction analysis or cepstral processing.

The traditional approach to deriving a phonetic representation from the acoustic features is by segmentation and labelling. This is usually achieved by first classifying the sound at each time slice (every 10 or 20 ms) into a small number of acoustic categories. These may be steady–periodic, changing–periodic, noise, silence etc. Adjacent slices of the same type are then coalesced into phonemic-sized segments (Fig. 4.17). The features present in each segment are used to categorise the segments with phoneme-like labels. A steady–periodic segment with a low first formant frequency and a high second formant frequency, for example, might be labelled as an /i/ vowel. Sometimes a number of consecutive segments represent a phoneme unit. A period of silence followed by a noise burst followed by a changing–periodic segment may be produced by a voiceless plosive. The mechanism for categorising the segments may be a set of production rules.

This process, segmentation and labelling, is very error prone. The acoustic manifestations of phonemes are subject to co-articulation effects which are very context dependent. Consequently a number of techniques have been developed for representing the possible errors in the output.

The simplest technique is to provide an error set: a matrix of the most likely inputs of the acoustic processor which may produce a given output. This error set can be obtained experimentally.

The disadvantage of this technique is that it only uses the acoustic data to estimate the most likely phoneme; the alternatives are predetermined. A better representation is the phonetic lattice. This is a two-dimensional structure giving the n most likely phonemes at each point in time. The usefulness of this representation can be increased by calculating a confidence measure for each output. This can be derived from the goodness of fit of each set of acoustic features to some ideal description.

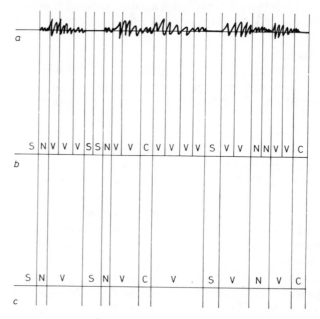

Fig. 4.17   *An example of the segmentation of continuous speech*
Each interval of the waveform *a* is first classified as steady periodic (V), changing periodic (C), noice (N) or silence (S) as shown in *b*. Similarly labelled adjacent segments are then coalesced into phone sized units as shown in *c*

It has been argued that the process of segmentation and labelling is inappropriate as an interface between acoustic data and linguistic knowledge (Green and Wood, 1984). Acoustic data consist of physical quantities whereas linguistic knowledge is symbolic. A new form of data structure is required which matches these incompatible knowledge sources. Green and Wood have proposed a 'speech sketch' for this structure, analogous to the 'primal sketch' employed in computer vision (Marr, 1982). The speech sketch is matched to the symbolic representation by a frame structure.

Another approach is to hypothesise the sequence of phonetic elements and then use a synthesis-by-rule algorithm to predict the acoustic data (Paliwal and Rao, 1982; Bridle and Ralls, 1985). Alternative hypotheses can be evaluated, comparing their predictions with the actual acoustic data. One advantage of this approach is that the characteristics of the speaker can be built (or trained) into the speech-by-rule system to cope with the multi-speaker problem.

4.3.2.2 Lexical knowledge
The task of the other sources of knowledge is to transform the phonetic string

or lattice into an acceptable sequence of words. A lexicon is obviously useful in this process. Word candidates from the lexicon can be matched against parts of the lattice, some measure of the goodness of fit can be derived, and the word sequences which best explain the acoustic data can be chosen.

In order to perform this operation, the lexicon must contain all the words in the vocabulary of the recogniser together with a phonemic or phonetic representation. An indication of the parts of speech which each word can be used as is also useful, as this knowledge can be helpful to the syntactic processor.

Many words may be spoken in different ways depending upon their usage. For example, the word 'the' is normally pronounced /ðə/ but it is pronounced /ði/ is the next word begins with a vowel (or if the next word is emphasised), and 'object' is pronounced /ɒbdʒIkt/ when used as a noun and /əbdʒekt/ when used as a verb. These differences in pronunciation can be listed or they can be represented by a network.

4.3.2.3 Phonological knowledge
Phonological rules express the systematic ways in which the pronunciation of words or phonemes may change with their environment. This knowledge can be used to reconcile the results of the acoustic–phonetic classification with the 'ideal' forms stored in the dictionary. If these rules are general it is more efficient to store this knowledge separately rather than to keep alternative forms of every word in the dictionary.

Context-dependent phonological rules can be formulated for vowel reduction ('spectrogram' is normally pronounced /spektrəgræm/ not /spektrəʊgræm/) and deletion ('boundary' is usually pronounced (baʊndri/ not /baʊnderi/). Phonological rules can also apply across word boundaries as well as within words. There are two forms: elision, or consonant deletion (The sequence 'six seven' is normally pronounced /sIksevn/ or even /sIsevn/ but not /sikssevn/.); and sandhi, or consonant insertion (The word 'how' is pronounced /haʊ/and 'are' is pronounced /a/ but 'how are you?' is pronounced /haʊwaju/.). An account of the use of phonological knowledge in speech recognition is given by Shoup (1980).

4.3.2.4 Prosodic knowledge
Prosodic knowledge can be used to locate the stressed syllables in an utterance and to segment the utterance into syntactic phrases. It can also be used to help to decide whether an utterance is interrogative or affirmative.

Prosodic features such as stress, juncture and intonation must be derived from physical estimates of energy, duration and fundamental frequency, so some of the problems which are encountered in acoustic–phonetic processing will also be found in prosodic processing. It is known that increasing the duration and intensity of a syllable will make the syllable more likely to be perceived as stressed (Fry, 1955) but it is difficult to know that the duration and intensity have been increased unless the syllable has been identified. It is also known that the fundamental frequency changes most rapidly during stressed syllables (Fry 1958).

Lea (1980) has suggested that prosodic knowledge could be employed in speech recognition in two ways. It could be used for disambiguating hypotheses made by other processors. If the phrase 'they are flying planes' was detected, prosodic knowledge could be used to decide whether the meaning was best represented by (they are flying) (planes) or by (they are) (flying planes). Prosodic knowledge could also be used in a processor by itself. Lindsay (1984) has followed this suggestion and has shown that the intonation contours of simple phrases can be identified with the five tones of Halliday (1963). These tones, in turn, relate to semantic labels such as 'reservation', 'emphatic statement', etc. (see Section 2.4.7). These labels can be checked against the semantic content of an utterance as deduced by other processors using other sources of knowledge.

4.3.2.5 Syntactical knowledge

The grammar of the language, expressed in a suitable form, is obviously a useful knowledge source. A number of grammars exist which allow sentences of various degrees of complexity to be analysed. If it is known that the spoken language conforms to one of these, then this syntactical knowledge can be used to restrict the sequences of permissable words.

A slot and frame grammar is perhaps the simplest form of grammar. This restricts the utterances to standard sentence frames in which only certain words can vary. For example, an air traffic controller might use the following frame to tell a plane that another is in its vicinity:

'There is a plane   miles from you, at   o'clock.'

Any number may be substituted in the first slot, and 1–12 in the second.

The recognition task is then reducd to the recognition of single words, except that the positions of the slots need to be spotted. Also the context may cause the physical manifestation of a word such as 'two' to be different in 'two miles' from that of 'two' in 'two o'clock'.

The next level of complexity is described by a finite-state grammar. This is sometimes known as a type 3 grammar (Fu, 1982). It may be expressed as a network of states in which the next state depends upon the last n states (Fig. 4.18). In practice n is very often set equal to 1.

More general grammars may be implemented to describe the syntax of an utterance. The next level is called a context-free, or type 2, grammar. In this, each node in the network represents a larger unit than a word, such as a phrase, but it has not been found capable of capturing the full complexity of natural English.

The most complex syntactic structures which have been utilised in speech-recognition systems are context-sensitive, or type 1, grammars which have been implemented as augmented transition networks, or ATNs (Woods, 1974). These are like finite-state grammars except that the nodes can contain special transitions which are like instructions to enter a sub-routine. This feature is useful for dealing with clauses. ATNs are of about the same complexity as transformational grammars (Chomsky and Halle, 1968), but the knowledge is expressed in a more useful form for automatic speech recognition.

Unrestricted grammars are known as type 0 grammars (Fu, 1982).

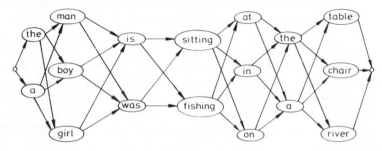

Fig. 4.18 *Network representation of a finite-stage grammar where n = 1*
Each state depends only on the previous state

4.3.2.6 Semantic knowledge

Semantic knowledge can be used in two ways. If a word is recognised this can be used to suggest other words to search for. One way of doing this is to store a kind of thesaurus. Each entry is followed by a list of common phrases in which that word is used. If the word 'computer' is detected then phrases such as 'digital computer', 'analogue computer', 'computer program', 'computer system', etc. could be searched for. Instead of storing this knowledge as a list, it is more efficient to store it as an associative semantic network (Woods, 1974).

Another way in which semantic knowledge can be employed is for deciding among similar-sounding word candidates. In the sentence 'The cavalry formed a ⟨word⟩' where the ⟨word⟩ candidates are 'soup' and 'troop', the semantic knowledge can be used to select 'troop.'

Semantic knowledge can also be combind with syntactic knowledge. In HEARSAY II (Hayes–Roth *et al.*, 1978) a semantic template grammar is employed. A semantic template is a set of semantically equivalent phrases. These are stored as the nodes of a network, and any path through the network forms an acceptable sentence. One path might be 'tell X about Y' where X and Y are semantic templates. X might represent the set ⟨me, us, him, her⟩ and Y the set ⟨ships, planes, submarines, helicopters⟩. In this application the semantic knowledge can be used to hypothesise the form of the sentence and other sources of knowledge, such as acoustic–phonetic, can be employed to choose among the alternatives.

4.3.2.7 Pragmatic knowledge

Whereas semantic knowledge is available at all times, pragmatic knowledge depends upon the current situation. It is not possible to discuss pragmatic knowledge except in the context of a given application. An example which is often quoted is the use of the board position in a chess game. The set of most likely next moves can be hypothesised from this, and hence the likely next utterance of the chess-playing-program's opponent can be guessed.

Pragmatic knowledge is usually available in a dialogue situation after the first few exchanges. Once the interrogator has asked a question, and the computer has confirmed what he wants to know, the choice of subsequent questions is narrowed.

If it is the computer which is asking the questions, the range of answers is often very small. Many computer programs are organised so that the man–machine interaction takes place by means of menus. The same organisation can be used, with advantage, when speech input and output is used. The computer asks 'What do you wish to do next?' and then lists a number of choices. The speech recogniser then expects one of these choices to be spoken, and this greatly simplifies its task.

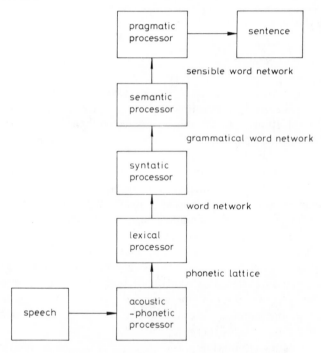

Fig. 4.19 *Hierarchical, bottom-up system of knowledge sources*

4.3.3 System organisation
The simplest organisation is to arrange the knowledge sources in a hierarchical manner (Fig. 4.19). The acoustic–phonetic processor produces a phonetic lattice which is passed to the lexical processor. This generates a network of possible word matches, which is passed to the syntactic processor. The network is pruned so that only those branches which are grammatically correct remain. The semantic processor then removes those branches which it considers to be non-

sensical, and if any remain, the pragmatic knowledge of the current situation is used to choose the most likely spoken utterance.

In practice it was found that this system organisation is inefficient. The flow of information is from the bottom up. A great many hypotheses, which are seemingly unlikely but which may be correct, have to be retained and tested at each stage. A more efficient use of hierarchical organisation is for the information to flow from the top down (Fig. 4.20). Pragmatic knowledge is used to suggest hypotheses which are put into sensible, well-formed sentences by the semantic, syntactic and lexical processors. These sentence candidates are then tested against the acoustic–phonetic data and the most likely one is chosen.

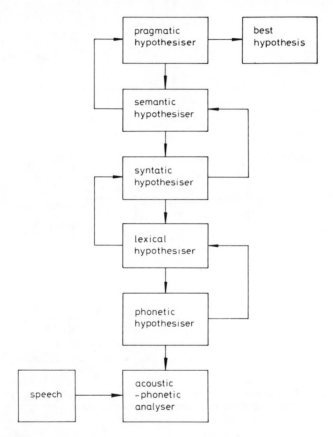

Fig. 4.20 *Hierarchical, top-down system of knowledge sources*

Instead of connecting the knowledge sources in a fixed order, with each only communicating with its neighbours, they can be organised so that they can all communicate with each other. One way of doing this is by means of a 'blackboard' (Reddy *et al.*, 1973). Each processor uses its source of knowledge about the spoken utterance by reading the suggestions that the other processors write on the blackboard, and then testing and refining these suggestions in the light of its own knowledge (Fig. 4.21).

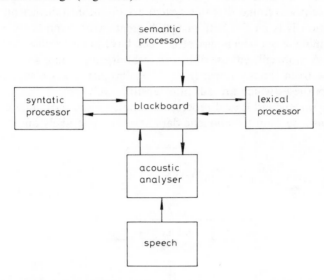

Fig. 4.21 *Heterarchical, or blackboard, system of knowledge sources*

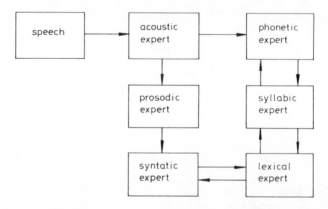

Fig. 4.22 *Society of experts*
The syllabic expert can communicate with the lexical expert about the structure of words. However, it has no direct knowledge of syntax

Another possible way of organising the sources of knowledge is to integrate them by compiling them into a single but large network. Recognition of a sentence then consists of searching for the path through this network which is most consistent with the received acoustic data. This form of system organisation has been used successfully in Dragon (Baker, 1975) and Harpy (Lowerre, 1976).

Yet another form of organisation has been suggested by De Mori and LeFace

(1985). The blackboard scheme is quite general and allows each source of knowledge to communicate with all of the others. In the particular case of speech recognition this communication is too rich. Instead a 'society of experts' is proposed in which each expert is as independent as possible and only communicates with experts who use related knowledge. The organisation of a society of experts is shown in Fig. 4.22.

Chapter 5

Speech-recognition algorithms

5.1 Speech analysis

A number of algorithms which have been developed for speech recognition will be described next. Some indication of their performance is given where appropriate. The structure of this Chapter is similar to that of the last. First, algorithms for speech signal analysis are described, then algorithms for speech-pattern matching, and finally algorithms for speech understanding.

5.1.1 Spectral analysis

One of the first processes in the recognition of speech is often spectral analysis. This may be performed by a filter bank or by a fast Fourier transform algorithm. A number of suitable FFT algorithms are presented in a collection of programs for digital signal processing edited by Weinstein *et al.* (1979).

An algorithm which is intended to produce very fast programs at the expense of instruction memory and program complexity is presented by Bergland and Dolan (1979). Several versions are given which trade memory for speed.

Most FTT algorithms require the number of data points to be a power of two. This results in the most efficient algorithms. However, Singleton (1979) presents an algorithm which permits other numbers of points. In general, the larger the prime factors of this number, the less efficient the calculation will be in terms of the number of operations per output point.

There are other techniques for performing spectral analysis. Algorithms for the periodogram method and the correlation method are presented by Rabiner, Schafer and Dlugos (1979).

More sophisticated algorithms which attempt to remove the effects of the glottal source from the vocal tract filter function by means of cepstrum analysis or linear prediction analysis may be employed. Gray and Markel (1979) present an algorithm for obtaining spectral estimates from linear prediction coefficients, and Tribolet and Quatieri (1979) present an algorithm for computing the complex cepstrum.

5.1.2 Formant tracking algorithms
It is fairly easy to track the formants in a sonagram by eye if the spoken phrase being analysed is known. It is much more difficult to perform this task if this information is not available. A machine required to track the formants is usually in this position.

There are four main sources of difficulty:

(i) When two formants come close to one another they coalesce to form a single peak in the spectrum. An algorithm which counts peaks from the lowest frequency upwards, and assigns the formants accordingly, will take such a peak to represent a single formant and so name the formants above wrongly.

(ii) In the spectra of many vowels, particularly open vowels, a peak often appears in the low-frequency region which is caused by the glottal source rather than the vocal-tract filter. In other vowels this peak combines with the first formant.

(iii) In some consonants, particularly nasals and laterals, antiresonances (zeros) occur in the spectrum as well as formant resonances (poles). These sometimes coincide in frequency with the formants and so reduce the energy at these positions. This may be sufficient to mask the peak.

(iv) Finally, as the intensity of the formants decreases, particularly during consonants, some peaks become insignificant before others so that a peak-picking algorithm will fail.

Nevertheless the simplest algorithm for formant tracking is one which picks the peaks in the power spectrum at successive points in time. This algorithm can be improved considerably by taking note of the peaks at neighbouring points.

There are variations of this algorithm which yield better results. One alternative is to obtain a power spectrum after spectral smoothing as described in Section 4.1.6. Another is to compute the transfer function of the linear prediction filter, then pick the peaks in this. More exact, but more computationally expensive algorithms exist for finding the poles of this filter. A model of speech production consists of a glottal source driving a series of resonators tuned to the formant frequencies. The linear prediction synthesis model consists of an error signal exciting a complex, multipole filter. If the poles of this filter are identified with the formants, their frequencies can be determined by finding the roots of the resulting equations (Markel and Gray, 1976).

Having obtained the formant frequencies in each time frame, the formant trajectories may be estimated by means of an algorithm presented by Markel (1972). Let N_p be the number of peaks in frame k. A nearest-neighbour criterion is defined by

$$d_{ij} = |F_i'(k) - F_j(k - 1)| \tag{5.1}$$

where $F_j(k - 1)$ is the jth formant frequency of the previous frame and $F_i'(k)$ is the ith frequency estimate for the present frame.

In the frequency region 0–3 kHz, $N_p = 3$ about 85–90% of the time for male voices. In this case the formants are assigned to the peaks. If $N_p = 1$, which occurs less than 1% of the time, the nearest-neighbour rule is used to assign this single peak and the other formant slots are filled from the previous frame.

For the cases $N_p = 2$, corresponding to one omission and one insertion of the peaks, more complex rules are invoked. For $N_p = 2$ the best peaks are assigned from the nearest-neighbour rule, and the other slot is filled by copying from the previous frame. For $N_p = 4$ the best peaks are assigned using the nearest-neighbour rule.

This algorithm works from left to right. More sophisticated algorithms, such as those reported by Ainsworth (1970) and McCandless (1974), work from anchor points. These are defined as high-energy points in the voiced regions. The formant frequencies are estimated at the anchor points, where the estimates are expected to be accurate, then the algorithm branches out in both directions in order to follow the formant trajectories.

5.1.3 Fundamental-frequency estimation

The development of algorithms for estimating the fundamental frequency of speech waveforms has occupied an important place in speech research for many years. A comprehensive survey is given by Hess (1983). He points out that most PDAs (pitch determination algorithms) consist of a preprocessor, the algorithm, and a postprocessor as shown in Fig. 5.1. The preprocessor consists of some device for reducing the effects of the formant frequencies, such as a low-pass filter, or enhancing the effects of the fundamental, such as centre clipping. The postprocessor is used for smoothing the output of the algorithm and for correcting any gross errors made by the algorithm. Again a low-pass filter can be used for smoothing. A special kind of filter, known as a 'median of n' filter, has been found useful for correcting the occasional errors made by even the best pitch-determination algorithms (Gold and Rabiner, 1969).

Fig. 5.1 *Structure of speech fundamental-frequency-estimation algorithms and devices*

Pitch-determination algorithms can work in either the time domain or the frequency domain. Some, although they operate on the time waveform, have properties similar to those which operate in the frequency domain. These different types of algorithms will be considered in the following Sections.

5.1.3.1 Time-domain algorithms: The simplest time-domain algorithm consists of a low-pass filter preprocessor followed by a zero-crossing detector. This algorithm will only work if the fundamental frequency is sufficiently different from the formant frequencies. As this is often not the case with female voices, and with many male voices articulating high-pitched /i/ or /u/ vowels, this algorithm is unsatisfactory.

An improvement on this method is to employ a threshold crossing rather than a zero-crossing detecting algorithm. This too, however, can fail if the amplitude of the signal falls below the threshold. It is therefore advisable to employ an adaptive threshold which is proportional to the amplitude of the signal.

Instead of using threshold crossings to determine the periodicity of the waveform, and hence its fundamental frequency, other features of the waveform may be employed. Obvious features are the peaks of the waveform. One such algorithm, first introduced by Gruenz and Schott (1949), is illustrated in Fig. 5.2. A new waveform (Fig. 5.2*b*) is produced which follows the speech signal until a peak is reached. It then decays exponentially until it crosses the speech signal again. If the resulting waveform is differentiated, a new signal (Fig. 5.2*c*) is produced with pulses at the beginning of each glottal cycle, but with some additional pulses present. If this process is repeated, as shown in Fig. 5.2*d* and *e*, a signal is produced which has pulses at the start of each glottal cycle. The time intervals between these pulses can then be used to estimate the fundamental frequency of the speech wave.

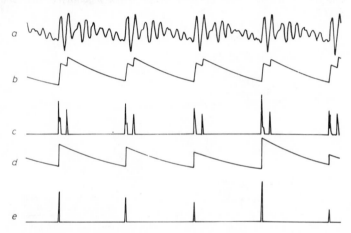

Fig. 5.2 *Fundamental-frequency estimation by peak picking*
The waveform (*b*) is derived from the speech signal (*a*) by means of a function which follows upward movements of the speech signal until a peak is encountered and then decays exponentially until it crosses the speech signal again. The waveform (*b*) is differentiated to produce the pulse train (*c*). This process is then repeated, producing the waveforms (*d*) and (*e*). The fundamental frequency is derived from the time intervals between the pulses in (*e*)

A more complex time domain algorithm was presented by Gold and Rabiner (1969). They realised that some features of the speech wave are good period markers in some conditions wheres others are better in other contexts. In order to extract the best measure in all conditions they obtained six estimates in parallel. The period markers they used are shown in Fig. 5.3. M1 is a pulse at each maximum of the wave and has a height equal to the distance from the axis to the peak. M2 also occurs at the maxima but its height is equal to the vertical distance from the last minimum to the current maximum. M3 is the vertical distance from the last maximum to the current maximum. M4, M5 and M6 occur at the minima of the speech wave and are the equivalent distances relative to these minima.

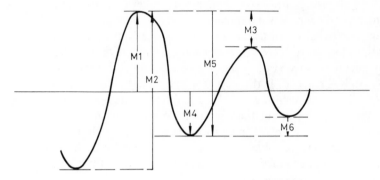

Fig. 5.3 *The period markers used in the pitch-determination algorithm of Gold and Rabiner (1969)*

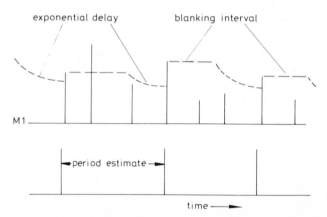

Fig. 5.4 *The periods between each of the markers shown in Fig. 5.3 are estimated by a blanking interval, during which the markers are ignored, followed by an exponential decay until the next marker is encountered*

A period extractor then operates on the period marker in each channel. This consists of a peak picker, followed by a blanking interval and an exponential decay, as shown in Fig. 5.4. The period estimates are then the time intervals between the pulses in each channel.

In order to select the most likely period a 6 × 6 matrix of values is formed. The first row contains the six current estimates from the parallel channels. Rows 2 & 3 contain the previous and penultimate estimates. Rows 4 & 5 contain the sums of rows 1 & 2 and 2 & 3, respectively. Row 6 contains the sums of the first three rows. Each value in row 1 is correlated with the other 35 values within a certain tolerance, and the value showing the maximum correlation is selected.

A similar type of fundamental-frequency-estimation algorithm has been described by Tucker and Bates (1978). In this algorithm an adaptive centre clipper is used to remove the minor maxima and minima of the speech wave. This reduces the number of peaks and so simplifies and speeds the execution of the main algorithm. A different set of waveform features is used in this algorithm. These include the amplitude and width (time between axis crossings) of each peak, together with its energy, polarity and a shape factor.

This algorithm was designed for estimating the pitch of musical sounds and it is claimed that it operates over a range of 40–2400 Hz. This is much more than is required for speech processing.

5.1.3.2 Frequency-domain algorithms: Instead of estimating the fundamental frequency of a speech signal by searching for periodicity in the time waveform, fundamental frequency may be found by first transforming the signal into the frequency domain.

If the speech waveform is perfectly periodic and the analysis window width is an exact multiple of this period, a line spectrum results. However, as speech is not perfectly periodic and as its fundamental frequency is not known, a continuous spectrum results which contains ripples at each of the harmonics. The fundamental frequency can be determined from the spacing of the harmonics if they are sufficiently visible.

An algorithm for estimating fundamental frequency from the spectrum has been suggested by Schroeder (1968). The spectrum is compressed along the frequency axis by dividing it successively by the integers 2, 3, 4 etc. The compressed spectra are then added together. The result is a function with an enhanced peak at the fundamental frequency.

Another technique for estimating fundamental frequency from the spectrum is cepstral processing (Noll, 1967). First the Fourier transform of the speech waveform is computed, then the logarithm of this transform is obtained. Finally the inverse transform of the log transform is calculated (Section 4.1.6).

The effect of the logarithmic transformation is to enhance the fundamental frequency relative to the formant frequencies. The cepstrum, which has the dimension of time, has a number of short-duration peaks, corresponding to the formants, near to the origin, and a single long-duration peak, corresponding to the fundamental frequency, separated from them. The fundamental frequency can be estimated from the position of this single peak.

5.1.3.3 Other algorithms: A number of other techniques have been employed for estimating the fundamental frequency of a speech wave. One such is autocorrelation analysis. Suppose a speech signal, $s(t)$, is digitised, and the resulting samples are $x(n)$ where the sampling interval is T, and the sampling times are $t = nT$, where n are integers. The autocorrelation function is then given by

$$\text{ACF}(k) = \sum_{n=1}^{N} x(n)x(n + k) \tag{5.2}$$

where there are N samples. In other words, the autocorrelation function is obtained by multiplying the speech signal by a delayed version of itself. The delay, k, is known as the lag.

For a periodic signal the autocorrelation signal will exhibit peaks at lag values equal to this periodicity. From the intervals between the peaks the fundamental frequency can be computed.

In practice it has been found that a more useful function results if the sampled waveform is first multiplied by a smooth function such as a Hamming window in order to reduce the effects of discontinuities. The performance of this algorithm can also be improved if the signal is first preprocessed by centre-clipping (Rabiner, 1977). This removes some of the effects of the formants.

The autocorrelation function requires many multiplications, which slows the execution of the algorithm on most digital computers. A similar algorithm, which executes faster because it involves subtractions instead of multiplications, is one based on the average magnitude difference function (Ross *et al.*, 1974). This is defined by

$$\text{AMDF}(k) \;=\; \sum_{n=1}^{N} |x(n) - x(n + k)| \tag{5.3}$$

where $x(n)$ is the sampled waveform, N is the number of samples, and k is the lag, as above. The AMDF exhibits minima at lag times equal to the periodicity of the signal.

Other methods of fundamental-frequency estimation are based on linear prediction analysis. Linear prediction assumes that the current value of a sampled waveform, $x(n)$, can be predicted from the past p samples according to

$$x(n) \;=\; \sum_{k=1}^{P} a_k x(n - k) + e(n) \tag{5.4}$$

where a_k are the prediction coefficients and $e(n)$ represents the error signal.

Algorithms have been developed for estimating the coefficients a_k in such a way that the error signal $e(n)$ is minimised (Markel and Gray, 1976). The error signal is small for the smooth portions of the speech waveform, but increases at the discontinuities. These discontinuities in voiced speech normally occur at the beginning of each glottal cycle. Hence the periodicity of the error signal can be used for estimating fundamental frequency.

The SIFT algorithm (simplified inverse filter transformation), introduced by Markel (1972), uses linear prediction analysis. The signal is low-pass filtered at 800 Hz, and then digitised at 2 Hz. The linear prediction coefficients, a_k, are then computed. As there are never more than two vocal tract resonances below 1 kHz, four coefficients are sufficient (Markel and Gray, 1976).

The coefficients are then used to predict the speech signal according to

$$x'(n) \;=\; \sum_{k=1}^{P} a_k x(n - k) \tag{5.5}$$

The error signal is computed from the difference between the original and the predicted waveforms. Autocorrelation is then performed on the resulting signal, and the fundamental frequency estimated from the periodicity of the ACF.

5.1.4 Endpoint detection

One problem in speech recognition is to detect the presence of speech in background noise. This is sometimes referred to as endpoint detection. Correct location of the beginning and end of an utterance minimises the amount of subsequent processing, and has been found to be important in improving the accuracy of recognition of isolated words.

Rabiner and Sambur (1975) have developed an endpoint detection algorithm which works well with tape-recorded signals and with speech spoken directly into a computer in an acoustic environment where the signal/noise ratio is 30 dB or better. The algorithm is based on two measures: short-time energy and zero-crossing rate. The algorithm is self-adapting in that the decision thresholds are computed directly from measurements made on the first 100 ms of the recording interval, where it is assumed that no speech is present.

Rabiner and Sambur list the situations which are likely to cause problems for an endpoint detection algorithm. These include:

(i) Weak fricatives such as /f,θ,h/ at the beginning or end of an utterance

(ii) Weak plosive bursts such as /p,t,k/

(iii) Final nasals

(iv) Voiced fricatives at the ends of words which become devoiced

(v) Trailing of certain voiced sounds, such as the final /i/ in 'three' becoming unvoiced.

The algorithm of Rabiner and Sambur was implemented in digital form. The speech was high-pass filtered at 100 Hz and low-pass filtered at 4 kHz, and then sampled at 10 kHz. The speech 'energy' at each point was defined as

$$E(n) = \sum_{i=-50}^{50} |s(n + i)| \tag{5.6}$$

where $s(n)$ are the speech samples. This defines the energy as the sum of the magnitudes of each 10 ms of speech. The zero crossing rate was defined as the number of zero crossings in each 10 ms interval.

The statistics of the background noise were measured during the first 100 ms of recording. These included the average energy, and the average and standard deviation of the zero crossing rate. The energy function for the entire interval was next computed, and the peak energy determined. A threshold was then found which was the lower of 3% of the peak energy and four times the 'silence' energy.

The algorithm begins by searching for the point at which this threshold is crossed. This is labelled as the start of the utterance unless the energy falls below this threshold before it rises to five times it. A similar algorithm estimates the location of the end of the utterance. As these are rather conservative estimates of the endpoints, it is expected that the interval between these points will contain the speech. However, in situations like those listed above some speech may fall outside these limits. To test for this, the zero crossing rates are compared with that of 'silence'.

The resulting algorithm was found in formal tests to make no gross errors (a weak fricative was detected if one was present), but the exact endpoints did not always correspond with those found by direct observation of the waveform.

For telephone speech, with a 3 kHz bandwidth, the use of zero crossings is not effective, so other endpoint detection algorithms must be employed. Lamel *et al.* (1981) performed a comparison of three types of endpoint detectors. They refer to these types as explicit, implicit and hybrid detectors. The algorithm of Rabiner and Sambur (1975) described above is an example of an explicit detector. An example of an implicit endpoint detector is a dynamic programming pattern-matching algorithm, as described in Section 4.2.8, in which each element of the template, including its endpoints, is compared with each element of the unknown pattern. The endpoints are implicitly defined as a result of the recognition process.

An example of a hybrid endpoint detector is given by Lamel *et al.* (1981). The first stage is an adaptive level equaliser which normalises the energy to the background noise level. Next, a number of thresholds are defined, and these are used to detect the locations of pulses of energy where speech sounds are likely to be present. The word endpoints are then estimated from the energy pulse endpoints by combining those pulses which are likely to belong to words. The following assumptions are made:

(i) The word whose endpoints are to be determined consists of one or more pulses.
(ii) The pulse with the maximum energy will always be part of the spoken word.
(iii) The larger the gap between two pulses, the less likely that these pulses will be part of the same word.
(iv) Pulses separated by greater than 150 ms are unlikely to both be part of the spoken word.

Based on these assumptions, the energy pulses are grouped into combinations of word endpoint pairs, and ordered in terms of likelihood. Each endpoint set is then used by the recogniser to determine the word with the lowest distance score. If the resulting distance is too large, the recogniser takes the next likely set of endpoints and again determines the word with the lowest distance score. The process is repeated until a reliable distance score is obtained.

Lamel *et al.* (1981) compared the performance of explicit, implicit, and hybrid endpoint detectors. They used a vocabulary of 39 words (the letters of the alphabet, the digits, and the words 'stop', 'error' and 'repeat') recorded by ten problematic speakers who habitually produced clicks, pops, lip smackings and heavy breathing. The recogniser employed a dynamic time-warping alignment procedure and 12 speaker independent reference templates per word produced by statistical clustering (Rabiner *et al.*, 1979) (see Section 4.2.5). The endpoint detectors were evaluated in terms of their recognition accuracy and rejection rate (i.e. when no sufficiently low distance score was obtained).

The explicit detector produced a 68·8% recognition accuracy and a 29·1% rejection rate. The implicit detector produced a recognition accuracy of only 29·4% demonstrating how susceptible DTW recognisers are to artefacts such as clicks if no provision is made to allow for them. The hybrid endpoint detector had a 74·9% recognition accuracy and less than 0·5% rejection rate.

5.1.5 Noise compensation
Background noise, as well as making the endpoints of an utterance difficult to detect, also interferes with the speech signal, making the recognition task more difficult. As speech recognition in the quiet is not an easy task for a machine, little research has yet been directed towards the even more difficult task of speech recognition in noise.

There has, however, been a good deal of work on the effects of noise on speech recognition by humans, and on the use of signal-processing techniques to compensate for the effects of noise. The effect of noise on speech communication has recently been reviewed by Ainsworth (1985), and a collection of papers on speech enhancement has been edited by Lim (1983).

Different types of noise have different effects on speech communication. In the quiet the speech level needs to be about 35 dB above the threshold of hearing for 50% of consonant–vowel–consonant syllables to be correctly identified. When white noise is added the level of the speech needs to be increased in order to maintain the same intelligibility. In the range 40–100 dB the level of the speech must be increased by an amount equal to the intensity of the noise (Fletcher, 1953). With periodically interrupted noise the intelligibility of the speech depends on both the intensity of the noise and the frequency of interruption (Miller and Licklider, 1950). The least disruption occurs at an interruption frequency of about 10 Hz. The greatest effect on intelligibility is obtained by adding speech from another talker. Carhart *et al.* (1975) found that adding one extra talker was equivalent to increasing the noise level by an additional 6·2 dB, adding two talkers was equivalent to 7·2 dB, and three equivalent to 9·8 dB. Thereafter adding additional talkers had less effect, with 64 being equivalent to a noise increase of only 3 dB.

The effects of quantisation noise and additive white noise on linear prediction analysis have been investigated by Sambur and Jayant (1976). They found that linear prediction analysis is fairly immune from DPCM quantisation, but the effects of DM quantisation are more severe and the effects of additive white noise are most serious.

Lim (1978) has proposed an algorithm for enhancing speech degraded by additive white noise by means of a correlation subtraction method. The short-term spectral magnitude is estimated from the noisy speech. It was found that, although this subjectively reduced the noise and improved the speech quality, it did not improve the intelligibility of the speech.

The waveforms of voiced sounds are approximately periodic, so their spectra contain harmonics. On the other hand noise is aperiodic. Hence some form of comb filtering may reduce the noise whilst preserving the signal. An algorithm based on comb filtering was presented by Frazier *et al.* (1976) and evaluated by Lim *et al.* (1978). Another algorithm in this class was presented by Parsons (1976). Although these algorithms are potentially applicable to many types of additive noise, including the case of competing speakers, they do not apply to unvoiced speech which is generally weaker than voiced speech and so suffers more from the effects of noise. Also they require accurate fundamental frequency estimation which is difficult in the presence of noise. Subjective tests show that so far these algorithms improve neither the intelligibility nor the quality of the speech.

Another approach attempts to exploit an underlying model of speech production. Lim and Oppenheim (1978), for example, present several algorithms for estimating the parameters of an all-pole model of the vocal tract. These parameters are then used for synthesising the speech wave. A similar algorithm which estimates the fundamental frequency as well as the linear production parameters was presented by Kobatake *et al.* (1978), and another devoted to estimating the fundamental frequency of degraded speech was presented by Wise *et al.* (1976). Informal listening tests indicate that speech quality is improved by these algorithms, but improvement of speech intelligibility is doubtful.

Humans have the advantage of two ears when listening to speech in a noisy environment. Improvements in speech-recognition accuracy might be possible if two microphones with different levels of speech and noise were employed. Widrow *et al.* (1975) have shown that intelligibility can be dramatically improved by their algorithm if one channel contains signal and noise and the other contains only noise which is correlated with the noise in the first channel. In practice, however, it is difficult to obtain a second channel which contains no speech. If it does, it will attempt to cancel the speech in the first channel.

A new application of this algorithm has recently been discussed by Harrison *et al.* (1986) in which an acoustic barrier exists between the microphones. In this case one microphone was placed inside the face mask of the pilot of an aircraft and the other outside. An improvement of 11 dB in signal/noise ratio was reported.

It seems, therefore, that at present there are few algorithms that are capable of improving the intelligibility of speech corrupted by noise, and which might be usefully applied to speech recognition by machine. The way in which humans group speech sounds and separate them from noise and other voices is being investigated (Section 2.4.6), and this should result in signal-processing algorithms which will improve the performance of automatic speech recognisers.

An alternative approach has been suggested by Bridle *et al.* (1984). Instead of removing the noise, those parts of the signal which appear likely to have been corrupted by noise are prevented from contributing to the recognition process. The noise spectrum is estimated when no speech is present. Those regions of the speech spectrum which are less intense than the corresponding regions of the noise spectrum are marked, then during the recognition process marked regions contribute a constant amount to the distance calculation between the test utterance and the templates. It was found that this algorithm made no difference in a digit-recognition task when the signal/noise ratio was 9 dB, but it improved the recognition score from 44% to 77% at 3 dB.

5.1.6 Reverberation reduction

In addition to being degraded by extraneous noise, speech signals are usually distorted by reverberation. As well as the direct path from the mouth of the speaker to the microphone, there are also indirect paths from objects and from the walls of the room. The signal at the microphone contains many echoes delayed by a few milliseconds up to a few seconds. The early echoes are due to single reflections from objects near the speaker or the microphone. They give the speech a hollow quality. The later echoes are due to multiple reflections from the walls of the room. They are weaker than the original source and are sometimes heard as distinct echoes.

Reverberated speech can be modelled as speech convolved with the impulse response of the reverberating environment, so one approach to reducing reverberation is to deconvolve the reverberated speech to separate the individual components. Neely and Allen (1979) have adopted this approach and developed an algorithm in which the reverberating impulse response is first estimated from the reverberated speech and then the estimated impulse response is used to reduce the reverberation by inverse filtering. Unfortunately this algorithm is only applicable in rooms with very small reflection coefficients.

Another approach is to first estimate the speech model parameters taking into account the presence of reverberation, and then synthesise the speech waveform from the estimated model parameters. Allen (1974) adopts this approach. His algorithm is reported to reduce reverberation in some cases, but the accuracy of the estimated parameters is not sufficient to generate high-quality speech.

An algorithm by Mitchell and Berkley (1970) attempts to reduce the late echoes by centre-clipping. It appears to be effective. Flanagan and Lummis (1970) present an algorithm for reducing the effects of early echoes. This requires two or more microphones. It is based on the idea that an early echo cancels some frequencies in each channel and that specific different frequencies are cancelled in different channels. Each channel is divided into many frequency bands by a filter bank, then the channel with the greatest energy in each band is selected. It is assumed that the channel having the greatest energy will be the one least affected by reverberation, so this method reduces the effects of early echoes.

Although this method reduces some reverberation it is not very successful in actual room environments because it does not deal with late echoes. Allen *et al.* (1977) have produced a successful algorithm by combining the two methods discussed above. However, some results by Bloom (1980) indicate that the speech intelligibility is not improved by such processing.

5.1.7 Vector quantisation

In Section 4.1.7 a number of techniques for computing the linear prediction coefficients of a speech signal were outlined. Linear prediction analysis was developed originally as a technique for coding speech signals for efficient transmission. This technique is particularly appropriate for coding speech digitally as an alternative to the analogue coding used in channel-vocoder systems.

One of the consequences of using digital systems is that the word length, or number of bits, required to code each coefficient has to be considered. In the original formulations each coefficient was quantised separately, so this was known as scalar quantisation.

An alternative method of quantising linear prediction coefficients has been developed by Buzo *et al.* (1980). This is known as vector quantisation (VQ), and was originally suggested for communication systems by Shannon (1960). If each interval of speech can be represented by a frame of k coefficients, then that interval can be represented by a point in k-dimensional space. If this space is divided into B cells, then each cell can be identified by a vector of b bits where $B = 2^b$. The relation between the centroid of each cell and its address is known as a codebook. In vector quantisation each frame of k coefficients is transmitted by a vector of b bits, the codeword, representing the address of the cell in which the linear prediction coefficients fall. The size of the codeword is sometimes known as the 'rate' of the codebook.

By choosing the co-ordinates of the centroids so that the distortion between the original speech and that synthesised from the linear prediction coefficients of the centroids is minimised, considerable savings in transmission capacity may be obtained. This is achieved by having a non-uniform distribution of cells throughout the vector space such that those areas where the density of the frames is greatest contain the most cells.

Buzo *et al.* (1980) employed an iterative technique to design the codebook. They used the Itakura–Saito distortion measure (see Section (4.2.4) to compute the distances between frames (Itakura and Saito, 1972). This measure is analytically tractable, computable from sampled data, and subjectively meaningful.

Two methods are proposed for computing the cell structure. In one, the centroid of all of the frames is first computed. Then each of the coefficients of this is multiplied by 0·99 and 1·01 to produce two new frames. The distortion between each frame and both of these new frames is computed and each frame is assigned to the cell giving the minimum distortion. The centroids of these new cells are then computed. This process is then repeated until B cells ($= 2^b$) have been generated or until the average distortion is sufficiently low.

An alternative is to select the frame at the greatest distance in the vector space from the overall centroid, then select the frame at the greatest distance from this frame. The distortions of all the frames are computed relative to these distant frames and assigned to one of two cells based on these. The centroids of these new cells are computed, and the process is repeated until a sufficient number of cells have been generated. It is not known at present which of these methods is most efficient, but both are computationally expensive.

Experiments have been performed by Buzo *et al.* (1980) to compare the channel capacity required by scalar and vector quantisation schemes for a given level of distortion. It was found that a 10 bit codebook VQ scheme had approximately the same amount of distortion as a 37 bit frame scalar quantisation scheme.

Voiced and voiceless speech waveforms have different-shaped spectra, and so have different distributions in the LPC frame space. Juang *et al.* (1982) have shown that even more efficient transmission can be obtained by designing separate codebooks for voiced and voiceless speech. No extra bits are required because this information is already provided in linear predictive coding schemes for synthesising the excitation function.

5.2 Speech pattern matching

One way of recognising a word is to compare it with a set of known words, or templates, stored in a machine, and to choose that word which it matches best. This method is only practical for isolated words, or discrete utterances, and only then when the vocabulary is reasonably small. The techniques which have been developed for these circumstances are reviewed in the next Sections.

5.2.1 Time normalisation

In general, as mentioned in Section 3.2.2, the same word spoken on different occasions, even by the same speaker, will exhibit variations. One of the major variations is the duration of the word. This poses a problem for a pattern matcher which is required to compute the distance between an unknown word and a set of word templates, as it will not normally be possible to align both the beginning and the end of the word with the templates.

The simplest solution is to employ linear time normalisation. That is to expand or compress the duration of each word so that it is equal to some fixed value such as the average length of the templates. This technique was tried by Denes and Mathews (1960) and found to increase the recognition score of isolated digits. The problem with linear time normalisation, however, is that, although it allows the endpoints to be aligned, it does not guarantee that the best match between the internal features of the words will be achieved.

A more general solution is non-linear time normalisation. This may be achieved by dynamic programming techniques (Section 4.2.8). This was first applied to speech signals by Velichiko and Zagoruyko (1970) and Sakoe and Chiba (1970, 1971).

An optimal match between two sequences of feature vectors (e.g. spectra or linear prediction coefficients)

$$A = a_1, a_2, \ldots a_i, \ldots a_I$$

$$\text{and } B = b_1, b_2, \ldots b_j \ldots b_J$$

is obtained by mapping one on to the other by means of the warping function

$$F = c(1), c(2), \ldots c(k), \ldots c(K) \tag{5.7}$$

where $c(k) = (i(k), j(k))$. This is illustrated in Fig. 5.5.

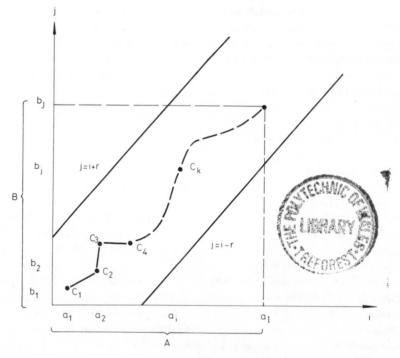

Fig. 5.5 *Warping function between the sequence of feature vectors A and the feature vectors B*

Sakoe and Chiba (1978) suggest a number of restrictions on the warping function:

(i) *Monotonicity*

$$i(k - 1) \leqslant i(k) \text{ and } j(k - 1) \leqslant j(k) \tag{5.8}$$

(ii) *Continuity*

$$i(k) - i(k - 1) \leqslant 1 \text{ and } j(k) - j(k - 1) \leqslant 1 \tag{5.9}$$

(iii) *Boundary conditions*

$$i(1) = 1, j(1) = 1 \text{ and } i(K) = 1, j(K) = 1 \tag{5.10}$$

(iv) *Adjustment window*

$$|i(k) - j(k)| \leqslant r \tag{5.11}$$

where r is an appropriate positive integer called the window length; this length depends on the timing difference between the words.

(v) *Slope constraint*: The slope of the warping function should be neither too gentle nor too great. If it is too gentle the warping function will not be able to adequately map one pattern against the other, and if it is too steep it may cause an unrealistic correspondence between a very short pattern and a relatively long one.

Sakoe and Chiba (1978) tested their algorithm with data consisting of Japanese digits and 50 Japanese place names spoken six times by two male and two female speakers. The first utterances of each word were used as the templates and the remaining five as the unknown patterns. When the adjustment window length and the slope constraint were optimised they obtained error rates of 0·2% with the digits and 0·8% with place names. This compared with 0·87% and 5·9%, respectively, using linear time normalisation with the same data.

Several authors have suggested modifications to the warping-function restrictions in order to improve the performance of the algorithm. For example, Paliwal *et al.* (1982) used a modified adjustment window as shown in Fig. 5.6. Their adjustment window is given by

$$|i(k) - j(k)/s)| \leqslant r \tag{5.12}$$

where s is the slope of the line joining the beginning point $(0,0)$ and the end point (I,J). This places the adjustment window symmetrically about the mean path. It is claimed that this removes the necessity for a slope constraint and allows a shorter adjustment window length. This both reduces the amount of computation and improves the recognition accuracy.

Rabiner *et al.* (1978) suggest other modifications to the adjustment window. They point out that a consequence of the window length and the slope constraint is that the adjustment window is actually a parallelogram as shown in Fig. 5.7a. For this to work well both the beginnings and the ends of the template and the unknown word must be accurately known. As this is not always the case (see Section 5.1.4), they suggest using an adjustment window of the shape shown in Fig. 5.7b in which there is a possible range of mismatch between the boundary points of the templates and the test words of up to 75 ms.

Rabiner *et al.* also investigated the effect of placing the adjustment window symmetrically about the locally optimum path as shown in Fig. 5.7c.

They found that the unconstrained algorithm (Fig. 5.7*b*) generally gave the best results and the locally constrained algorithm (Fig. 5.7*c*) the worst. They point out, however, that no knowledge concerning the end of the utterance is used in the locally constrained algorithm so that gross endpoint errors, which were eliminated for the other algorithms, may have had a deleterious effect.

Das (1982) has also investigated the effects of adjustment-window conditions on the performance of dynamic time-warping algorithms. Like Paliwal *et al.* (1982) he found that a 'band' dynamic programming algorithm was superior to a parallelogram-based algorithm, but the performance of the parallelogram algorithm could be improved by employing an endpoint detection algorithm to optimise the match at the utterance boundaries.

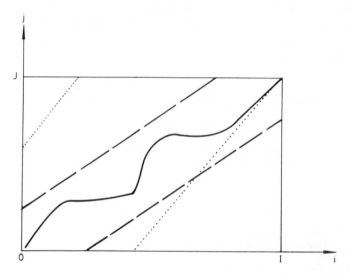

Fig. 5.6   *The adjustment window used by Paliwal et al. (1982) (– – –) compared with that of Sakoe and Chiba (1978) (. . .). The solid line is the warping function*

Another modification was introduced by Das (1982). Speech can be considered to consist of steady-state segments and transitions between these steady-state segments. The steady-state segments contain redundant information, so the transitions contain more information relevant to recognition. In order to increase the importance of the transitions in the operation of the dynamic programming algorithm, the transitions can be expanded. This can be achieved by computing the distances between successive frames and flagging those differences which exceed a threshold. Additional frames can then be inserted between the flagged frames by interpolation. This 'smoothing' process was found to reduce the number of recognition errors.

Myers *et al.* (1980) developed an algorithm in which the templates and the test utterances were first linearly normalised to a standard duration and then compared by a dynamic programming algorithm. They compared the performance of this algorithm with a number of other formulations and found it to be at least as good as the best of the others. In addition the standard durations had advantages for practical implementations.

Another form of preprocessing prior to dynamic time warping has been suggested by Kuhn and Tomaschewski (1983). They employed a procedure called 'trace segmentation' which maps the variable number of input spectral frames into a fixed number of frames with equal spectral change between adjacent frames. Template and test utterances are then aligned with a very narrow adjustment window. It is claimed that this leads a reduction in recognition error rate by a factor of 2 to 5, a reduction of computation by a factor of 3 to 20, and a reduction of memory required for the templates by a factor of 2 to 15. Other techniques for reducing computation and memory requirements have been suggested by Tappert and Das (1978).

A different approach to reducing the amount of computation has been proposed by Brown and Rabiner (1982). Their approach is based on the well-known techniques for a directed search through a grid to find the shortest path (Nilsson, 1970; 1981). This procedure can lead to a reduction in computation by a factor of 3.

One of the problems with dynamic time-warping algorithms is that differences in the durations of parts of words are deliberately ignored even though they may have phonemic significance. Moore *et al.* (1982) point out that the principal difference between words such as 'league' and 'leek' is the duration of the vowel. They show that by measuring the local timescale variability and incorporating this knowledge as an additional constraint in the dynamic time-warping algorithm a considerable reduction in recognition error can be achieved.

5.2.2 *Codebook recognition*

A different approach to isolated word recognition was introduced by Shore and Burton (1983). Instead of time aligning the templates and test utterances, they dispensed with time information altogether. Their approach is based on vector quantisation (Section 5.1.7). Instead of designing a codebook from a long sequence of speech, as is done in speech coding for low-bandwidth transmission, a separate codebook is constructed for each word in the vocabulary from a number of repetitions of that word. When an unknown word is received, vector quantisation is performed with each codebook and the unknown word is classified by choosing that codebook which gives the lowest average distortion per frame of speech.

In the design of the codebooks Shore and Burton (1983) employed the Itakura–Saito distortion measure (Section 4.2.4) and a number of variants (Itakura, 1975). They compared two types of clustered codebooks: fixed size and fixed distortion. In fixed size codebooks the number of clusters is specified in advance and is the same for each codebook. In fixed distortion codebooks the number of clusters is increased until the distortion falls below a threshold. Shore and Burton also compared these clustered codebooks with unclustered codebooks which contain a codeword for every frame in the training sequence.

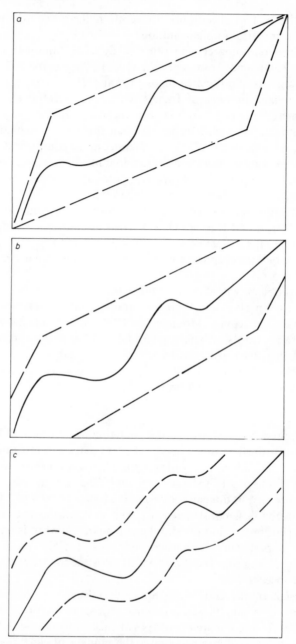

Fig. 5.7 *Adjustment windows investigated by Rabiner et al. (1978)*
  a Parallelogram adjustment window
  b Parallelogram adjustment window with endpoint mismatch
  c Locally constrained adjustment window

They tested their system with the TI database (Section 7.1.4) which consists of the ten digits 0 to 9 and ten control words spoken by a large number of men, women and children. In speaker-dependent studies they found that recognition performance increased as the number of linear prediction coefficients was increased up to 14, but it remained constant with a further increase. Recognition performance also improved as the number of codewords per codebook increased up to 64 (the largest number used), and it was better with fixed size than fixed distortion codebooks for a given average distortion. With the parameters optimised the algorithm achieved an average recognition accuracy of 99·2% with the full TI database and 99·7% with the digit subset in speaker-dependent mode. With a speaker independent system using eight male speakers these figures dropped to 88% and 95%, respectively.

One way of retaining some of the information concerning the sequence of spectral frames in a word is to segment that word into a number of sections and then design a VQ codebook for each section. A number of algorithms based on this approach have been investigated by Burton *et al.* (1985). They refer to sequences of codebooks as multisection codebooks.

A separate multisection codebook is designed for each word in the recognition vocabulary by dividing the words in the training sequence into equal-length sections and designing a VQ codebook for each section. Unknown words are classified by dividing them into sections, performing vector quantisation on each section, and finding the multisection codebook which yields the smallest average distortion.

In order to divide a word into sections the endpoints must be known. Burton *et al.* (1985) determined the locations of these with an algorithm based on the ideas discussed in Section 5.1.4. They then normalised each word into 24 frames and investigated the effect of the compression factor – the number of frames spanned by a codebook. With fixed-size codebooks they found that section codebook rates of 3 and 4 gave about the same recognition accuracy as an unclustered codebook, but these rates were significantly better than a rate-2 codebook. Compression factors of between 3 and 6 gave the best results.

Multisection codebooks appear to improve speaker-independent recognition. For male speakers and the 20-word TI database the recognition accuracy in increased from 88% with single-section codebooks to 97% with multisection codebooks. A recognition accuracy of 97·7% was achieved for combined male and female speakers using the 10-digit vocabulary.

The single-section vector-quantisation approach tries to model each vocabulary word as a discrete memoryless source. Multisection vector quantisation is a way of incorporating memory. It can be viewed as a one-step Markov model with transition probabilities that are either 0 or 1 for moving to the next state or section. This approach appears to give good results, but improvements might be obtained by developing more general probabilistic models.

5.2.3 Statistical modelling

One way of dealing with the variations in the productions of words is by means of statistical models. A single production of a word generates a sequence of feature vectors such as spectra or frames of linear prediction coefficients. Other productions of the same word generate similar, but different, sequences. The underlying model can be thought of as a sequence of states, representing the feature vectors, and transitions between these states (Fig. 5.8). The variations in the productions are encompassed in the transition probabilities between these states.

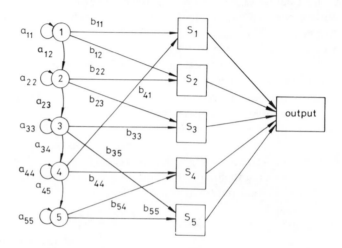

Fig. 5.8 *A five-state hidden Markov model showing the transitions between the states a_{ij} and the symbols b_{ik}*
Only the output symbols s_k can be observed

If such a model is available for each word in the vocabulary, a recogniser can be designed which compares the production of an unknown word with each of the statistical models, and chooses that model which best matches the production. Dynamic programming algorithms (Sections 4.2.7 and 4.2.9) can be employed to efficiently determine the best match. Speech-recognition algorithms based on these principles have been investigated for whole words by Bakis (1976), for sub-words by Jelinek (1976) and by others.

One implementation of an isolated-word recogniser based on statistical modelling was made by Rabiner *et al.* (1983). This employed the vector-quantisation algorithm of Juang *et al.* (1982) to reduce the speech waveforms to sequences of vectors, and the re-estimation algorithm (Section 4.2.9) to train the hidden Markov models. In recognition mode a Viterbi algorithm was used to determine the distance score between the unknown utterance and each of the word models (Fig. 5.9).

A number of different Markov model structures were investigated including an unconstrained model (Fig. 5.10*a*) in which any state could go to any other

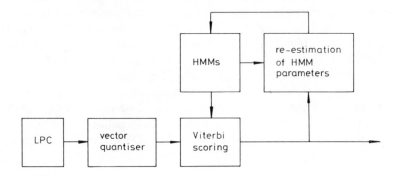

Fig. 5.9   *Training the hidden Markov models*

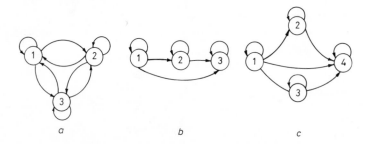

Fig. 5.10   *Different configurations for a three-state Markov model*
   a Unconstrained
   b Constrained serial
   c Constrained parallel models

state, a serial model (Fig. 5.10*b*), and a parallel model (Fig. 5.10*c*). Rabiner *et al.* found that the serial model produced a lower error rate than the unconstrained model, but that the serial and parallel models produced similar error rates. They concluded that no advantage was to be gained from the additional complexity of the parallel model. They also investigated the effects of varying the number of states in the serial model. They found that the error rate decreased as the number of states was increased to about 5 or 6 with a statistical fluctuation thereafter.

One of the advantages of statistical recognisers over conventional dynamic time-warping recognisers is that variations among speakers can be incorporated in the statistical model. However, clustering techniques (Section 4.2.8) can be introduced into dynamic time-warping recognisers using several templates per word in order to allow them to operate with multiple speakers. It is therefore of interest to compare the performance of a hidden Markov-model recogniser with that of a time-warping recogniser using the same speech database.

Rabiner *et al.* (1983) have performed such a comparison. They used an HMM algorithm with a constrained serial structure with five states, preceded by a VQ algorithm with a 6 bit codebook. Its structure is shown in Fig. 5.11. They compared the performance of this with an LPC/DTW recogniser (Rabiner and Levinson, 1981). Each word was isolated by an endpoint detector (Lamel *et al.* (1981), segmented into 45 ms frames spaced 15 ms apart, then an 8-pole linear prediction analysis was performed by the autocorrelation method. The templates for the DTW algorithm were formed by a clustering procedure (Rabiner *et al.*, 1979). This algorithm produced about 12 templates per word with the training data employed. The structure of the LPC/DTW recogniser is shown in Fig. 5.12.

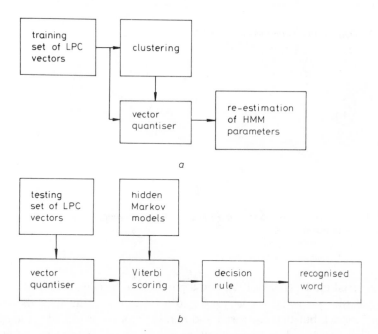

Fig. 5.11   *Isolated word recognition based on HMM*
a The vector quantiser and the word models are trained
b Each test utterance is quantised and compared with each model, then a decision rule is applied to recognise the word

Two databases were used to test the recognisers. One, TS1, consisted of the ten digits each produced once by 100 adult speakers. The other, TS2, consisted of 200 digits produced by each of ten speakers. The two recognisers described above were tested together with an LPC/DTW recogniser which also incorporated the VQ used with the HMM/VQ recogniser.

The results showed that with the TS1 database the recognition scores were

96·3% with HMM/VQ, 98·5% with LPC/DTW and 96·5% with LPC/DTW/VQ. With the TS2 database the recognition scores were 92·8% with HMM/VQ, 98·7% with the LPC/DTW and 95·5% with the LPC/DTW/VQ recogniser. Thus the multiple template DTW system shows a slight superiority over the HMM system, though it is not clear from these results whether this is due to the use of VQ in the HMM system.

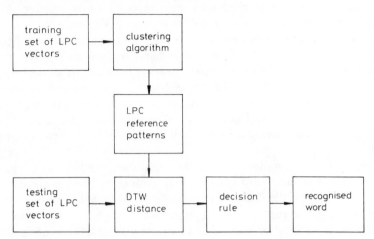

Fig. 5.12   *Structure of the LPC/DTW speech recogniser*

As mentioned earlier, recognition by means of a dynamic time-warping algorithm is computationally expensive as the distance calculations have to be made during the classification process. Hidden Markov models require much computation during the training phase when the models are built, but much less so during classification provided the number of states is much less than the number of frames of speech. Rabiner *et al.* (1983) show that the computation and storage requirements of the HMM system are an order of magnitude less than those of the DTW system.

HMMs are not adequate for modelling duration contrasts such as occur in pairs of words such as 'league – leek' and 'pod – pot'. Russell and Moore (1985) describe a modification, which they call hidden semi-Markov models (HSMM), which reduces the recogntition error rate with such word pairs from 26·5% with HMMs to 14·7% with HSMMs.

5.2.4 Speaker independence
In the production of a word by many speakers there is variation in spectral content as well as in the timings of acoustical events (Peterson and Barney. 1952). It is caused mainly by the different-sized vocal tracts of the speakers. This spectral variation can be dealt with explicitly by frequency normalisation or implicitly by clustering or statistical modelling. These two types of processing are independent, so normalisation can be performed to reduce the variability before the clustering algorithm is applied.

A linear normalisation algorithm has been applied to vowel identification by Gerstman (1968). He employed the frequencies of the first two frequencies of the extreme vowels /i,u,ɑ/ to normalise the formant frequencies of the other vowels. This algorithm succeeded in greatly reducing the overlap between vowel categories in the Peterson and Barney data.

This algorithm, however, requires the identification of the vowels /i/, /u/, and /a/ in order to be able to cope with the vowels of a new speaker. A linear normalisation algorithm was proposed by Wakita (1977) which does not require this information. This algorithm employs linear prediction analysis to estimate vocal-tract length, then normalises the formant frequencies of each vowel in such a way that the vowel appears to have been produced by a vocal tract of a standard length. This technique has the advantage of dealing with the variations of a single speaker during the productions of different vowels due to the movement of the larynx (Fant, 1960). Wakita showed that this algorithm increased the recognition score from 78·9% to 84·4% with American-English vowels.

An even more successful normalisation procedure has been investigated by Suomi (1984), but his algorithm was tested with eight Finnish vowels; so the results may not be directly comparable. Suomi applied a phsychoacoustic model, forming vowel spectra with a phon/bark scale instead of the more usual dB/Hz scale. Identification was achieved by comparing unknown spectra with a set of template spectra. In order to normalise an unknown vowel its spectrum was matched against each template in two stages. First the spectrum in the 2–6 bark region was slid across the template in order to find the minimum distance, then a similar procedure was carried out in the 7–16 bark region. Using male-produced templates and female test spectra this normalisation procedure increased the recognition score from 73·2% to 88·1%.

One of the reasons why linear normalisation algorithms are only partly successful is that the mapping of the spectra of male to female productions of the same vowel is non-linear (Fant, 1975). The procedure of Suomi (1984) partly compensates for this by employing different linear normalisations in different parts of the spectrum. A more general technique is to employ a dynamic programming algorithm to determine the non-linear mapping. This procedure is called frequency warping, analogously to time warping.

Paliwal and Ainsworth (1985) investigated the behaviour of several dynamic frequency-warping algorithms. They found that whereas these algorithms can successfully transform the spectrum of a vowel produced by one speaker into that of the same vowel produced by another speaker, they can also transform it into the spectrum of a different vowel. They concluded that dynamic programming algorithms applied in the frequency domain in the same unconstrained way as they have been applied in the time domain do not improve vowel recognition.

The database employed by Paliwal and Ainsworth (1985) to test their algorithms consisted of the 11 British-English vowels spoken by four male and four female speakers. The wide variation in vowel spectra is illustrated by recognition scores of only about 33% when female test vowels were matched against male templates, or vice versa. This score was about the same whether or not dynamic frequency warping was employed. However, by employing asymmetric, vowel-dependent warping windows it was found that this score could be increased to about 60% by dynamic warping (Ainsworth *et al.*, 1984).

Matsumoto and Wakita (1979) have also investigated dynamic frequency-warping algorithms. They employed a warping window derived from the shortest and longest vocal tracts expected (Fig. 5.13). Using a database of American-English vowels they also found dynamic frequency warping to be of little use. With male templates and female test vowels they obtained a recognition score of 63·8% by simple matching and 63·9% with frequency warping. By applying an algorithm to eliminate the effects of the differing glottal-source spectra, the recognition accuracy increased to 76·1%. When spectral compensation and frequency warping were applied the recognition score was 84·3%.

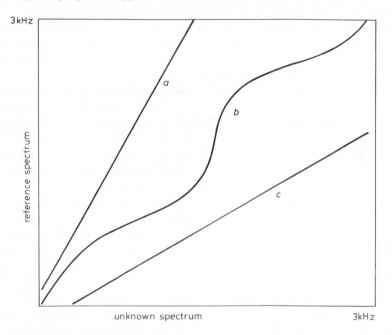

Fig. 5.13 *Dynamic frequency warping to match spectra produced by vocal tracts of different lengths*
a Longest vocal tract
b Warping function
c Shortest vocal tract

Another technique for determining the transformation between words produced by different speakers is to analyse the statistical relationships between time-aligned portions of words. This approach was taken by Hunt (1981) and applied to the voiced and voiceless parts of words. He found little difference between the effects of linear and non-linear transformations.

Instead of attempting to reduce speaker variability by normalisation, an alternative approach is to characterise the variability by means of mutliple templates for each item in the vocabulary. The templates to be used can be chosen by clustering techniques (Section 4.2.8).

Rabiner *et al.* (1979) developed an algorithm for speaker-independent recognition of isolated words based on this principle. They used the dynamic time-warping algorithms described by Rabiner *et al.* (1978) (Section 5.2.1) to time-align frames of linear prediction coefficients derived from productions of the words. This data was then used to form clusters (Rabiner *et al.*, 1979), and the production nearest the centre of each cluster was chosen as the template to represent that cluster. It was found that about 12 clusters per word were required to represent all the data adequately.

With single-template matching algorithms the decision as to which word was spoken is usually made by a nearest-neighbour or minimum-distance rule (Section 4.2.4). With multiple templates more sophisticated decision rules can be implemented. Rabiner *et al.* employed a K-nearest-neighbour rule in which the vocabulary item whose average distance of the K nearest neighbours to the unknown word is minimum is chosen as the recognised word.

The recognition algorithm was tested with a database of 39 words (the letters of the alphabet, the digits, and the words 'stop', 'error' and 'repeat') produced by 100 speakers. With the constrained endpoint dynamic time-warping algorithm (Rabiner *et al.*, 1978), a $K = 2$ nearest neighbour decision rule, and 12 templates per vocabulary item, a recognition accuracy of 79·2% was obtained using the clustering algorithm. With the same conditions, but with randomly chosen templates, the recognition accuracy was only 69·9%.

In order to compare the system with speaker-dependent word recognisers, experiments were performed with a subset of the database containing only the digits. An accuracy of 98·2% was obtained which was comparable with any speaker-dependent system yet investigated up to that time.

5.2.5 Connected-word recognisers

Although some isolated-word recognisers have attained high accuracies they are unsuitable for use in many applications. Inserting pauses between words is a most unnatural way of communicating. Utterances consisting of strings of digits, such as telephone or credit-card numbers, are usually spoken as groups of 2 to 5 digits with pauses between the groups but not between the digits within a group. For this reason algorithms which deal with connected words, such as short strings of digits, have been developed.

The simplest approach is to segment the sequence of words, and then apply an isolated word-recognition algorithm. This approach was adopted by Sambur and Rabiner (1976). However, segmentation into words is a difficult problem because of co-articulation effects at word boundaries. Sambur and Rabiner designed a special segmentation rule for their specific vocabulary, but it was not possible to generalise this rule to apply to arbitrary vocabularies.

An alternative approach is to combine segmentation with recognition using a dynamic programming algorithm. The patterns to be matched consisted of a test utterance, containing a string of words, and a set of word templates. For small numbers of words in the test utterance and vocabulary (such as 2 or 3) it is possible to concatenate in all possible orders to form a set of connected word templates, then to apply dynamic programming to determine the sequence of templates which best match the test utterance (Fig. 5.14). For larger strings and bigger vocabularies, the amount of computation involved with this approach rapidly becomes prohibitive.

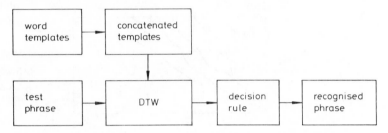

Fig. 5.14 *Connected word recogniser based on matching phrases constructed from all possible word orders*

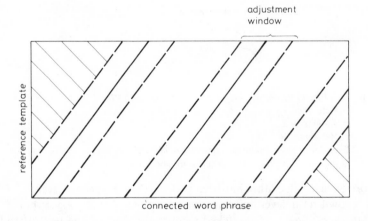

Fig. 5.15 *Two-level connected word algorithm (Sakoe, 1979)*
Partial distances are computed for the phrase against each template by moving the adjustment window as shown. The sequence of words is determined by performing DP matching on the partial distances

Sakoe (1979) has developed a 2-level dynamic programming algorithm which deals with this problem. In this algorithm every template is matched against the test utterance using all possible start points and end points, yielding a matrix of partial distances. This is the word-level matching part of the algorithm. In the second, or phrase, level the optimum sequence of templates is determined from these partial distances by once again applying dynamic programming (Fig. 5.15).

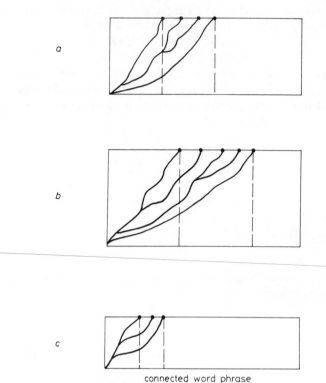

connected word phrase

Fig. 5.16   *Level-building connected-word recognition algorithm (Myers and Rabiner, 1981)*
   a Reference 1
   b Reference 2
   c Reference *N*
   Each template is matched against the start of the phrase in the first level of the algorithm. The possible endpoints are shown

A more efficient algorithm has been proposed by Myers and Rabiner (1981). This is known as a level-building dynamic time-warping algorithm. In this algorithm each template is matched against the start of the test utterance as shown in Fig. 5.16. This gives a range of points where the next word in the sequence might start. The process is repeated by matching each template against the test utterance from each point in this range. The paths are further constrained by the warping window as shown in Fig 5.17. This process is continued until the end point of the test utterance is reached. The sequence of templates is then determined by backtracking from the end of the test utterance to its beginning following the optimum path. This algorithm achieves a similar accuracy to that of Sakoe (1979), but at considerably less computational effort.

An even more efficient algorithm has been investigated by Bridle and Brown (1979). This is known as the one-stage algorithm. It was originally proposed by Vintsyuk (1971), and has been compared with other connected word algorithms by Ney (1984). Each template is matched against the first part of the test

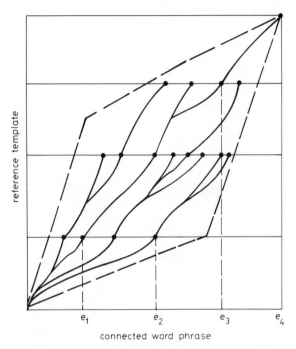

Fig. 5.17   *Possible paths through a four-level phrase with a parallelogram warping window*
The endpoints e_i of the words in the connected phrase are determined by backtracking

utterance and the optimum path yielding the minimum distance score is determined as in isolated word recognition. Each template is then matched against the test utterance starting at the point at which the last template match ended (Fig. 5.18). Computation proceeds for all templates in parallel, in one pass through the test utterance. This process continues until the end of the test utterance is reached. At this point the best score corresponding to the word at the end of the test utterance is selected. The sequence of templates which leads to this score is chosen as the string of words in the input pattern.

Ney (1984) shows that the 1-stage algorithm requires only about 4% of the computation required by the 2-level algorithm of Sakoe (1979), and about 25% of that of the level-building algorithm of Myers and Rabiner (1981). In addition the 1-stage algorithm uses only about 10% of the storage requirements of the other algorithms.

One of the advantages of both the 1-stage algorithm and the 2-level algorithm is that syntactic constraints (Section 4.3.2) may easily be incorporated. The

points in the test utterance where one template changes to another are determined as part of the optimisation process. If certain word orders are unlikely,
or prohibited, appropriate weights can be inserted in the distance calculations.

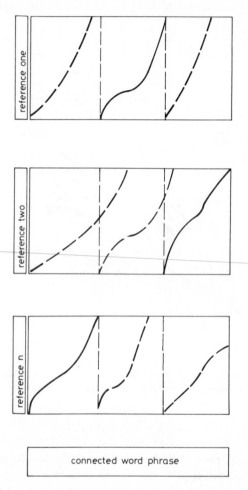

Fig. 5.18   *One-pass connected word algorithm (Bridle and Brown, 1979)*
    a Reference 1
    b Reference 2
    c Reference *N*
    The least-cost paths are shown by the solid lines and the others by dotted lines

5.2.6 Sub-word pattern matching

So far in this Chapter the smallest linguistic unit which has been considered is
the word. This simplifies the recognition problem by reducing it to pattern
matching, but leads to difficulties when the size of the vocabulary is increased.

    An alternative approach is to segment each word into smaller units, identify each of these units, then employ the sequence of these units to recognise the word. The question then arises, as discussed in Section 3.2.1, as to what units should be employed.

The largest linguistic unit below that of the word which is suitable for this purpose is the syllable. One approach to isolated word recognition might be to record one or more examples of each syllable in the language, and then employ one of the connected word algorithms described in Section 5.2.5. However, it is estimated that there are about 10 000 syllables in spoken English (Moser, 1969), so the training procedure would be rather lengthy. In addition, the computation required to match each syllable of the test word against 10 000 templates would be prohibitive.

One way of reducing the number of units is to use demisyllables (Section 3.2.1). There are only about 2000 of these. Fujimura *et al.* (1977) have successfully concatenated such units in order to synthesise speech. They have shown that the number of units can be further reduced by segmenting into demisyllables and affixes. This reduces the number of units to about 1000 demisyllables and five affixes.

An isolated word-recognition system based on demisyllables has been investigated by Rosenberg *et al.* (1983). It consisted of a lexicon and a demisyllable inventory. It was designed to recognise the 1109 words employed in Basic English (Ogden, 1930). Each entry in the lexicon consisted of three parts: an orthographic transcription of the word, a phonetic transcription and a demisyllable transcription. There were two types of entry for each word. The primary entry corresponded to a carefully articulated pronunciation, and the other entries consisted of less careful pronunciations. The demisyllable transcriptions were obtained from the phonetic transcriptions by applying the syllabification rules of Kahn (1980).

The demisyllable inventory was constructed from linear prediction coefficients derived from 1000 recorded words which contained all the demisyllables. Stressed demisyllables were selected from CVC monosyllabic words, and unstressed demisyllables were obtained from polysyllabic words. Initial demisyllables consisted of the region from the start of the syllable to 60 ms after the start of the transition or the onset of voicing. Final demisyllables consisted of the remainder of the syllable.

Fig. 5.19 is a block diagram of the demisyllable-based word recogniser. An unknown word is isolated by an endpoint detector and a linear prediction analysis is performed. The unknown word is then matched against each word in the lexicon. The templates are constructed from the demisyllable inventory using the level-building technique of Myers and Rabiner (1981), and matched against the unknown word by a dynamic time-warping algorithm.

The system was tested in speaker-dependent mode with the 1109 word vocabulary of Basic English spoken by two male speakers. The results showed an error rate of 20–30%. A comparison was made with a wole-word recognition system using the same data. This system produced error rates of 10–15%, but required considerably more storage for the templates. It was estimated that the storage requirements of the demisyllable-based system become less than that of a whole-word system for vocabulary sizes in excess of 500 words.

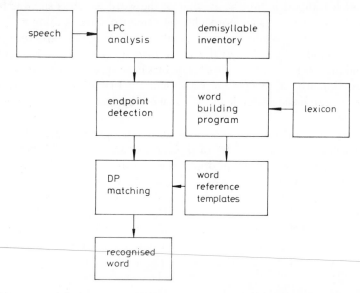

Fig. 5.19   *Demisyllable-based word recogniser (Rosenberg et al., 1983)*

A different approach to word recognition via syllables has been described by Zwicker *et al.* (1979). They also provide an interesting form of preprocessing based on psychoacoustic concepts. They employ a 24-channel critical-band filter bank, and derive measures of loudness, spectral pitch, roughness and timbre from the output of this.

The positions of the syllabic nuclei in the utterance are first identified by looking for peaks in the loudness function. As the loudness of strong fricatives may be greater than that of weak vowels, a modified loudness function was employed in which the loudness of the low-frequency channels was enhanced relative to the high-frequency channels. The number of syllables in a word was correctly identified about 96% of the time by this means. Discriminant functions were employed to identify the vowels by classifying the loudness patterns of the channels at the peak of each syllable. About 70% of the vowels were correctly identified.

The next problem is to identify the prevocalic and postvocalic consonant clusters. This was achieved by assuming that the minima in the modified loudness function were the sylllable boundaries. The consonant clusters were identified by taking nine equally spaced frames between the syllable boundary and the syllable peak, and then computing the Euclidean distance in a multidimensional space between these frames and templates derived from reference utterances. The consonant cluster was identified by choosing the one having the minimum distance from the test frames. If there were two minima between the syllable peaks these calculations were performed for both minima, and the cluster giving the least distance from both of them was chosen. Separate templates were employed for prevocalic and postvocalic clusters so that only phonologically acceptable sequences were chosen.

The system was tested with the names of 236 German cities spoken three times by a single speaker. About 77% were recognised correctly. An incorrect number of syllables was responsible for only about 3.5% of the errors.

Another algorithm which uses sub-word pattern matching has been developed by Vysotski (1984). This employs a fairly crude acoustic analysis to first segment the speech signal into four broad phonetic classes:

s_0: unvoiced pause
s_1: fricative-like segment
s_2: transition segment
s_3: vowel-like segment.

A number of parameters are then measured depending on the type of segment. These parameters represent the characteristics of each segment such as the maximum values of the energy and zero crossing rate, the locations of these maxima, and the duration of the segment with respect to that of the entire utterance. During the training phase the means and standard deviations of these parameters are estimated. A word thus consists of a sequence of segments, with each segment being characterised by the values of its parameters. A word in the vocabulary may have one or several reference prototypes depending on the variations encountered in its pronunciation.

In recognition mode, the test utterance is segmented and the parameter values estimated as in the training mode, then the distance between the test utterance and each of the reference prototypes is calculated.

A 20-word vocabulary produced by 27 male and 13 female speakers was used to train the system. The system was then tested with five male and six female speakers, only one of whom contributed to the training. The results showed an error rate of less than 5%.

A sub-word pattern-matching algorithm based directly on phoneme segments has been proposed by Kopec and Bush (1985). This has been used for isolated digit recognition, but is a network-based system similar to Harpy (see Section 5.3.3).

The digits are first segmented by means of three prominent acoustic events: the boundary between voiced and voiceless speech, the boundary between speech and silence, and the local minimum in the third formant of /r/ in 'zero'. These achieved the necessary segmentation of the digits except between the vowels, diphthongs and semivowels. The boundaries between these were obtained by dividing the interval into a pair of segments with a prescribed duration ratio.

A pronunciation network for the set of 11 digits (1–9 plus 'oh' and 'zero') was formed by combining the sequences of segment labels for each of the individual digits as shown in Fig. 5.20.

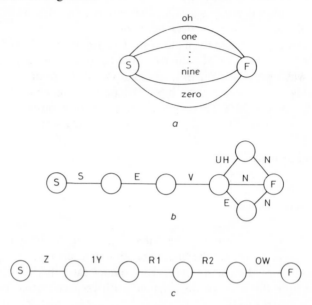

Fig. 5.20   *(a) Isolated digit pronunciation network*
(b) Pronunciation network for the word 'seven' showing alternative pronunciations
(c) Pronunciation network for the word 'zero' showing /r/ represented by a sequence of elements

Each of the branches of the pronunciation network is associated with a pattern matcher. These were based on vector quantisation of linear prediction spectra similar to the VQ-based whole-word system of Burton *et al.* (1985). Each segment class was represented by one, two or three vector-quantisation codebooks. The pattern matcher returns a distance score representing the distortion introduced by vector quantisation of that segment with the codebook.

An unknown utterance is recognised by finding the path through the network corresponding to the minumum matcher score. This is obtained by means of a dynamic programming algorithm similar to that proposed by Bridle *et al.* (1982).

The performance of the system was evaluated using the TI database (Leonard, 1984). In speaker-independent mode with the 11 digits, a recognition score of 99·1% was achieved. With the 10-digit subset the performance was 99·5%.

5.2.7 Large vocaculary systems

In some circumstances, although words may be spoken in isolation, a large vocabulary is needed. In such intances it is impractical to employ pattern-matching techniques with every word because of the computation required. It is therefore instructive to examine whether the search space can be reduced before pattern matching is employed.

Pisoni *et al.* (1986) have found that simply knowing the number of phonemes in a word is a powerful constraint. They found that with a 126 000-word pronouncing dictionary, knowledge of the length of an isolated word reduced the search space to 6324 candidates. In automatic speech processing, however, segmentation into phonemes is itself a problem, so reliable estimates of word length are difficult to obtain.

Pisoni *et al.* (1986) have also shown that if the phonemes are classified as either consonants or vowels the search space is much further reduced. They estimated that the size of the sets of word candidates, averaged across different word lengths, decreased to 109. This brings the recognition problem within the scope of pattern matching techniques.

Although the segmentation problem has not been solved, much information can be readily obtained concerning the identification of the individual phonemes. In many cases it is relatively easy to distinguish a voiced consonant from a voiceless one, for example, or that a sound segment is a plosive or a nasal (Section 2.4.9). Shipman and Zue (1982) have shown that, if every phoneme in a word can be identified as belonging to one of six manner classes (vowel, plosive, nasal, semivowel, voiced fricative or voiceless fricative) then a 20 000 word vocabulary (Webster's Pocket Dictionary) reduces to an average set size of just two candidates. Pisoni *et al.* (1986) obtained similar results with their 126 000-word vocabulary. Using the same six manner classes the average candidate set size was reduced to 5·5 words.

5.3 Speech-understanding systems

In the recognition of continuous speech it is not usually necessary for an exact transcription of the spoken sentences to be derived. It is normally sufficient for a sentence with the same meaning to be obtained. For this reason speech recognisers which deal with continuous speech are often known as speech-understanding systems.

Words in continuous utterances are much more difficult to recognise than isolated words. Co-articulation effects take place at word boundaries as well as within words, making each word context dependent. The word boundaries themselves are often not apparent from the acoustic signal. Words are pronounced differently depending upon their position in the sentence and their degree of stress.

On the other hand, the sequence of words in a sentence is not arbitrary. It should conform to the grammar of the language. The words must relate to each other and to the situation in which the sentence is used in such a way that the sentence makes sense. Also the prosody must conform to certain rules if the sentence is to be understood. It should, therefore, be possible to use these sources of knowledge in order to decode the seemingly imprecise acoustic signal which is received.

A number of speech understanding systems have been constructed and tested. Several of these will be described in some detail.

5.3.1 Blackboard systems

One way in which human experts interact to solve a complex problem is by means of a blackboard. One expert writes the facts, as far as they are known, on the board. Another expert, perhaps a logician, suggests some relation between these facts and presents a tentative solution. Another expert, perhaps a psychologist, explains that because of human nature the first hypothesis is unlikely and suggests an alternative. Yet another expert, a scientist with skills in a related field, presents another point of view and suggests more tests. Gradually the best possible explanation of the facts emerges on the blackboard. This supplies the motivation for the HEARSAY II speech-understanding system (Reddy *et al.*, 1973).

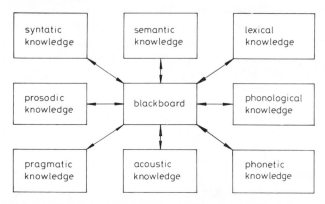

Fig. 5.21 *Structure of the HEARSAY speech understanding system*

An outline of the system is given is given in Fig. 5.21. The knowledge sources, parametric, phonetic, phonemic, phonological, lexical, syntactic and semantic, all communicate with each other by means of the blackboard. The system was first simulated on a large general-purpose computer, then later each knowledge source was programmed on a separate minicomputer and the processors were connected via a network.

The heart of the system is the blackboard. This is a two-dimensional structure with the dimensions being time from the start of the utterance and level (Fig. 5.22). There are eight levels representing different descriptions of the utterance.

The parametric level holds the most basic representation of the utterance. It is the only direct input to the machine from the acoustic signal. Several different parameters have been used including the energies in the channels of a one-third octave filter bank measured every 10 ms, linear prediction coefficients, and wide-band energies and zero crossing counts.

At the segmental level frames having similar acoustic characteristics are combined into phonetic-sized units. Several different ways of segmenting the utterance may be hypothesised and presented simultaneously on the blackboard at this, and other, levels.

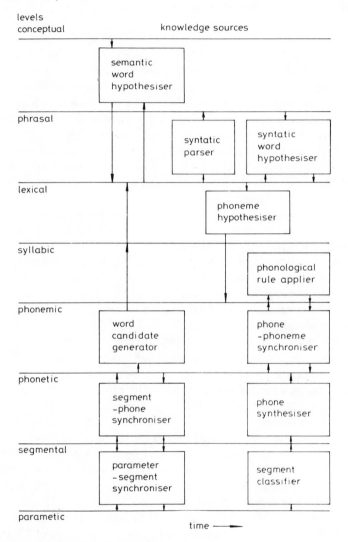

Fig. 5.22 *Structure of the blackboard*

At the next level, the utterance is represented by a phonetic description. Sequences of segments representing a single phone are combined and a fairly detailed allophonic label is given to each segment. Again, alternative hypotheses may be present at the same time.

The surface-phonemic level occurs next. This gives a description of the utterance in terms of phoneme-like units, together with stress markers and an indication of word and syllable boundaries. This representation is not hypothesised from the lower phonetic level, but from the lexical (Fig. 5.22).

The next three levels, syllabic, lexical, and phrasal, are self-explanatory. The conceptual level provides the link with the task which the recogniser is required to perform. In a data-retrieval situation this might represent the relationship between the concepts in the database.

The general principle by which the experts (knowledge sources) operate is 'hypothesise and test'. Data is read from one level and used to form a hypothesis. This hypothesis is written at another level, and used by another expert in turn as its data. The mechanism by which the hypotheses are formed is that of production rules. When certain conditions are satisfied an action results. This action may satisfy a condition for another rule to operate, or it may be a hypothesis which can be written on the blackboard.

The flow of information is very complex as the system is data driven. Initially a spoken utterance causes data to be entered at the parametric level. The segmenter·classifier reads the parametric data and writes its hypotheses at the segmental level. The phone synthesiser uses this as data and writes at the phonetic level. These processes may be interspersed by the parameter-segment synchroniser or segment-phone synchroniser (Fig. 5.22) checking, and possibly making adjustments to, the boundaries.

The word-candidate generator reads the data at the phonetic level, groups the phones into syllables, then writes at the syllabic level. It then hypothesises words and writes the word candidates at the lexical level. The word candidates are given a credibility rating, which depends on how well they fit the data, and are arranged accordingly on the blackboard (Fig. 5.22). The beginnings and endings of the words, with appropriate tolerances, are also indicated.

At this stage the phoneme hypothesiser can read the word candidates and write the appropriate phonemes at the surface-phonemic level. These may be modified by the phonological-rule applier. The phone-phoneme synchroniser can then operate, and this may enable any of the experts mentioned so far to revise their hypotheses.

Once data is written on the blackboard at the lexical level, the syntax experts can be brought into action. The syntax and semantics of HEARSAY II are combined in a semantic template grammar (Hayes–Roth *et al.*, 1978). The syntax-word hypothesiser reads the word candidates and searches through the network which embodies this grammar in order to determine the path with the best match. There will inevitably be gaps at the lexical level at this stage, and the syntax-word hypothesiser can suggest new word candidates to fill these gaps. These new word candidates will be written at the lexical level and will trigger the phoneme hypothesiser into action and, in due course, the other lower level experts will modify their hypotheses and change the credibility ratings at the lexical level.

Data from the lexical level will also interact at the conceptual level and the semantic-word hypothesiser may cause further modifications at the lexical level.

Complex systems such as HEARSAY II pose many problems. It is obviously only sensible for one process at a time to read or write on the blackboard. This can be achieved by a system of interlocking. On the other hand, especially if a network of processors is involved, the system is more efficient if each expert can perform its operations in parallel with the other experts (Fennel and Lesser, 1975).

One of the advantages of the blackboard organisation is that each knowledge source can be modified and extended independently. If the system were to be modified for a new task, the semantic template grammar would need to be changed, but the lower phonetic levels need not be altered. If the system were to be modified for a new language, the phonological rules would need altering as well as the experts using lexical and syntactical knowledge.

5.3.2 Controller systems

Another way in which a group of experts can solve a problem is used in law courts and in committees. The judge, or the chairman, asks each of the experts to present his evidence or opinion. In a court a fixed order of procedure is used, but in other organisations the chairman decides at each point in time which of the experts is likely to present the most relevant evidence, and invites him to have his say.

A speech-understanding system based on this form of organisation has been developed by BBN. It is called HWIM (hear what I mean). A block diagram of the system organisation is shown in Fig. 5.23. It will be seen that the flow of information is partly bottom-up and partly top-down with the control module both receiving and transmitting information.

In order for the controller to be able to assess the evidence received from the different knowledge sources, it is necessary to employ some uniform scoring system. In HWIM this is done by means of an application of Bayes' theorem. The probability that a hypothesis H_i about what was spoken is correct given the evidence E_j:

$$Pr(H_i/E_j) = Pr(E_j/H_i)Pr(H_i)/Pr(E_j) \tag{5.13}$$

That is, the probability of the hypothesis being true given the evidence is equal to the probability of the evidence given the hypothesis multiplied by the *a priori* probability of the hypothesis divided by the *a priori* probability of the evidence.

When there are several types of evidence, either each from different knowledge sources or all from the same knowledge source, this equation becomes:

$$Pr(H_i/E_{j1} \& E_{j2} \& . . E_{jn}) = (Pr(E_{j1}/H_i)/Pr(E_{j1}))(Pr(E_{j2}/H_i/Pr(E_{j2}))$$

$$. . . (Pr(E_{jn}/H_i)/Pr(E_{jn}))Pr(H_i) \tag{5.14}$$

if the different pieces of evidence are independent.

With this scoring system the validity of different hypotheses can be compared in the light of the available evidence.

The various knowledge components of the system are shown in Fig. 5.23. The parametric speech analyser accepts a digitised speech waveform (0–5 kHz) and performs a 13-pole linear prediction analysis (Makhoul, 1975) using a 20 ms Hamming window. Formant frequencies are estimated from the poles of the linear prediction filter and fundamental frequency is computed by a centre-clipped autocorrelation algorithm (Gillman, 1975). Other parameters such as energies, zero crossing rates, and a spectral slope measure are also obtained. All parameters are computed at 10 ms intervals.

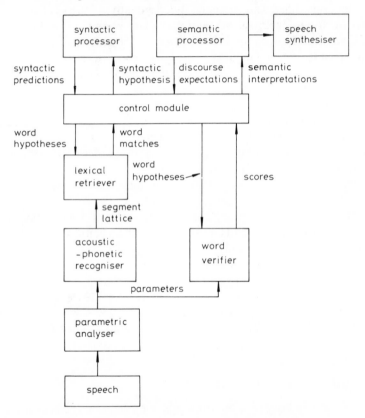

Fig. 5.23   *Structure of the HWIM speech-understanding system*

The acoustic–phonetic recogniser operates on the paremetric data to produce a phonetic lattice (Schwartz and Zue, 1976). It performs three tasks: segmentation, labelling and scoring. The segmentation and labelling tasks are performed by 35 acoustic–phonetic rules embodied in a computer program. The rules are applied iteratively producing first a gross segmentation and labelling which is later refined to produce phoneme-like segments. The results are returned as a phoneme lattice with several alternative labels for each segment. The score is computed for each label as the likelihood of the phoneme given the evidence (Schwartz, 1976).

The lexical retriever embodies the lexical and phonological knowledge. It consists of a tree-structured dictionary which merges common parts of similar words as shown in Fig. 5.24. The dictionary contains phonological knowledge by means of word-boundary rules. Different paths through the network are followed depending on the word sequence. For example, the word 'last' will be /last/ in the sequence 'last one' but /las/ in 'last six' as shown in Fig. 5.24.

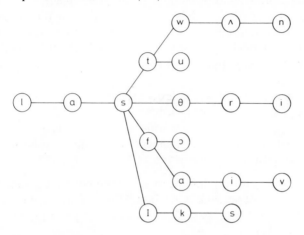

Fig. 5.24 *Fragment of a tree-structured pronunciation dictionary showing the word 'last' followed by the digits 'one' to 'six'*

The output of the lexical retriever is a sequence of words which best matches the phoneme lattice. The lexical retriever can be used in several ways. It can list all the words with matches in isolation, or it can find words adjacent to previously found words.

The word verifier is used to check any hypothesised word (Cook, 1976). It looks up the pronunciation of the word in a dictionary, modifies this to take account of any context, generates a time-varying spectral representation by means of a speech synthesis-by-rule program (Section 2.3.2), then compares this with a region of the parametric representation of the spoken utterance. This comparison uses a spectral-distance metric and a dynamic programming algorithm (Itakura, 1975).

The syntactical component embodies syntactical, semantic and pragmatic knowledge. It contains a parser built around an augmented transition-network grammar (Woods, 1975). Its function is to judge whether a given word sequence is grammatically correct, to predict possible extensions of the word sequence, and to build a formal representation of the utterance.

The task of HWIM was to give assistance in managing a travel budget. It could answer questions such as 'Give me a list of all trips taken' and 'How much is left in the budget?' All this knowledge is built into the semantic component. It uses a semantic network to represent travellers, destinations, meetings, trips, budgets etc. This network is used to generate the answers to the questions, and to assist the semantic component in verifying that the hypothesised word sequences are sensible in a travel budget context.

The control module embodies the strategy for understanding the utterance. One control strategy which has been investigated is as follows:

(i) Use the lexical retriever to scan the phoneme lattice for word matches independent of context, and place these on an event queue.

(ii) Select the event with the highest score and present this to the syntactic component. If this event spans the whole utterance a model of the utterance will be returned. If this model is grammatically unacceptable, the hypothesis will be rejected. If the event only spans part of the utterance, a proposal for expanding it will be returned.

(iii) Send the new proposal to the lexical retriever to test its likelihood using word-boundary phonological knowledge.

(iv) Rescore the events in the queue using the word verifier.

(v) Check to see if the limit on the number of evaluations has been reached, and if so stop. If not return to step (ii).

This control strategy ensures that the interpretation of the utterance will be the first one found, but not necessarily the best. However, as the most likely events are always selected for processing first, the best interpretation of the evidence will probably be selected.

5.3.3 Integrated systems

Another way to use knowledge sources to solve a problem is to integrate them in a unified structure. The Harpy speech-understanding system (Lowerre, 1975) employs this method.

In such a system the constraints imposed on the knowledge sources may be more severe than with the system considered so far. However, the performance of the Harpy system suggests that this speech-understanding algorithm might find practical utility in some task domains.

The structure of the system is a network. Each source of knowledge, syntactical, lexical, junctural and phonemic, is expressed in the form of a network, then these networks are integrated into a single large network. Each path through the network represents an utterance which could be recognised by the system. In the recognition phase, an unknown utterance is matched against the network in such a way that the path through the network which gives the best match is determined. The sequence of words corresponding to that path is then taken as the spoken sentence.

The syntactic knowledge is embodied in a finite-state grammar. A simple example is shown in Fig. 5.25 (Lowerre and Reddy, 1980). Sentences such as 'Please help me' and 'Please show us everything' are legal in this language.

The lexical knowledge is represented by a pronunciation dictionary with alternative pronunciations of each word expressed as a network. These pronunciation networks attempt to include phonological word-boundary effects. For example, /z/ in 'please' may be voiced, devoiced or mixed depending on the following word.

Although the possible variations in pronunciation at word boundaries are included in the dictionary, the actual sequences that are permitted at word boundaries are governed by juncture rules. The network for 'help' will contain paths corresponding to /hel/ and /help/, but the first will be selected by the juncture rules if the following word is 'me' and the second if the next word is 'us'.

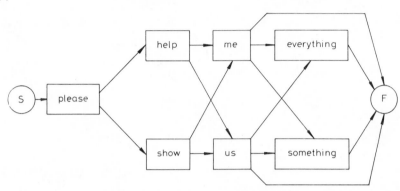

Fig. 5.25 *An artificial language showing syntactic knowledge embodied in a finite-state grammar*

Finally phonetic knowledge is represented by the range of durations permitted for each phone and by the phone templates. The phone templates are represented as a transformation of linear-prediction coefficients. The durations are determined empirically. The phone templates are determined automatically by asking a speaker to repeat about 20 predefined sentences which contain all the phones used in the language. The Harpy system analyses these sentences using speaker-independent templates to identify the location of each word, then generates a speaker-specific template for each phone by averaging the data obtained from each occurrence of that word.

Once all the knowledge sources have been defined, the next stage is to compile these into a network. First the grammar definition is used to compile a word network. This is processed until all the redundant paths have been removed. The pronouncing dictionary is then used to compile a phone network for each word of the language, and these are integrated into the word network. The phone characteristics, templates and durations are inserted, and the juncture rules are applied at word boundaries. Finally any new redundant paths are removed.

This process is computationally intensive. It took over 13 hours on a DEC 10 system for a document-retrieval language with a 1011-word vocabulary to be compiled (Lowerre and Reddy, 1980). The resulting knowledge network contained about 15 000 states.

An unknown utterance that is to be recognised by the system is first digitised and its endpoints are determined. It is then segmented into phonetic units by a recursive segmentation algorithm (Gill *et al.*, 1978). The spectral characteristics of each segment are computed at its midpoint, and the matching process begins.

The goal of the recognition algorithm is to determine the sequence of phones which represents the best acoustic match to one of the paths through the network. This is achieved using a combined dynamic programming and beam search technique.

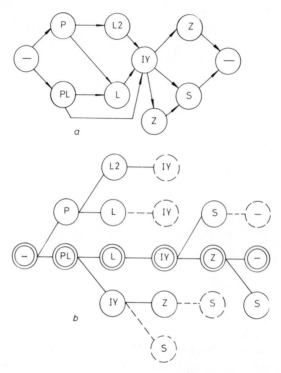

Fig. 5.26 *Structure of an integrated speech-understanding system such as HARPY*
a Alternative pronunciations of the word 'please' embodied in a network
b Recognition by a beam search through the network

The first segment is matched against the phones at the start of the network. and the best match and those having a score within a specified amount of the best match are recorded. The next segment is then matched against the phones of the network which follow those that were retained (Fig. 5.26), and again only the best match and the near optimal matches are retained. The cumulative matching scores are recorded, and used in the next stage. This process continues until all of the segments have been used and the end of the network has been reached.

The path through the network having the lowest score is then taken to represent the spoken utterance. The word and phone sequence of this path is determined by simple backtracking along this optimal path from the endpoint.

Chapter 6

Architectures

The algorithms discussed in the previous Chapter need to be implemented in suitable hardware in order to be used. In some cases simply programming them on a general-purpose digital computer is sufficient, but many of them are computationally expensive. In such instances it is necessary to implement them in specially designed hardware for them to operate in real time.

6.1 Preprocessing hardware

The first stage in the speech-recognition process is usually the parametrisation of the acoustic signal. This is sometimes performed after digitisation, but for reasons of speed the parameters are often extracted by special hardware. In the past this was necessary in order for reasonable lengths of speech to be processed without taking an inordinate amount of time. As computers became faster it became common practice for parametrisation to take place after digitisation. However, with the advent of fast processors designed specifically for signal processing it is again becoming worthwhile to perform preprocessing externally from the system used for recognition.

6.1.1 Analogue preprocessing

The most common form of analogue preprocessing hardware is a filter bank. Often the analyser of a vocoder system is used because it is known that this retains sufficient information about the speech signal for it to be resynthesised sufficiently accurately for the resulting speech to be understood.

A typical vocoder is described by Holmes (1980). This implementation has 19 overlapping frequency bands. The centre frequencies and bandwidths of the filters are given in Table 4.1. Sometimes third-octave filter banks are employed. The relationship between the centre frequencies of these follow a logarithmic scale (Pols *et al.*, 1969). In other instances critical-band filter banks have been used which attempt to model the frequency characteristics of the human auditory system (Zwicker *et al.*, 1979).

In the past attempts have been made to track formant frequencies and other parameters by analogue means. Munson and Montgomery (1950), for example, prefiltered the speech signal into ranges appropriate to the individual formants. The zero crossing rates and amplitudes in each range were measured in order to estimate the formant parameters. This method suffers from the disadvantage that the formant frequency ranges overlap. A more elaborate system was implemented by Chang (1956) in which the zero crossing rate in the first formant filter was used to adjust the cut-off frequency of the second formant frequency.

Two methods of tracking formants based on short-time spectral analysis have been designed and implemented in hardware by Flanagan (1956). One was based on locating the points of zero slope in the spectrum and the other on the detection of local spectral maxima. Both methods used a filter bank to obtain the spectrum of the speech signal. More sophisticated formant trackers have also been developed by Shearme (1959), Holmes and Kelly (1960) and Stead and Jones (1961).

6.1.2 Digital hardware

In recent years a number of digital signal processors have become available which seem ideally suited for preprocessing speech signals. They are essentially general-purpose digital processors which have special features which make them suitable for real-time signal-processing applications. They differ from more usual processors in being extremely fast, especially at multiplication, and in having a relatively small amount of, but fast, memory. In addition, they have an instruction set which speeds the execution of digital signal-processing algorithms.

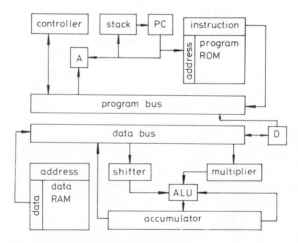

Fig. 6.1   *Schematic diagram of a digital signal processor*

One such digital signal processor is the Texas Instruments TMS320. A simplified block diagram of its architecture is shown in Fig. 6.1. It is constructed with MOS technology and is capable of executing five million instructions per second. The TMS320 has separate program and data memories and buses which enables instruction fetch and execute to overlap. The device contains a hardware multiplier which can perform a 16 × 16 bit multiplication in 200 ns.

The instruction set consists mainly of single-cycle instructions specially tailored for digital signal processing. Many algorithms involve a sum of products operation. The TMS320 can execute pipelined multiply-and-accumulate instructions at a rate of 400 ns each. The sample-delay operation, which is needed in autocorrelation and linear prediction analysis, is performed by a single instruction.

There are other features which make the device suitable for signal-processing applications. Arithmetic overflow can cause special problems. In the TMS320 overflow can be set to load the largest or smallest representable value (whichever is appropriate) into the accumulator. This has a similar consequence to saturation in analogue systems.

There are, of course, other digital signal processors available besides the TMS320. Some of these which are suitable for speech-recognition algorithms are described by Quarmby (1986).

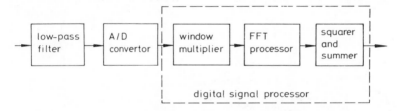

Fig. 6.2 *Real-time spectral analysis performed by a digital signal processor*

A digital signal processor may be programmed to perform an FFT in real time. The basic system is shown in Fig. 6.2. An antialiasing filter and an A/D convertor produces a digital representation of the speech signal in the buffer register. The signal is windowed by multiplying successive points by a window function stored in memory. This operation takes place whilst the buffer register is being filled with the next frame. The FFT is computed from the windowed data, then the power spectrum is obtained by squaring and adding the real and imaginary coefficients. A 256-point FFT can be performed in about 16 ms, leaving time for other operations to be carried out and the power spectrum obtained in real time (Magar *et al.*, 1982).

6.2 Dynamic programming processors

Dynamic programming algorithms require the execution of many thousands of simple operations. If a test word, half a second long, is to be matched against a vocabulary of 100-word templates of the same length, and each word is represented by a sequence of spectral feature vectors measured every 10 ms, then 250 000 operations are required in order to calculate the distance matrices alone. This means that dynamic programming algorithms run slowly when implemented on sequential machines. The speed could be increased considerably if some of the operations were carried out in parallel.

There are at least three ways in which the speed of dynamic programming processors can be increased. One way is to build special-purpose architecture. This approach has been taken in the Marconi SR–128. This system can cope with a maximum of 240 templates and has a response time of 50 ms. Another way is to employ a number of independent, but interlinked, microprocessors. This approach is taken in the Logica Logos system (Peckham *et al.*, 1982). A third way is to build special-purpose LSI chips containing arrays of simple processors (Burr *et al.*, 1984).

6.2.1 Multiprocessor systems

Dynamic programming operations can be speeded up by utilising a number of general-purpose microprocessors to make the calculations in parallel. One such system is Logos (Peckham, 1982). Its architecture is shown in Fig. 6.3.

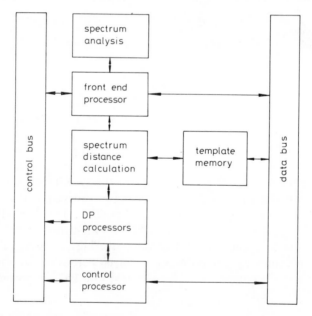

Fig. 6.3 *Architecture of the Logos speech recogniser*

The incoming speech signal is passed through a 20-channel hardware filter bank. The output of this spectrum analyser is sampled by an 8086 microprocessor every 10 ms. A sequence of feature vectors is stored. A buffer allows up to 5 ms of speech to be stored to allow re-runs of recognition on the same data.

This microprocessor controls the front-end processor (FEP) which also incorporates the spectrum-distance calculations. Each input frame is compared with the template frames using a spectral-distance metric. This gives a measure of the dissimilarity between the frames. Using special-purpose hardware with a pipelined architecture, the distance calculation module (DCM) makes a frame comparison every 4 microsec. This requires fast static RAM for the storage of the templates. Because of warping-window constraints not every input frame needs to be compared with every template frame. If only 10% of the frames are compared and each template consists of an average of 25 frames, it is possible for 1000 templates to be compared at an input frame rate of 100 Hz.

Logos employs the connected-word algorithm of Bridle and Brown (1979). It is a one pass algorithm, so 'partial traceback' makes it possible to input speech continuously and recognise words as they are spoken. The calculations for the individual templates are independent, except at the beginnings and ends of templates; so in the present architecture the template processing can be shared between several dynamic programming processors (DPPs). Each DPP performs the calculations for a subset of the vocabulary. The processing that involves the interaction between the templates is handled by the control processor (CP) which also controls the FEP (Fig. 6.4).

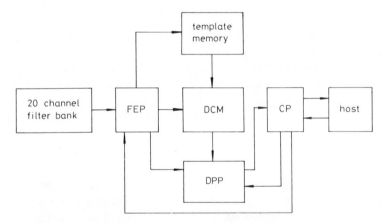

Fig. 6.4 *Functional view of Logos*
Spectra from the filter bank are passed to the distance calculation module (DCM) by the front end processor (FEP). The DCM computes the distances between the features of the input spectra and those of the stored templates and passes the results to the dynamic programming processors (DPPs), which calculate the cumulative distances and choose the minima. The system is controlled by the control processor (CP) which also communicates the results of the recognition to the host computer

The DPPs are special-purpose boards based on the 8086 16-bit processor, and the CP and FEP are standard 8086 single-board microcomputers. This allows changes to be easily made to the system for particular applications.

In normal operation the FEP runs continuously, filling up the speech buffer. The CP periodically reads a data frame from the speech buffer and transfers it to the DCM for processing. The DPPs are loaded by the CP at the beginning of a frame and then started. Each DPP executes the dynamic programming algorithm for the templates assigned to it.

As the templates end, partial recognition results are stored. The CP combines the partial recognition results. When all the templates have ended a score is passed to the next templates allowed by the syntax, so that these templates become the next candidates for recognition. The syntax employed depends on the application.

A somewhat different approach to multiprocessor systems has been taken by NEC. A signal processing device (μPD7764) has been produced which is specially designed for speech recognition (Quarmby, 1986). It contains two processors, the D-processor and the G-processor, which work independently in a pipelined structure. Both have their own RAM and so may be programmed independently.

The D-processor contains two subtractors and two adders. It is a distance-measuring processor, and is good at performing operations such as:

$$d = \sum_{i=1}^{N} (T_i - R_i) \tag{6.1}$$

The G-processor is a more conventional processor and is intended for running the dynamic programming algorithm.

It is claimed that the device can be connected to a digital signal processor programmed to perform spectral analysis to form a speech-recognition system which can be used either as an isolated word recogniser with a vocabulary of 340 words or as a connected-word recogniser with a vocabulary of 40 words. In both instances a recognition accuracy of 99% and a response time of 0·3 s is claimed.

6.2.2 Systolic arrays

Another form of architecture which has been proposed for implementing dynamic programming algorithms is a systolic array structure. A systolic array consists of a matrix of processing elements with each element connected to its near neighbours. Each processor performs its operations independently, except that at each clock interval it receives input from some of its neighbours and transmits output data to others. Information flows through the system at regular intervals in much the same way as blood flows through the body at each beat of the heart.

A systolic array suitable for implementing dynamic time-warping algorithms has been described by Burr *et al.* (1984). It consists of an array of $m \times n$ processors (Fig. 6.5). The test word contains m feature vectors and each reference template consists of up to n feature vectors.

Most of the dynamic programming algorithms described in the literature can be implemented on such an array. Consider the algorithm of Sakoe and Chiba (1978). In this algorithm the local distance between each frame of the test word and the reference template is calculated from

$$d(i, j) = \sum_k [T(i, k) - R(j, k)]^2 \tag{6.2}$$

where $[T(i, k)]$ is the ith feature vector frame of the test word and $[R(j, k)]$ is the jth frame of the reference template.

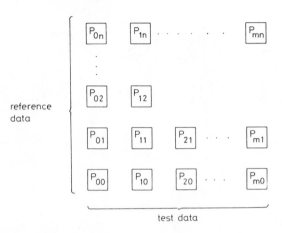

test data

Fig. 6.5 *A systolic array of processors*

Once the local distances have been computed, the cumulative distance is calculated from

$$g(i, j) = \min \begin{cases} g(i, j - 1) + d(i, j) \\ g(i - 1, j - 1) + 2d(i, j) \\ g(i - 1, j) + d(i, j). \end{cases} \tag{6.3}$$

In Fig. 6.6 a processing element capable of computing these functions is placed at each point in the array. These elements are connected together as shown in Fig. 6.6. The test and reference feature vectors are pipelined to the rows and columns of the array.

As a simplified example suppose the array consists of 4×4 elements. A test word $[c_i]$ is to be matched against two templates $[a_j]$ and $[b_j]$, each of which contains four frames. The frames are sent to the array as shown in Fig. 6.6.

In the first time interval, the first frame of the test word c_0 and the first frame of one of the reference templates a_0 are sent to processor P_{00}. In the next time interval the distance between these, A_{00}, is computed, and c_0 and a_0 are passed to the processors P_{10} and P_{01}, respectively. At the same time the second feature vector frames c_1 and a_1 are sent to these processors. A sequence of the activity of each of the processors is shown in Fig. 6.6. The cumulative distance function for the first template appears at processor P_{33} after eight intervals, and for the second template after ten intervals. If the overall minimum cumulative distance is chosen from the cumulative distances appearing at the top right processor, the

142   Architectures

template showing the optimum match will be identified as soon as the last template has been processed.

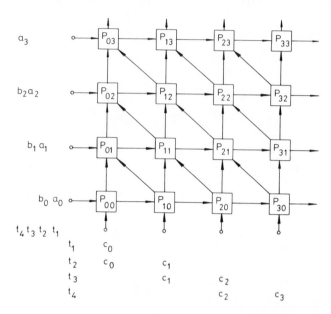

Fig. 6.6   *A test pattern $C(c_0, c_1, c_2, \ldots)$ is matched against the reference patterns $A(a_0, a_1, a_2, \ldots)$ and $B(b_0, b_1, b_2, \ldots)$ by the systolic array of processors P_{ij}*

It will be seen from Fig. 6.6. that the activity in the processors moves diagonally across the array. Burr *et al.* (1984) suggest that this phenomenon can be used to reduce the size of the array. The outputs from the upper right-hand processors can be fed back into the ones in the lower left as shown in Fig. 6.7. The data recirculates and the processors are used more efficiently. Furthermore the size of the array need no longer be the same as the test words and reference templates. This is particularly useful when one pattern is very long and the other is short, as in word spotting.

Sakoe and Chiba (1978) found that the optimal time-registration paths formed by matching different utterances of the same word were close to the diagonal. It is only necessary, therefore, to consider the local distance functions which lie within a small window either side of the diagonal. This allows a systolic array to be designed in which the length of the diagonal can be reduced. If these ideas are taken to their limit a four-processor array configuration is arrived at as shown in Fig. 6.8. Although the processors are used more efficiently in this configuration, the overall processing speed for a given input pattern and set of templates will be reduced compared with a full array.

Burr *et al.* (1984) report that they are designing a systolic array containing 128 processors in an 8 × 16 configuration. The system is designed to run with a

5 MHz clock and with 2 Mbytes of RAM to allow a 1000-2000-word template dictionary.

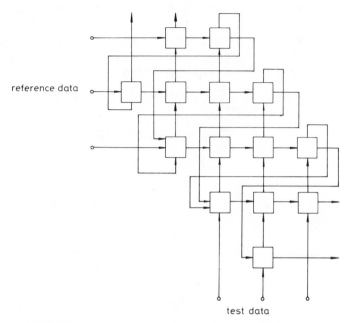

reference data

test data

Fig. 6.7 *The outputs of the processors are connected back to the inputs in order to limit the size of the systolic array*

A full array using 40 nine-dimensional feature vectors per word and a window 10 processors wide would require 400 processors. This would produce a new result every 40 μs, and have a throughput of 25 000 matches per second. An 8 × 16 reduced array, requiring five repositionings to span the 40 × 10 diagonal region would run at approximately one-fifth of that rate or 5000 words/s. This compares with a conventional design implemented on a sequential machine by Ackenhusen and Rabiner (1981), which, using the same example of 40 nine-dimensional feature vectors, achieved 40 word comparisons in 0·3 s.

Systolic-array architecture can be extended to the implementation of conencted word-recognition algorithms (Section 5.2.5). Wood (1985) has reviewed the algorithms of Banatre *et al.* (1982), Myers and Rabiner (1981), Sakoe (1979), and Bridle *et al.* (1982). He suggests that the algorithm and the architecture should be considered together as the choice of algorithm can significantly affect the architecture.

Banatre *et al.* (1982) describe an architecture to implement their algorithm which is based on similar ideas to Burr *et al.* (1984). This is shown in Fig. 6.9, and consists of three arrays: an isolated word dynamic time-warping array, a minimising array, and a phrase-level array. The isolated word array has a two-dimensional structure and calculates isolated word matches. The second array takes the isolated word scores (cumulative distances) and computes the minimum over all templates. The third array calculates the phrase-level match. The disadvantage of this architecture is the large number of processing elements required.

Wood and Urquhart (1984) suggest that a more efficient architecture could be designed to implement the algorithm of Bridle *et al.* (1982). This algorithm is more sequential because of its single-pass nature.

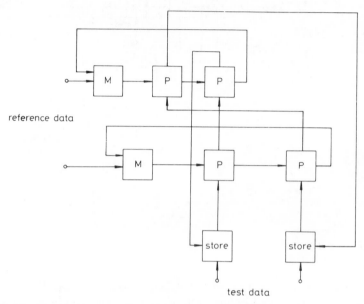

Fig. 6.8 *A systolic array consisting of four processors*

The architecture is a linear chain of processing elements as shown in Fig. 6.10. The length of the chain is determined by the longest template. The frames of the test word enter the left-hand end of the chain sequentially and meet each of the fraïnes of the reference templates as they pass along the chain. At each processing element the local distance between the frames is computed and added to the local minimum to form the cumulative distance. This is placed in a stack for use with the next input frame. The size of the stack is equal to the number of words in the vocabulary. The distances are used to find the overall minimum cumulative distance and the endpoint score (if the present template frame is an endpoint). Each processing element performs the same operations simultaneously and passes these distances to the next element on the right for updating the next frame. When all the template frames have passed through, the last processing element contains the overall cumulative distance and the endpoint score. These are passed to the left-hand end of the chain as initial conditions for the start of the next input frame. The label of the best matching template is passed to the host computer. When the last frame of the test word

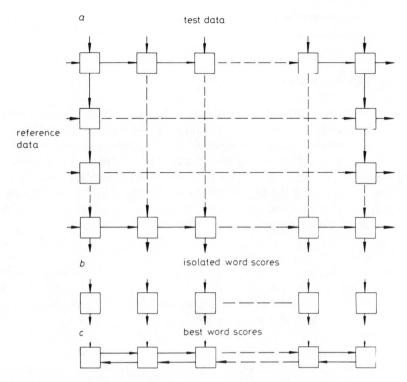

Fig. 6.9 *Architecture for a connected word recogniser (Banatre et al., 1982)*
a Isolated word DTW array
b Minimising array
c Phrase level array

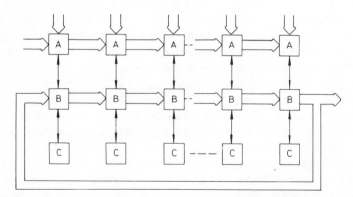

Fig. 6.10 *Systolic architecture for the one-pass connected-word recogniser of Bridle and Brown (1979)*
A: Systolic distance calculator
B: DP matching element
C: DP score stack

has been processed the host will have received a string of labels corresponding to the best matching phrase.

6.3 Knowledge-based systems

Several knowledge-based systems have been described in the previous Chapter. Some of the knowledge processing algorithms of which they are composed are very computationally expensive and run slowly on general-purpose computers. If they are to operate in real time special architectures will need to be developed.

It might be argued that designing architectures for knowledge-based systems should be delayed until the algorithms themselves have stabilised. However, faster ways of executing the algorithms are desirable at an early stage if the performance of the algorithms is to be optimised and evaluated.

6.3.1 Computational requirements

The computational requirements are very dependent on the type of knowledge being processed. This in turn is related to the level of description of the speech. Bisani (1985) has discussed the characteristics of the processing required at three typical levels: parameter extraction, acoustic–phonetic analysis, and word and sentence recognition.

The lower levels, parameter extraction and phonetic analysis, require fast arithmetic. This can be achieved by digital signal processors for parameter extraction and, possibly, by systolic array processors for phonetic analysis. The arithmetic needs for sentence recognition are currently less demanding. On the other hand, word and sentence recognition requires efficient symbol processing.

One way of measuring the amount of processing required for speech recognition is in millions of instructions per second of speech, or MIPSS. Bisani (1985) estimates that parameter extraction requires about 30 MIPSS whereas acoustic–phonetic analysis needs only 0·5 MIPSS. The amount of computation required for sentence recognition depends on the number of words in the vocabulary and the branching factor (see Section 7.2.3). For a vocabulary of 1000 words or less and a low branching factor (less than 10) about 3 MIPSS are needed, but for the same-sized vocabulary and a high branching factor some 30–300 MIPSS might be required. With large vocabularies, of the order of 10 000 words, about 15 MIPSS might be required for low branching factors, and 100–1000 MIPSS for high branching factors.

The amount of memory required for both parameter extraction and phonetic analysis is less than 64 kbytes. However, Bisiani suggests that at least 0·5 Mbytes are necessary for sentence recognition with a 1000-word vocabulary and 5 Mbytes or more will be required for sentence recognition with a vocabulary of 10 000 words.

It is only possible to make accurate estimates of computational requirements for a task when the algorithms for performing that task have stabilised. This is currently the case for parameter extraction, but not for knowledge processing at the higher linguistic levels. Consequently the estimates given above should be regarded as tentative.

There have been few attempts to design architectures specifically for processing speech knowledge. One exception is a systolic machine designed to hypothesise the existence of words in a phonetic lattice. This is described in the next Section. There are, however, a number of new architectures of a general nature which are being designed and built to aid in the solution of problems in artificial intelligence. Some of these may prove useful for implementing knowledge-based speech-recognition algorithms.

6.3.2. Systolic machines

Frison and Quinton (1985) have proposed a systolic architecture for implementing an algorithm for spotting words in a string of phonemes obtained from a phonetic analyser.

Let the phoneme string be $X = [x_1, \ldots, x_n]$ where x_1 etc. are the phonemes, and let $Y = [y_1, \ldots, y_m]$ be the phonetic transcription of a word. The algorithm computes the probability, for every substring $[x_k, \ldots, x_{k+p}]$, that this substring was produced by pronouncing the word Y.

It is assumed that the phonetic analyser can make three kinds of errors (Green and Ainsworth, 1972; Buisson *et al.*, 1974; Bahl and Jelinek, 1976):

(i) it may insert phonemes with a probability p_i; a phoneme x is inserted with probability $q_i(x/y)$

(ii) it may omit phonemes with a probability p_0

(iii) it may substitute phonemes with a probability p_s; a phoneme x is substituted with a probability $q_s(x/y)$.

Let $L(i, j)$ be the likelihood that the phonetic analyser produces $[x_1, \ldots, x_j]$ by analysing $[y_1, \ldots, y_i]$. $L(i, j)$ will be the sum of three terms, $L_i(i, j)$, $L_o(i, j)$ and $L_s(i, j)$, which correspond to x_j inserted, y_i omitted, and x_j substituted for y_i. These quantities are given by:

$$L_i(i, j) = L(i, j - 1)p_i(y_{i+1})q_i(x_j/y_{i+1})$$

$$L_o(i, j) = L(i - 1, j)p_o(y_i)$$

$$L_s(i, j) = L(i - 1, j - 1)p_s(y_i)q_s(x_j/y_i) \tag{6.4}$$

By computing these quantities for every value of i and j, the probability of Y given the phoneme string X is obtained. This computation is time consuming if performed serially.

The systolic solution proposed by Frison and Quinton (1985) is to employ one processor for the calculation of every $L(i, j)$. Each processor has three inputs and three outputs. In order to compare every word in the vocabulary with every substring in the phoneme string, the patterns representing the words and the phoneme string are pipelined into the network in much the same way as the feature vectors are supplied to the systolic array of Burr *et al.* (1984) described in Section 6.2.3.

Frison and Quinton (1985) report that a multiprocessor system consisting of 89 processors is being constructed in 5 micron NMOS VLSI technology. Each processor contains an arithmetic unit for addition, subtraction and incrementation, working memory, and a look-up table module for logarithms (used to reduce multiplications to additions for speed). Each processor contains approximately 12 000 transistors.

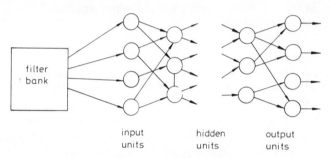

input   hidden   output
units   units   units

Fig. 6.11   *Architecture for a hypothetical Boltzmann machine speech recogniser*
Each of the connections has a variable weight whose strength alters with the local activity

It is estimated that with a 500 ns clock cycle the basic program of each processor will be executed in about 50 μs, so that the array will be capable of processing a vocabulary of about 2000 words in real time.

6.3.3 Language-oriented machines

Instead of designing an architecture to implement a particular algorithm, an alternative approach is to design an instruction set which is suitable for implementing a particular class of algorithms. This is part of the philosophy used in the design of digital signal processors. It is also the basis of current LISP machines (Greenblatt *et al.*, 1980).

LISP machines are good for executing some word and sentence level algorithms. They are particularly useful as they enable new algorithms to be implemented and tested quickly.

Prolog machines have also been suggested as a means of implementing speech-recognition algorithms (Warren, 1982). However, their usefulness has not yet been established.

Another possibility is the use of production-system machines such as DADO (Stolfo *et al.*, 1983). These are currently too slow for the problems encountered in knowledge-based speech recognition if a real-time response is required. Although their structure is suitable for implementing complex knowledge-based algorithms, the process of execution is essentially sequential so that improvements in speed are only likely to come from general hardware developments.

6.3.4 Parallel machines

One way of speeding the execution of an algorithm is to divide its operation into several parts and to run these simultaneously on a number of processors. The extent to which this is practical depends a good deal on the communication required between the subdivisions of the algorithm.

The HEARSAY II speech-understanding system has been implemented on a network of processors (Fennel and Lesser, 1975). It was found that the recognition time for a given utterance decreased as the number of independent processors on which the knowledge sources were implemented increased. A limit was reached at about eight processors, and thereafter the speed of recognition remained constant at about one-quarter of that obtained with a single processor. The problem is that the hypothesise and test paradigm on which HEARSAY II is based is essentially sequential so that a limit on the number of processes which can be performed in parallel is soon reached.

There does not seem to be any possibility of increasing the recognition speed of blackboard systems merely by adding more processors in parallel. It is possible that better performance could be attained by designing special architectures for each of the knowledge sources. The word hypothesiser could be made to run faster by implementing its algorithm on a systolic array as described in Section 6.3.2. As yet no special architectures have been developed for the other knowledge processors.

6.3.5 Networks of processors

Another architecture which is being considered for speech recognition is one which embodies a Boltzmann machine (Hinton *et al.*, 1984). This is a distributed network of processors which is in some ways like a systolic array. However, unlike a systolic array the activity does not flow through the network in regular beats.

The processors are connected to their neighbours as shown in Fig. 6.11. Each processor is a two-state unit which may be either on or off. The state of each unit at a given time depends on the signals it receives from its neighbours. These signals also depend upon the strengths of the connections between the units.

A crucial problem which must be solved in such a machine is how to develop a suitable algorithm for adjusting the strengths of the connections. Hinton *et al.* (1984) have discovered a way of doing this which depends only on the states of the local units. It thus becomes possible to construct such a machine in VLSI technology.

The use of Boltzmann machines architectures in speech recognition is only beginning to be investigated (Bridle and Moore, 1984), and its practical utility is not yet known. It is possible that other forms of adaptive parallel distributed processsing networks such as multi-layered perceptions may be more appropriate for speech recognition (Peeling *et al.*, 1986).

Chapter 7

Performance assessment

There are at least three reasons for wishing to assess the performance of a speech recogniser. Firstly the user of a recogniser wishes to be assured that it is capable of performing the task which he requires to be done. Secondly the designer of a system involving a speech recogniser needs to know its performance in order to integrate it into the system. Thirdly research workers need to be able to assess the performance of different algorithms in order to make comparisons and assess progress. Unfortunately assessing performance is not a simple matter as recognition accuracy depends not only on the algorithm employed but also on many other factors including the speaker, the size and content of the vocabulary, the noise environment, and the syntax employed in a particular application.

7.1 Recognition performance

In the last few years a number of groups have been formed with the specific intention of recommending techniques and standards for assessing recognition performance. These include the Speech Technology Assessment Group (STAG) of the Institute of Acoustics in the UK, the IEEE Working Group on Speech I/O Performance Assessment in the USA, and one aspect of the GRECO organisation in France. These groups are in the process of working towards standards for databases and drawing up guidelines for conducting tests to assess the performance of speech recognisers and synthesisers.

7.1.1 Performance measures
The basic measure of performance is the percentage recognition rate or the recognition accuracy. This is defined as

$$\text{Recognition rate} \;=\; \frac{\text{No. of correctly recognised words} \times 100}{\text{No. of test words}} \quad (7.1)$$

The recognition rate by itself, however, is virtually meaningless. Any report of the recognition rate of a system should also include a description of the database employed, the background noise level and type (white noise, impulsive etc.), and any transmission channel noise. If the database is not standard its description should include the vocabulary, the number of speakers and their dialects, and the microphone and recording conditions.

In order to facilitate comparisons between different speech-recognition systems the standard deviation of the recognition rate should also be given. With the use of statistical tables it will then be possible to decide whether a recogniser with a reported recognition rate of 99·2% really does have a superior performance to one quoted as having a recognition rate of 98·8% with the same database.

word recognised

	1	2	3	4	5	6	7	8	9	0	NR
1	10										
2		9	1								
3			8								2
4				7	3						
5					6				3		1
6						10					
7					1	9					
8								10			
9					4				6		
0										10	
NS	1			2							

(rows labelled "word spoken")

Fig. 7.1 *Confusion matrix for a digit recogniser with a recognition score of 85%* NS shows the number of times that a word was recognised when none was spoken, and NR shows the number of times that there was no response when a word was spoken

For many applications an anaylsis of the errors is important. These may be of three types. First there is the substitution rate, which gives the number of times one word is confused with another (such as 'five' misrecognised as 'nine')

$$\text{Substitution rate} = \frac{\text{No. of substituted words} \times 100}{\text{No. of test words}} \tag{7.2}$$

One way of presenting the actual substitutions is by means of a confusion matrix. In this, the responses are plotted against the intended words as shown in Fig. 7.1. Any cell containing a non-zero entry shows the number of times a given reponse was obtained for a given input. A perfect recogniser will produce a confusion matrix with entries only along the diagonal.

In a particular application if the number of substitutions is considered too large for any vocabulary item, it may be possible to redesign the vocabulary by substituting a word with a similar meaning but with a different acoustic structure for that item.

As well as substitution errors, some words may produce no response. These can be characterised by the measure

$$\text{Deletion rate} \quad = \quad \frac{\text{No. of deleted words} \times 100}{\text{No. of test words}} \tag{7.3}$$

Also, particularly if the noise level is high, responses may be obtained when no word was spoken. These can be measured as

$$\text{Insertion rate} \quad = \quad \frac{\text{No. of inserted words} \times 100}{\text{No. of test words}} \tag{7.4}$$

The error rate is then the sum of the substitution rate, the deletion rate and the insertion rate.

7.1.2 Rejection rate

In many speech recognisers a reject facility is included. This is sometimes implemented by considering the distance of the input pattern from the nearest template. If this distance is greater than a threshold, the input is ignored. If a reject capability is employed, the following measure is important

$$\text{Rejection rate} \quad = \quad \frac{\text{No. of rejected responses} \times 100}{\text{No. of test words}} \tag{7.5}$$

In any report about tests with a recogniser, the setting of the reject threshold or the rejection criteria should be recorded.

In some applications it is important that as few incorrect recognitions (substitutions) as possible should be made. The number of substitutions can often be reduced by increasing the reject threshold, but at a cost of missing some of the spoken words (Wilpon and Rabiner, 1983). If no response is obtained, the word can be repeated more carefully.

7.1.3 Human equivalent noise ratio

In the past the performances of many speech recognisers have been evaluated with a variety of vocabularies, and their recognition rates reported. However, recognition rates depend crucially qn the vocabulary employed, so how can the performances of different recognisers be compared? Moore (1977) has suggested that one way to do this is to compare them with the behaviour of a reference human speech recogniser.

He employed a multidimensional scaling technique to obtain, from vowel (Pickett, 1957) and consonant (Miller and Nicely, 1955) confusions in noise, two distance matrices representing the dissimilarities between vowels and between consonants. These can then be used to compute the perceptual distances between the words of an arbitrary vocabulary for any signal/noise ratio.

In order to compare a speech recogniser with this model, the performance of the recogniser is simulated with the model by varying the noise level until the same recognition rate is obtained as with the recogniser. If only a small amount of noise is necessary to simulate the performance of the recogniser, the recogniser must be performing well, whereas if much noise is required the performance must be poor. The amount of noise is termed the human equivalent noise ratio (HENR), and can be used to compare the performance of recognisers tested with different vocabularies.

However, if there was a fault in the recogniser misleading results might be obtained with some vocabularies. For example, suppose the machine was incapable of distinguishing between the fricatives but was tested with a vocabulary of words containing no fricatives. An abnormally low value of HENR would result. A significance factor, therefore, has to be added indicating the comprehensivenes of the set of words in the test vocabulary.

The HENR does not give any indication of whether the machine is operating like a human. To indicate this a second parameter is required. Such a parameter may be calculated from a confusion matrix. The obtained confusion matrix is subtracted from the one predicted by the model. If the difference is large the recogniser does not behave like a human, but if it is small the recogniser can be said to be behaving in human fashion.

A suitable measure of the difference between two matrices is the 'stress' (Kruskal, 1964). This is the square root of the sum of the squares of the differences between corresponding elements of the two matrices.

A similar approach to comparing speech-recognition systems by evaluating them separately against a standard has been proposed by Chollet and Gagnoulet (1982). They present a reference system that could be run on a variety of databases to determine quantitatively their relative difficulty.

7.1.4 Databases

When constructing a database for assessing speech-recognition performance it is necessary to realise the differences which exist between speakers. As well as the obvious differences between male and female speakers and the different regional accents, there are also differences in the consistency with which people speak. Some people will produce a similar acoustic signal, with minor variations, each time they are asked to pronounce a given word, whilst others will produce acoustic signals which exhibit major differences. It is relatively easy to obtain high recognition rates, especially with speaker-dependent systems, with the former type of speaker but not with the latter. Consistent speakers are sometimes referred to as 'sheep' and inconsistent speakers as 'goats'.

Smith *et al.* (1986) have investigated the performance of a DTW algorithm (Sakoe and Chiba, 1978) with a database of the digits produced by 40 normal speakers of British English. They measured the consistency of the templates and the performance of the algorithm. The consistency of the templates was defined in terms of the mean inclass spectral difference (MID) and the mean outclass spectral distance (MOD). MID is defined as the average distance between pairs of samples of the same class measured along the optimum time registration path (Section 4.2.8). MOD is defined similarly for pairs of samples taken from different classes.

They found a correlation of 0·39 (significant at the 1% level) between the recognition error rate and MID, and a correlation of 0·687 (significant at the 0·1% level) between error rate and MID/MOD. They also found a high correlation between the mean and the variance of the error rates. Such measures as MID/MOD could be used to calibrate databases to show that the speakers included were a representative sample of the population as a whole.

Databases should contain examples of male and female produced speech. Many algorithms appear to perform better with male speech, but this could be a reflection of the preprocessing and parametrisation involved. The frequency of the fundamental is mostly below that of the first formant for male voices, but not for female voices. This makes the first formant frequency of male speech easier to estimate. Performance measurements obtained with male speakers should not, therefore, be extrapolated to female speakers.

Databases should also contain examples of different regional dialects. The TI database (Leonard, 1984) contains speakers from 22 different American cities. It is not yet known whether there is any significant difference in the performance of speech recognisers with respect to regional dialects (or even different languages), but the availability of databases with suitable numbers of speakers from each region will allow this question to be addressed. A multilingual digit database has been constructed (Bridle, 1983) produced by 19 speakers from NATO countries. It contains 9600 spoken digits by both native and non-native speakers.

When a database is produced the conditions under which it was recorded should be specified. This specification should include the signal/noise ratio, the type of background noise, whether an anechoic chamber was employed, the type of microphone and its position relative to the mouth of the speaker, and the recording bandwidth. If digitisation is employed, the sampling rate should be specified.

Controlled recordings may be made in an anechoic chamber with negligible background noise. In order to obtain performance measures in noisy conditions, various types of noise are often added at a later date. It must be remembered, though, that a person will often speak differently in a high-noise environment in order to make himself understood. Adding noise to a recording made in the quiet may not produce the same recognition rate as a live assessment made in noise. It may, therefore, be sensible to include speech recorded in a noisy environment in a database.

If the database is to be made available to other groups, the recording material must be specified. In the past analogue recordings on quarter-inch magnetic tape at 7·5 ips have been the standard. This provides a signal/noise level of about 60 dB. Recently digital recordings using Beta or VHS video cassettes have become more common. This is sometimes referred to as PCM/VCR technology. Sampling rates range from 10 to 20 kHz at 14 or 16 bits per sample. With this technology signal/noise ratios of 80 dB or greater are feasible. Other advantages accrue from digital recordings. Multiple copies can be made without degradation, and the entries may be tagged so that sub-databases may easily be assembled.

In the design of a speech database there is the final problem of what words to include. Ideally the database should reflect the vocabulary used in the application, but with the diversity of applications increasing (Chapter 8) this is clearly impossible in general.

Many databases include the spoken digits. When error rates were of the order of a few percent the digits formed a useful vocabulary. With claimed digit error rates of less than 1% such databases become less useful. A huge amount of data must be processed before meaningful results are obtained.

More difficult vocabularies include the spoken letters of the alphabet. This vocabulary contains many rhyming sounds (e.g. A, J, K and B, C, D, E, G, T, P, T, V) which are difficult to distinguish. In addition they are all, with the exception of W, monosyllables and so are not likely to be typical of the vocabulary used in a practical application. Many databases compromise by including the ten spoken digits, which are fairly standard and can be used for comparison purposes, and about ten other words, often referred to as 'control' words such as 'stop', 'go', 'delete' etc., which are typical of words used in applications.

The design and construction of a speech database is an enormous task. Suppose there is a vocabulary of 20 words. If they are to be used to train and test a recognition system about 10 repetitions of each list is required. Ideally many more repetitions should be included, spoken on different days so that some indication of variation over time can be measured. Each list should be recorded with the words in different orders so that context effects are balanced. About five orders might be sufficient, making a total of 1000 tokens per person.

Suppose that speech from five regions is to be investigated, together with the effect of the sex of the speaker. At least 10 speakers are required in each category. This makes a total of 100 speakers, and 100 000 word tokens in the database. This is for a very small vocabulary of isolated words and only one recording condition!

A number of speech databases have been constructed and descriptions of these are given by Baker *et al.* (1983). The *de facto* standard which has been used in a number of studies is the TI database (Doddington and Schalk, 1981). This consists of 20 digits and command words spoken in isolation in a quiet sound booth into a boom-mounted cardioid microphone by 16 speakers. Each word was repeated 16 times, making a total of 5120 word tokens.

A more comprehensive database has also been constructed at Texas Instruments (Leonard, 1984). This database contains 11 digits (1–9 plus 'zero' and 'oh') spoken by approximately equal numbers of men, women and children from 22 different American cities. This database contains 75 400 word tokens.

One of the largest speech databases has been constructed by the US Federal Aviation Administration. It contains 350 000 word tokens spoken by 5000 speakers over dialled-up long-distance telephone lines. The words include the digits, the international phonetic alphabet ('alpha', 'bravo', 'charlie', . . .'zulu') and 32 control words.

A British-English-speech database has been produced at RSRE (Deacon *et al.*, 1983). It contains an anglicised version of the diagnostic rhyme test (DRT) (Voiers, 1977), the digits 0–9, the 26 letters of the alphabet, and the 60 most frequent words used in telephone conversations. The DRT consists of 100 pairs of monosyllabic words which differ only in the first phoneme.

The database contains 16 lists with the words recorded in different randomised orders. In each list only one word of each pair in the DRT is included. The intensity level and the rate of speaking was controlled during the recording. The words are arranged so that isolated word-recognition tests or connected-word-recognition tests may be conducted.

The National Physical Laboratory in the UK and the National Bureau of Standards in the USA act as archives for speech databases.

7.1.5 Guidelines for performance assessment
A set of guidelines for assessing the performance of speech recognisers has been drawn up by the IEEE and the US National Bureau of Standards. These have been summarised by Baker *et al.* (1983) and Pallett (1985). The intent of these guidelines is to provide a benchmark for the comparison of performance characteristics. The main recommendations are as follows:

(i) *Speaker population*
The speakers should be representative of the user population. Their characteristics should be noted. These should include sex, age, dialect history, speaker training, speech science knowledge, speech idiosyncracies, and motivation and/or fatigue. The number of speakers should be large enough to statistically represent each significant speech characteristic of the population.

The acoustic environment for the speaker and the channel over which the data is transmitted should simulate the operational environment. Important characteristics are the speech signal/noise ratio, the spectral content of the noise, the nature of the noise (steady state, impulsive), and a description of the noise source (factory noise, aircraft interior, office noise). The channel is characterised by its bandwidth, the transmission signal/noise, phase distortion and any channel limiting.

(ii) *Vocabulary*
The actual performance of any speech-recognition system is highly dependent upon the vocabulary. Both the number of words to be distinguished at any time

and the acoustic similarity of the words are critical factors. The number of words to be distinguished at each instant (the branching factor or active subvocabulary) is not the same as the total number of words in the vocabulary. A system with a vocabulary of several hundred words but with a branching factor of 5 is likely to perform better than a system with a 10-digit vocabulary each of which is equally likely at any time.

In syntactically constrained tasks, performance results should contain a complete description of the grammar, frequencies of the transitions from each task to the next, and the average branching factor.

(iii) *Testing methodology*

In designing performance tests, careful attention must be paid to the data, the training and testing procedures, and the documentation of the performance.

Enough data must be processed in order to obtain statistically meaningful results. It is good practice to maintain complete separation of the training and test data and to record them in different sessions, and if possible on different days. All data should be recorded in order to permit analysis and verification. If the effect of several parameters on the recognition rate is being investigated, only one parameter should be varied at a time.

Ideally several measurements should be made to characterise the performance of the system. These should include separate measurements for substitutions, deletions, insertions and rejections (for both in-vocabulary and out-of-vocabulary utterances). Errors due to speaker artefacts such as stammers, coughs, lip smacks etc. should be noted, as should the effects of speech which is too fast or slow. The effects of factors such as vocabulary size, syntax, dynamic range and noise tolerance should be documented.

7.2 Hardware specifications and performance

Speech recognisers, like all other electrical equipment, need to have their specifications documented in order to facilitate their connection to other equipment. The variable nature of speech, however, increases the complexity of this specification.

7.2.1 Acceptance tests

Before a speech-recognition system is accepted a number of tests should be carried out. For a speaker-dependent system which needs to be trained for each new speaker these tests can be quite time consuming.

First of all the amplitude and gain control settings should be checked with pre-recorded material. The recognition performance can also be checked with standard templates and pre-recorded speech to confirm that the hardware is functioning correctly.

Next tests with live speech should be carried out. The microphone should be correctly positioned near the lips of the speaker, and the gain control should be adjusted with normal-amplitude speech. In some systems the speech level and the background noise are measured and the gain control is set automatically.

Sometimes a continuously active microphone is employed, but other systems use a 'press-to-talk' microphone. The former is necessary if the hands are to be occupied with some task, but noises between the speech utterances may cause insertion errors. The latter has the advantage for isolated-word systems that there will always be a distinct silence between words, so that endpoint detection is simplified.

If possible it is useful to listen to the input speech prior to any signal processing in order to confirm that the speech is not being distorted. The proper connection of any peripheral equipment should be checked to ensure that no ground loops are introduced.

The next step is to train the system. This process is sometimes called 'enrolment'. It should be done according to the manufacturer's recommendations taking note of the number of training tokens and their order of presentation. Possible training procedures are:

(i) repeat each token the specified number of times (1111, 2222 etc.)
(ii) repeat the whole vocabulary (1234, 1234 etc.)
(iii) speak the tokens in random order (321432 etc.).

For isolated-word systems the minimum pause duration between words must be adhered to. It may be possible to adjust the rejection threshold at this point.

Once the system has been trained, it should be tested. If the recognition rate is much lower than expected this may not be due to faulty equipment or poor design. The speaker may be a 'goat'! The system should be retrained and tested with other speakers. The performance of recognisers based on statistical modelling can sometimes be improved by increasing the number of training tokens.

7.2.2 Diagnostics

Because of the variable nature of speech, speech recognisers are somewhat fault tolerant. When a fault develops the system often continues to work, but with an increased error rate. An increased error rate, however, is not necessarily due to an equipment fault. It may also be due to a change in the environmental noise level or to changes in the speaker's articulation.

If a fault is suspected a number of checks should be carried out. First check that the background noise is the same as it was during the acceptance tests. If it is significantly different the source of the noise should be identified and removed, or if this is impossible the system should be recalibrated.

The microphone and transmission channel should be checked by examining the speech level and waveform prior to signal processing. The gain setting may have changed or the addition of peripheral equipment may have increased the system noise.

The recogniser itself can be checked with recorded material. It is sometimes useful to obtain a confusion matrix as this often has diagnostic value. For example, if it is found that words containing fricatives are being confused this may be caused by a reduction in channel bandwidth.

If none of these checks reveal any problems, the cause of the increase in error rate may be a change in the speaker himself. This may be temporary due to a sore throat or a cold, or it may be permanent due to a change in attitude resulting in more informal articulation. The solution is to re-train the system.

7.2.3 Vocabulary size
There are two aspects to vocabulary size. The first is the total number of words, or the total duration of speech, which the system can hold. This is related to the amount of storage available and will usually be included in the manufacturer's specification. It can only be increased by the addition of extra hardware to increase the storage.

The other aspect is the number of alternative words which are possible at each point in time. This is known as the active subvocabulary, the branching factor or the perplexity (Jelinek *et al.*, 1977). For a given recognition algorithm this will depend on the acoustic similarity of the words. The specifications may give an average and a maximum value for this. The maximum value may be limited by processing time. The actual value will depend on the words used in a particular application. It may be possible to approach the maximum by choosing appropriate, acoustically dissimilar, polysyllabic words.

It is expected, and found to be the case, that the error rate measured with speech-recognition machines increases with vocabulary size. Surprisingly, however, human recognition performance is much less dependent on vocabulary size. Doddington (1980) reports that for human speech recognition the error rate was found to be 1% for a 50-word vocabulary, 1·2% for a vocabulary of 1500 words, and only 2·3% for a 26 000 word vocabulary.

7.2.4 Response time
The response time is a crucial factor in many applications, and so should be included in the specification. It will often be related to the branching factor as this specifies the number of comparisons that have to be made.

If the processing time is comparable to or less than the utterance duration, the system response may be described as 'real time'. Pallett (1985) has suggested a multiple of utterance duration as a comparative measure for other than real-time systems. He assumes that processing is initiated at the beginning of an utterance and completed with the return of the recognised word. Thus a twice-real-time system would take 900 ms (450 ms from the end of the utterance) to recognise a word of 450 ms duration.

7.3 System performance

When the speech recogniser has been found to work adequately with the vocabulary appropriate to the application, the whole system needs to be tested to confirm that speech is a useful input medium for the application. A training procedure needs to be established for the operators, and possibly a users' manual needs to be produced.

7.3.1 Usability

It is first necessary to try the system out with an operator who is familiar with speech recognisers in order to prove that the total system is capable of performing the required task. Any difficulties should be reported and the system should be changed to eliminate them. If possible this testing should take place in the environment where the system is to be used.

The operator should make deliberate mistakes and report the behaviour of the system. No system involving speech recognition is likely to behave perfectly all of the time, so procedures should be built into the system to ensure that recognition errors do not result in catastrophic failures.

7.3.2 Acceptability

The next stage is to test the system with the actual users. Being initially unfamiliar with speech recognisers they may speak less consistently and so produce more recognition errors. On the other hand they may be more familiar with the overall task and so may be able to work faster. Experienced inspectors on a production line, for example, generally know what faults to look for, so their utterances may be more rapid. If the response time of the recogniser is too great, the system response may be too slow.

Additionally the actual users may already have a vocabulary for performing the task which may be different from the vocabulary of acoustically dissimilar words produced by the designer. Some retraining of the system or the users, or both, may be necessary and compromises may need to be made.

7.3.3 Throughput

It must be remembered that speech input is acceptable only if it can be performed faster, more easily, or if no other method is available. If speech is replacing some other method of data entry it will be helpful if the time to perform the task can be measured before and after the introduction of the speech recogniser. It will then be possible to assess the value of introducing speech recognition. This should then provide guidance as to whether it is worthwhile introducing speech recognition into other operations.

One way of measuring throughput is in terms of transaction time (Peckham, 1986). This notion can be introduced with reference to banking. The time is takes to cash a cheque or make a deposit from start to finish is the transaction time. If the transaction time of an operation is measured with and without speech recognition the effectiveness of introducing speech recognition can be readily assessed irrespective of the response time and error rate of the recogniser. If the error rate is high so that many mistakes have to be corrected, the transaction time will be increased.

Applications

There are a number of actual and potential applications of automatic speech recognition. Some of these are viable at present, but others must await improvements in performance or reductions in cost. The factors which affect the introduction of automatic speech recognition will be considered in this Chapter.

8.1 Types of application

Some types of application require only a small vocabulary of isolated words spoken by a single speaker and are feasible today if economic conditions are favourable. Others require the understanding of speech from a wide variety of talkers and will only be possible in the future, if at all, after much research and development. Some applications require an immediate response, while in others a short delay is acceptable. In most applications a 100% recognition rate is desirable, but in some a small percentage of errors can be tolerated.

8.1.1 Data entry

The type of application which has the least stringent requirements is data entry. An inspector in a factory, for example, examines articles on a production line and makes a note by voice of any defects which need to be rectified. This allows him to use his hands in the examination without having to constantly keep picking up a pencil to make notes.

In data-entry applications an isolated word, speaker-dependent speech recogniser is usually acceptable. A small delay between the end of the utterance and the recognition decision can be tolerated. The acceptable performance level depends on the task. If this needs to be high, some form of feedback must be provided. This could be done visually, but it would require the eyes to be diverted from the examination; or it could be done auditorily by means of synthetic speech.

A typical example of the use of automatic speech recognition for data entry is described by Nelson (1985). Inspectors are required to look for defective solder joints, material defects and assembly errors on printed-circuit boards. This is normally done using both hands to manipulate the board whilst it is being viewed with a low-power microscope. Any errors which were found were previously entered into a document which was sent with the defective PCB to the repair section. After repair the PCB and its paperwork was returned to the inspector for verification that the discrepancies had been corrected. The defect information was then entered into a computer.

This process had a number of shortcomings. There were data inacurracies caused by faulty recording and indecipherable handwriting. Operator efficiency was diminished because of the constant need to switch between defect identification and recording. This also caused eyestrain. In addition the information concerning defects was not available for quality control until after the end of the cycle (which took from two days to two weeks).

The introduction of voice-data entry enabled the inspectors to enter the defect information directly into the computer whilst looking at the PCB. This had several beneficial effects. The number of recording errors was greatly reduced; operator productivity, which initially dropped by 10% when voice data entry was introduced, increased by 25% after a period of six weeks; and the defect information became available immediately for quality-control processing.

Other successful applications of voice-data entry have been in warehousing. For example, Rehsoft (1984) describes an application in which spare parts for all types of vehicles are kept in a large warehouse and each day many deliveries are dispatched to dealers throughout Europe. A computerised ordering system assembles lists of parts required by each dealer. A number of orders are combined in these lists so that convenient-sized loads are formed. The task of the operator is to collect the items in the list, weigh them, pack them into a box, and record their part numbers so that an invoice can be produced. In the old system several lists had to be produced manually and handed to a typist for entry into the computer system.

The efficiency of the operation was improved by voice-data entry. The operators were equipped with lightweight microphones and earphones connected to a small portable transmitter. This enabled voice communication to be made to a speech recogniser and computer via an FM radio link. Feedback to the operator was via a large VDU and by means of an ultrasonic device which could produce 'beeps' in the earphones. A connection was made between the weighing machine and the computer.

This equipment enabled the operator to pick up an item and enter its identification number directly into the computer by voice. He then placed it on the scales, and instructed the computer, again by voice, to weigh it. The item was then packed in the box for delivery. The computer indicated which items were needed, checked the lists and weights, and prepared the invoices. The necessity to type the data into the computer was eliminated. Also inquiries could be dealt with more rapidly as it was known which items had been packed for delivery as soon as they had been processed.

In applications such as these, speaker-dependent systems are acceptable, but in others speaker-independence is mandatory. Another application of voice-data entry is in the use of computers remotely controlled via a telephone. In such circumstances other forms of direct data entry are not practical. In such applications financial data is often involved, so a high level of accuracy is important.

8.1.2 Control

Applications involving control have very different requirements from those involving data entry. The most important requirements are a high recognition rate and a fast response time. In many potential control applications the accuracy is so high that voice control may never be appropriate. There might not be time to correct a response if a mistake is made before a disastrous situation developed.

Fortunately the other requirements for voice control are less stringent. Usually a small vocabulary suffices, and the system can be set up for a particular speaker. In addition the vocabulary can be chosen so that the words are maximally different from each other. All these factors can be made to contribute to high recognition accuracy.

An aeronautical application has been described by Taylor (1986). A system called EVA (Equipment Vocal pour Aeronef) is being developed for the French Air Force (Melocco, 1984). This has a vocabulary of 30 words which is sufficient to enable the pilot to change radiocommunication frequencies and to issue commands to the autopilot system. The system was operated in flight conditions with speeds ranging from 180 knots to Mach 1·5 and with load factors approaching 5 g at altitudes up to 45 000 feet. It was reported that recognition rates of 95–96% were achieved.

8.1.3 Communications

There are two types of applications of automatic speech recognition associated with communications. One concerns the routing of a message, and the other its contents.

At the transmitter a connection could be routed by a spoken command instead of a manual operation. This would require a high degree of accuracy and speaker independence. If speech recognisers were sufficiently inexpensive it might be practical to locate one in each telephone set, and train it with the voice of the person who normally used that set. This would circumvent the requirement for speaker independence, but would preclude the use of voice dialling in public telephones.

At the receiving end speech recognisers could, in principle, replace telephone operators. The recognisers could respond to both spoken names and extension numbers, and route the calls appropriately. In order to perform this operation successfully they would need to be speaker-independent and have a high recognition rate. They would not be tolerated if a large proportion of wrong numbers resulted. Simple dialogues could be developed to deal with engaged and unanswered numbers. This would be a great improvement over some present systems where the caller is simply abandoned.

One of the difficulties of applying speech recognition to communications is that speaker independence is normally required. However, in certain situations this is less of a problem than might be expected. Rosenberg *et al.* (1980) investigated the possibility of using spoken spelled names for directory inquiries. Previously Rosenberg and Schmidt (1979) had found that with a speaker-dependent system, although the recognition rate for the individual letters was only about 80%, the rate for identifying the correct directory listing was about 95%.

The letters of the surname (up to six) were spoken in isolation followed by the word 'stop', then one or more initials again followed by a final 'stop'. A speaker-independent recognition algorithm which employed clustering techniques (Rabiner *et al.*, 1979) was used to select the five best matches for each spoken letter. These were then used to obtain the best match to a name in an 18 000-entry telephone directory by means of a backtracking algorithm. With the parameters optimised the resulting letter error rate was about 30%, which might be expected because of the acoustic similarity of many spoken letters. However, the constraints of the directory produced a listing error of only 5%.

The other aspect of communications where speech recognisers might find application is in monitoring messages. The system would be programmed to spot certain words, and to alert an operator when these were recognised. The ability to do this would be useful in criminal investigations and intelligence work.

8.2 Application areas

The widespread use of automatic speech recognition is expected to follow the adoption of computers in various areas of human activity. In this section the potential uses of ASR will be considered. Those tasks which require speaker-dependent, isolated word recognition await only cost reduction for their introduction. Tasks requiring speaker independence and/or continuous speech recognition must wait for the development of better algorithms and, perhaps, hardware improvements.

8.2.1 Home applications

The use of ASR in the home is limited by the extent to which home appliances are centrally controlled. There is little point in saying 'on' to a central-heating boiler if it is necessary to walk to an outhouse where the boiler is located. Consequently most of the functions which could be controlled in the home by ASR could equally well be initiated by switches. However, banks of switches may be unacceptable in the sitting rooms of many households, whereas a small unobtrusive microphone is another matter.

Consider the house of the future in which all of the appliances of today are linked to a central computer. The heating will be turned on and off according to a program, but fine control and changes to the program could be effected by voice. A request could be made for the temperature of the bedroom or bathroom to be increased sometime before entering those rooms.

Many television sets have button-operated remote controls for changing the channel and adjusting the picture quality and sound volume. These functions could be voice controlled, and the same speech recogniser could be used as for controlling the heating system. This applies to many other consumer products (Brundage, 1985).

Once computers and speech recognisers and synthesisers are as common in the home as television sets, many other forms of entertainment may be developed. The established board games, such as chess and draughts, could be played by voice, with or without a human opponent.

Home databases could be developed which could be accessed by voice. For example, a diary of future appointments could be kept which could be accessed more rapidly than scanning the pages of a book. One advantage of such a computerised voice-operated diary is that it could be accessed remotely by telephone. Members of a family could all use the same diary and so avoid clashes of appointments.

The applications discussed so far only require small vocabularies and a limited number of speakers. These are well within the capabilites of present-day recognisers. When speaker independence is achieved a new range of applications becomes possible. Telephone-answering machines could be developed which were more intelligent. They could first attempt to establish the identity of the caller, then an appropriate response could be given. If the call was expected, a specific message could be relayed. If the call was not expected an invitation to leave a message could be given, as with current telephone-answering machines.

8.2.2 Office applications

In the office, too, voice-controlled telephone-answering machines could be used. First of all they could be used to route incoming calls. The calls could be directed to the appropriate extension either by number or name. It would be possible to reprogram the exchange by voice so that the calls were temporarily diverted during absences or meetings in other rooms. Alternatively message answering and recording facilities, similar to those mentioned in the previous Section, could be employed to deal intelligently with the call.

The main current uses of computers in offices are for word-processing and database applications. It has long been the dream of designers of speech-recognition systems to produce a machine which could type any utterance spoken into it. Such a machine would revolutionise offices. Unfortunately a continuous speech recogniser with an unlimited vocabulary and normal English syntax is required, which is not currently possible. Meisel (1986) has argued that it is practical to design a system with considerably less than 100% recognition accuracy, the output of which could be corrected by keyboard or speech editing.

He argues that in voice data-entry applications an error rate of less than 0·1% is the target, whereas there are some indications that an error rate rate of 5% or greater would be acceptable for a speech-to-text system (Meisel, 1984). He suggests that systems with such an error rate could be produced.

Bahl *et al.* (1984) have performed experiments in which users compared isolated-word and continuous simulated speech-to-text systems. They concluded that isolated-word systems are almost as acceptable as continuous ones. This may have been because the task of the users was to compose a short business letter or it may have been that the users were asked to correct recognition errors immediately they occurred. This study suggests, however, that even isolated-word recognisers may be acceptable for some office tasks.

A fundamental requirement of a speech-to-text system is a large vocabulary. The 1000 most frequent words make up about 75% of a typical text, but about 5000 words are required to cover 95%. The other 5% depend very much on the user, the subject matter and the style. A very large vocabulary, of the order of 100 000 words, is required. For a perfect recogniser 5000 words may be sufficient, giving an overall error rate of 5%. For a recogniser with an inherent error rate of 5% a very much larger vocabulary is required. This enlarged vocabulary, however, is likely to lead to an increased error rate.

One solution to this problem has been suggested by Kurzweil (1985). This is to provide a system with the 5000 most frequent words, but which is capable of handling a 10 000 word vocabulary. As new words are encountered they can be added to the vocabulary until 10 000 words are included. After this when new words are encountered unused words among the original 5000 can be deleted to make room for them. Thus a user-specific vocabulary will develop.

Another question which arises is whether a speech-to-text system needs to be speaker-independent. As most office systems will only be used by a few people a speaker-dependent mode of use is possible. However, the training (enrolment) time will be great for a large-vocabulary system, so speaker independence might be preferred. This of course will result in a higher error rate and increased editing. A possible compromise is an adaptive system which initially gives tolerable speaker-independent performance on a medium-sized vocabulary, but which stores speaker-dependent templates for those words which need to be edited.

In any large-vocabulary system the use of syntax is important, but with a speech-to-text system artificial syntax is not appropriate. A syntax which corrects recognition errors (and possibly bad grammar) may inadvertently change the meaning of some esoteric, but legal, constructions. Bahl *et al.* (1984) have investigated the use of syntax in an isolated word recogniser with a vocabulary of 2000 words. Without syntax the error rate was 20·3%, but with syntax this dropped to 2·5%.

The other problem with large-vocabulary speech-to-text systems is that of speed. Speech-understanding systems which involve many knowledge sources require vast amounts of computation. Eventually this computation may be performed in near real time by means of custom devices and parallel architectures, but in the meantime it is likely that systems will become available which exhibit satisfactory performance but only after a considerable delay. Provided this delay is not too great, speech-to-text systems should still be viable in an office environment. After all there is an inevitable delay in receiving a finished document with either a shorthand or an audio typist.

The other major office application concerns databases. There are two uses of speech recognisers: data entry and database inquiry. Entering data such as names and addresses of customers by voice is not practical, but entering numeric information such as quantities of goods bought and sold and invoice numbers is a possibility. This may not be worthwhile in a noisy office, but the possibility of entering orders and sales figures directly from a remote location by telephone has great potential.

Database inquiry is another potential office application. Languages with restricted syntax are often used for database inquiries, so this is an ideal application of speech recognition. The combination of telephone, speech recogniser and computer makes possible an inquiry system which would enable information about prices, delivery dates etc. to be obtained instantly at any time of the day or night from remote locations throughout the world.

8.2.3 Industrial applications

Because of the diversity of industrial processes many applications of speech recognisers have not yet been conceived. On the other hand, some applications are already being tested. For example, computer-controlled machine tools are programmed in the usual way via a keyboard. In a hostile environment this may not be convenient because the operator needs to wear protective clothing such as thick gloves. In such circumstances control of machines by voice may be a viable alternative. Rigoll (1984) describes an application of speech input to machine tools.

One use that speech recognisers have found in industry is in inspection and quality control. On a production line an inspector may be using his hands holding a manufactured article. When he discovers a fault he needs to write down, or type, the article number and the nature of the fault so that it can be rectified further down the line. This process can be speeded if the inspector can enter this data into a computer by voice. An added advantage is that the computer can assemble statistics about the faults so that the quality-control department can ensure that it has sufficient supplies of components so that the faults can be corrected without delay. This type of application has been described for the electronics industry (Nelson, 1985), and is becoming common in the automotive industry (Howie, 1986).

An example of ASR in a warehousing application has already been mentioned in section 8.1.1 (Rehsoft, 1984). Another example is given by Ashton (1985). Each day a technician would spend four hours checking cases which had been shipped to or were about to be shipped from a warehouse, and writing appropriate numbers in a report. He would then spend a further two hours typing this data into a computer terminal. By means of an FM link to a speech recogniser and synthesiser he was able to save the two hours at the terminal. There were additional benefits as well as this saving. As there was only one stage in entering the data into the computer and as the data was verified immediately by feedback from the synthesiser, the error rate of data entry was reduced. This led to a more efficient operation which benefited other processes in the organisation.

In some applications, such as CAD, it has been found advantageous to use speech input in conjunction with other devices such as a light pen or a mouse as well as a keyboard (Monahan *et al.*, 1985). Light pens or mice are best suited to the entry of graphical data, whilst other data such as identification labels can be entered by voice without the gaze being removed from the screen. Henderson *et al.* (1984) describe one such application involving the structural analysis of offshore platforms.

A similar situation occurs in modern map and chart making. If existing large-scale maps are digitised, new maps covering areas from several old maps can readily be produced. At the Department of the Hydrographer charts are laid on a digitising table and operators are able to enter data into the computer by voice without taking their hands off the equipment or their eyes off the chart (reported by Peckham, 1986).

Another application of voice-data entry, particularly in the retail industries, is inventory control. A stock taker counts the number of items on a shelf, writes this information in a notebook, the later types it into a computer where it is checked against sales figures and used to produce forecasts which are in turn used for ordering replacements items. If the stock taker can enter the data directly into a computer by voice, the whole process can be speeded.

Speech recognition has been used in industry for materials handling. Articles on a conveyer belt can be routed to appropriate destinations by controlling the sorting mechanism by voice.

8.2.4 Transport applications
There are two main areas of application of speech recognition relating to transport: those which involve the driver and those which affect the consumer.

The pilot of an aircraft uses his hands and feet for controlling the plane but he also needs to press switches to raise and lower the undercarriage, change radiocommunication channels, etc. On passenger aircraft these functions are normally performed by the co-pilot, but in emergencies and in solo aircraft they have to be carried out by the pilot. It is possible that some of these functions could be more easily initiated by voice, but great care must be taken. Certain characteristics of the voice change in stressful situations, and these may affect recognition accuracy. In a dire emergency, when the pilot is incapacitated, it is possible that an aircraft might be guided remotely by voice by the air-traffic controller.

The increased performance of aircraft has been paralleled by a proliferation of instruments in the cockpit. Attempts have been made to rationalise these instruments by combining their displays into a single unit containing a cathode-ray tube (Taylor, 1986). This CRT is surrounded by a great many keys which can be used to activate a number of functions. These units are known as control display units (CDU). Research is in progress to determine whether flight information is more easily accessed on a CDU by voice rather than by combinations of keys. An electronic flight information system (EFIS) was first controlled by voice in flight in 1982 (Cook, 1984). Speech was used to replace manual control of 16 knobs and buttons. Recognition error rates of only 2% were reported.

It is occasionally necessary for helicopters to hover over fairly small ships so that equipment or personnel may be landed or recovered. In such circumstances the pilot's hands and eyes are fully occupied. A flight-management system is being developed which will enable the pilot to control displays, tune radio frequencies and change navigation waypoints (Taylor, 1986).

Another application of speech recognition in the field of avionics is in the training of air-traffic controllers. This application is suitable because the vocabulary is well defined and the command language is structured. Currently the training is carried out using simulators. The trainee sits at a console equipped with a radar display and voice-communication links. A computer system contains a model of the surrounding airspace. The output of the model is presented to the trainee by means of a synthetic radar image and messages from people acting as aircraft pilots. Hobbs (1984) has developed a system where the acting pilots are replaced by a speech recogniser and synthesiser controlled by the output of the model.

Although the driver of a motor vehicle does not have so many tasks to perform as the pilot of an aircraft, nevertheless there are situations when his hands and feet are fully occupied with controlling the vehicle and he needs to perform some other operation. In heavy traffic, for example, he may run into a rainstorm and need to switch on the windscreen wipers. He could do this without taking his hands from the steering wheel if the wipers were voice operated (Brundage, 1985). Similarly he could operate his traffic indicators by voice when he wished to make a turn. When navigational aids are added to road vehicles they may be used more readily if they can be operated by speech. It is possible that the use of speech recognisers in vehicles could make a contribution to road safety. Naturally precautions would need to be taken to ensure that casual conversation and the car radio did not produce unintentional effects.

The other area of application concerning transport is in bookings and timetable inquiries. Computers are used extensively in modern airline reservations. In travel agencies bookings and inquiries are made by keyboards. With the use of speech recognisers any traveller with a telephone could have direct access to the reservation system.

With speaker-independent recognisers members of the public could have direct access to computers for both inquiries and bookings. This applies not only to airlines, but to railways and coach services as well.

8.2.5 *Applications in education*

The most obvious application of speech recognition in education is in computer-assisted learning (CAL). At present information about a topic is displayed on a screen, the student reads it, then a question is displayed to which the student responds by typing an answer. The next piece of information to be displayed depends upon the student's answer.

The possibility of using speech synthesis to present the information is being explored, but the response is via the keyboard. There is some virtue is this as it develops typing skills in the student, but the possibility exists of employing speech recognition. This form of response would be more natural, so the learning process might be speeded. By using verbal presentation and response CAL could be used with younger children, but the utility of this has yet to be demonstrated.

One area of education where speech recognition might be employed is in foreign-language learning. Studies with synthetic speech are revealing the acoustic features which native speakers of a language use to recognise the words of their language. Non-native speakers need to be able to produce these same acoustic features if they are to be understood. Special speech recognisers could be built which detect these features, and these could be incorporated in CAL systems which drilled the students in those words which they found dificulty in pronouncing correctly.

8.2.6 *Medical applications*

There are a number of areas of medicine where speech-recognition systems might find application. These might involve patients, doctors or laboratory applications.

One possibility, though not strictly speech recognition, is in screening patients for voice pathologies. Some diseases of the larynx affect speech signals and this could be detected by analysis techniques akin to those used in speech recognition. Machines could be built which would indicate those patients who should undergo further medical tests.

Systems could be developed which could be used for self-diagnosis. Some such systems have been investigated using VDUs in which patients describe their symptoms by responding to questions. This information can be used to arrange an appointment with an appropriate specialist. It can also be used to prepare a concise report for the specialist. Using speech recognition and synthesis this kind of preliminary examination could be conducted over the telephone. If such a system were properly organised, it could save time for both the doctor and the patient.

There has been some research into using expert systems for medical diagnosis. Expert consultants describe the tests they make on patients and the conclusions they draw from the results of these tests. All this information is fed into a computer. The computer system can then be used to guide less experienced medical personnel to achieve the same level of skill. It would be advantageous for the doctor to communicate with the computer by voice whilst he was conducting the examination. This should significantly reduce the time spent on the examination as the doctor, or his assistant, would no longer have to enter the information manually into the computer.

In medical laboratories many samples are analysed by examining substances under a microscope. For example, the number of corpuscles in samples of blood are routinely obtained by this method. This process cannot be automated because any unusual features need to be observed and recorded. The laboratory technician counts the number of corpuscles in a small area then records this number. Continually focusing the eyes on the specimen and then on the recording paper is fatiguing and causes eye strain. This task could be performed more efficiently if the data was recorded by voice so that the eyes could remain focused on the specimen.

8.2.7 Applications in public service

One of the earliest applications of speech recognition was in the postal service (Martin, 1976). Parcels were sorted by one man picking up a parcel and reading the destination aloud from the label. Another man then keyed this destination into a computer so that the parcel would be routed to the correct bag when the parcel was placed on a conveyor belt. By using a speech recogniser one man could carry out the whole operation in the same time which two previously took.

Another potential use of speech recognition in public service is in police work. As the police make more use of computers, database inquiries become important. Because of the mobile nature of police patrols immediate access to databases by voice over a radio link could save valuable time and improve efficiency.

8.2.8 Military applications

The potential use of speech recognition in combat aircraft is similar to its use in civil planes. The pilot, however, has to cope with higher speeds, fly closer to the ground, and to control his weapon systems. The additional channel provided by voice might provide him with an advantage over an enemy (Lea, 1979; Moore *et al.*, 1984; Melocco, 1984; White *et al.*, 1984; Taylor, 1986). Applications in fighter aircraft have been considered by Drennen (1980), in bombers by North and Lea (1982), in helicopters by North and Adist (1983), and in naval aircraft by Taggart and Wolfe (1981).

In warships speech recognition could be used to control weapon systems from the bridge. However, as defensive weapons are fired automatically when attacking missiles are detected, the use of voice control seems superfluous. In some naval situations it might be advantageous for the captain to control the helm, interrogate the navigational computer, and control the weapons by voice.

There is a possibility that artillery could be controlled by voice, but speech recognition is more likely to be used by the army to aid communications.

There is great potential for the use of speech recognition in intelligence work. Voice communication can be monitored by word-spottting systems, and human operators alerted when key words are recognised (Bridle, 1973; Wohlford *et al.*, 1980). This makes it possible to monitor many more channels with a given staff.

Finally speech can be used to assist astronauts in space. Astronauts wear bulky space-suit gloves which make accurate key strokes difficult. The use of speech recognition may overcome this difficulty (Taylor, 1986). In the Space Shuttle the crewman who operates the remote manipulator system (RMS), also controls the closed-circuit television system (CCTV). This leads to problems as the RMS needs both hands to manipulate it, but the television camera often needs to be controlled simultaneously. For this reason voice operation of the CCTV is being developed (Jordan, 1985).

8.2.9 Aids for the handicapped
Many of the uses of speech recognition described in the previous Sections could be used to aid the handicapped. The control of home appliances by voice could greatly add to the comfort and enjoyment of life by people with paralysed limbs (Fisher, 1986). A means of converting speech into writing would aid the deaf. Even if such a device were too expensive for individual purchase, it could be used for automatic subtitling of television programmes and films.

A system similar to that described for foreign-language learning could be used for training deaf people in speech production. The missing auditory feedback could be applied by visual means.

A good deal of mobility could be restored to people with paralysed limbs if they were supplied with a motorised wheel chair controlled by voice (Herscher, 1979). However, people who have limb-movement problems often also have speech problems (Rodman *et al.*, 1985). It might be possible to permit some disabled people to drive cars who are presently prevented from doing so, if some of the vehicle controls were voice operated.

As the use of computers becomes more widespread, the penalty for not being able to do so will become greater. People with imprecise control of their hands find it difficult to operate keyboards, but the use of speech may circumvent this difficulty.

8.3 Human factors

One of the many reasons for using speech recognition for interacting with machines is that speech is the natural mode of communication between humans. It is claimed that speech will allow persons who lack typing skills and technical training to use computers more easily. In such a situation great care must be taken to ensure that the computer's reactions match the person's expectations of it.

An early study of human behaviour in the interactive use of a simple spoken word recogniser was conducted by Addis (1972). A computer was programmed to act as a teaching machine which instructed the user about the system. It interacted with the user visually by means of a screen and auditorily by means of recorded messages and tone bursts. The user interacted with the system by means of a simple recogniser which detected the order of voiced and voiceless sequences in speech. The only words the user was supposed to utter were 'yes', 'no', 'stop' and 'wrong'. The machine could not distinguish between 'no' and 'wrong', but these were discriminated on the basis of context.

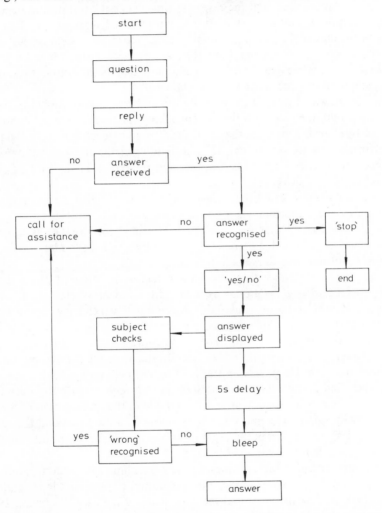

Fig. 8.1 *Flowchart of a simple speech-recognising system which contains appropriate actions in the case of misrecognitions (Addis, 1972)*

The system displayed information for the user to read, then checked that this had been understood by asking questions which called for a vocal response. The procedure for dealing with the answer is shown in Fig. 8.1. If the system recognised 'yes' or 'no' in reply to a question, it displayed that word on the screen. If the user did not contradict the machine by saying 'wrong' within five seconds, the system assumed that it had recognised the response correctly and indicated this by producing a confirmatory tone burst. The user could interrupt the system at any time by saying 'stop'.

The times taken for a vocal response to be made to the questions were measured. It was found that the response time was not constant but depended on the question. It was in the range 0–2·5 s with a mode at about 0·6 s. Response times to the checks (i.e. the user saying 'wrong' when the system typed 'yes' or 'no' incorrectly) were shorter than this, about 0·3 s. Users tended to check incorrect machine recognition with 'wrong', but usually they did not respond if the machine recognised what they said correctly.

The system was displayed at an exhibition and was used by 134 visitors. The teaching program ended with the system asking the user if he would allow his voice to be recorded for a database. Of the 89 who reached this far and agreed, 68 performed exactly as required, 12 made reading errors and 9 failed to operate the machine because they spoke too fast and their voices could not be distinguished from the background noise.

This study demonstrated that a large proportion of naive users can interact successfully with a machine via a speech recogniser. Most of them managed to adjust their voices so that the machine interpreted their replies as intended. Some, however, responded to machine errors by speaking louder and louder, which did not improve the recognition rate.

Underwood (1984) has discussed human factors in terms of physical, cognitive, social and organisational aspects. The physical aspects are the level, background noise and distortion of the speech signal, which have been discussed in previous Chapters. Cognitive aspects include the mode of man–machine interaction, the user's mental model of the machine, his short-term memory, and the interference of competing tasks. Social aspects affect the acceptability of speech recognition. Do people appear foolish when conversing with a machine, or do they find it prestigious to use such hi-tech. equipment? Organisational aspects concern the changes which will be made in the organisation as a result of introducing speech recognition. These should be anticipated and the system should be designed as part of the organisation as it will be after the introduction, not how it was before.

There are basically three modes of man–machine interaction: command mode, question-and-answer mode, and menu mode. Which mode is employed depends on the task involved and the experience of the user (Peckham, 1986). Command mode is usual for experienced users of a system. However, with voice-operated systems the number of potential commands at a given instant may exceed the branching factor. It will then be necessary to arrange the commands in a hierarchical structure so that the required operation can be accessed by a sequence of commands. As even experienced users occasionally have difficulty in recalling the whole repertoire of available commands, some form of help facility should be provided which can be accessed at any time.

Question-and-answer mode is more appropriate for inexperienced or occasional users of a system. This mode is often tedious for experienced users but it can be fairly error-free, especially if the only answers are 'yes' or 'no', and often leads to the shortest transaction time for naive users.

Menu mode is also often appropriate for inexperienced users. This is similar to question-and-answer mode but the list of possible answers is given. It is easy to incorporate small-vocabulary isolated-word recognisers in menu-driven systems. If the menu is presented auditorily, however, care must be taken to ensure that the time taken to present the list of items does not exceed the span of short-term memory.

Whatever the mode of interaction chosen, the appropriate use of feedback must be considered. In some circumstances the recognition of each word must be verified before any action is taken, but in others such a pedantic procedure would unnecessarily slow down the operation.

In a hands and eyes busy situation it is sometimes thought that speech provides an additional channel allowing extra data to be processed without interference with the primary task. Some experiments by Berman (1984) show that this is not necessarily true.

There are a number of models of human information processing. Broadbent (1971) suggested a model based on a single-channel processor which copes with a number of simultaneous tasks by time sharing. Experiments have not confirmed this. Another model is based on parallel processing (Kahneman, 1973). This would allow speech processing to take place in parallel with other information processing provided the total processing capacity was not reached. Schneider and Schiffrin have proposed an alternative model (Schneider and Schiffrin, 1977; Schiffrin and Schneider, 1977). Many highly practised, well-learned tasks can be performed with little conscious intervention. The model of Schneider and Schiffrin adds this facility to the model of Broadbent. It is an attractive model for advocates of automatic speech recognition, but unfortunately it cannot successfully explain dual-task interference.

The currently accepted model is similar to that of Kahneman, but with a reservoir of processing power associated with each input modality and encoding process (McLeod, 1977). The introduction of speech input or output may employ some underused reservoir, but in a dual-task situation it may also overload some encoding process causing task interference.

Berman (1984) has performed some experiments designed to investigate this model in speech-related tasks. In one experiment subjects were required to perform a visual search task and to simultaneously decide whether numbers presented auditorily were odd or even. They responded either manually or by speech. The auditory task slowed down the visual task, but there was no difference in the speed or accuracy of the digit classification when the response was manual or vocal. The implication is that a pilot flying a plane will have his visual attention interrupted whether he changes radio frequencies manually or by voice.

In a second experiment Berman examined the interaction between concurrent tasks when one was a psychomotor task and the other involved spatial or verbal encoding with a manual or vocal response. The psychomotor task was a tracking task using a joystick. The other task required pairs of letters, presented on the same display as the tracking task, to be classified 'same' or 'different' depending on geometric shape (spatial task) or letter name irrespective of upper or lower case (verbal task). Responses were made either by voice or by pressing buttons with the hand not involved with tracking.

It was found that spatial matches were faster than verbal matches, and manual responses were faster than vocal. However, when the tracking difficulty was increased from easy to difficult the reaction time of the manual response increased with the verbal task but not with the spatial task, whereas the reaction time of the vocal response increased with the spatial task but not with the verbal task. This experiment illustrates the complex interactions which occur in a high-workload multitask environment. A change from manual to verbal processing does not necessarily lead to an increase in operational efficiency.

A third experiment by Berman illustrates the effects of speech-related tasks on short-term memory. Subjects were required to enter a sequence of five digits, presented visually or auditorily, into a speech recogniser or a keyboard. After 15 seconds the sequence was presented again, either by the same or different modality, and the subject was required to state whether this was the correct sequence. During the 15 second period the subject was required to count backwards in threes from a cued starting number. The cue was either presented visually, and the subject wrote down the subtracted numbers, or auditorily, in which case the subject spoke the numbers. It was found that verification was slower when the interfering task was performed vocally. This experiment illustrates the additional difficulties which an operator may encounter if a task is changed from a manual to a vocal one.

In most situations in which speech recognition is employed an opportunity arises for the user to be trained. This time should be used to explain not only the use of the system, but also its limitations. For example, if a speaker-dependent recogniser is to be used it will probably only function satisfactorily when the user is in the same state as he was when the system was trained with his voice. Temporary conditions such as colds or sore throats may change the voice sufficiently for the error rate to increase to an unacceptable level. No amount of fault finding will discover this reason, but retraining the system may reduce the error rate to its former level. In military operations it should be noted that training missions may not simulate combat situations sufficiently for changes in the voice to be copied.

When a user is first introduced to a speech-recognition machine he will probably be somewhat in awe of it, and will speak slowly and distinctly. As he becomes more familiar with it, it is likely that he will become more careless in his speech habits. In order to guard against this it is advisable to retrain the machine at regular intervals.

8.4 System factors

When considering the application of speech recognition in a complex system an analysis of the system should first be performed. The overall task should be broken down into a number of subtasks. Where a subtask involves human interaction with a machine, the use of speech recognition can be considered.

If the subtask does not involce discrete manual action the use of speech recognition is probably not appropriate, and should be rejected. If the subtask is of this nature then the accuracy requirements and the time constraints should be estimated. These will help to decide whether any of the available recognisers are suitable for the task.

The actions being performed by the operator should be considered next. If the operator is communicating with other members of the working crew by voice, it may be confusing to interact with a machine by the same modality. However, if the hands of the operator are occupied with some other task, the use of voice may provide a valuable extra channel. In a high-workload environment this may not be so.

Table 8.1 *Some commercial speech recognisers available in 1984, together with their specifications and costs*

Manufacturer	Product	Active vocabulary	Connected word	Syntax	Cost, $US
Verbex	3000	120	yes	yes	30 000
Logica	Logos	≤ 1000	yes	yes	?
Threshold Technology	T-600	50	no	yes	14 000
Votan	VPC 6000	75	yes	yes	4500
Dragon Systems		64	yes	yes	3000
Texas Instruments	SCS	50	no	no	2600
Infovox	RA-101/PC	48	no	yes	1000
Scott Instruments	Shadow/VET	40	no	no	700

8.5 Economic factors

The cost of a speech recogniser is to a large extent related to its performance. A simple speaker-dependent isolated word recogniser can be purchased for a few tens of pounds, whereas a speaker-independent system with a low error rate, such as the Verbex 3000, costs tens of thousands of pounds. In between these two extremes there is a whole range of recognisers whose costs depend upon their performance (Table 8.1).

The economics of speech recognition depends upon the function that the recogniser is to perform. Peckham (1984) mentions that speech recognition has been accepted most readily where the cost is justified in terms of the increased productivity. One of the best examples is quality-control inspection. He suggests that users may be unwilling to pay much for speech recognition in multifunction terminals where speech is just another input mode. In certain applications, such as mobile phones where speech allows one hand to remain on the steering wheel, the extra cost can be justified. The economics of introducing speech in telephone exchanges is different from single-user systems as the cost can be shared among many users.

If the recogniser not only replaces a keyboard, but also the keyboard operator, the economics are again different. This is often the case if a speech recogniser allows a user to interact with a computer remotely via the telephone system. The savings then might involve the salary and overheads of an employee, which might make the use of a more expensive recogniser with a better performance an economic proposition. In fact, as the recogniser can operate 24 hours a day, seven days a week, the costs of several employees might be saved.

Besides the direct savings of using speech recognition, the enhanced services that could be provided should be considered. A 24-hour inquiry system may not reduce costs, but it may increase business. It may be helpful for people living in different time zones. If the cost of speech recognisers is reduced in the future, as seems likely as the applications increase, it may become worthwhile to use several recognisers accessing the same database, so that employees' and customers' time spent on inquiries can be saved.

Chapter 9

The future

9.1 Achievements

In the last decade machines which perform speech recognition have moved out of the laboratory and into the market place. Though it is still uncommon to find a speech-recognition machine in use, they exist and are being used in increasing numbers. The machines in the market place do not have all of the capabilities which are desired of them, but they are still useful in certain applications. Much remains to be done, but a number of substantial advances have enabled steady progress to be made and speech-recognition technology is becoming established.

One of the advances which allowed pattern recognition in general, and speech recognition in particular, to develop was the general availability of suitable digital computers. These enabled the algorithms to be developed more rapidly, and to be tested with large quantities of data. This development is still in progress, and advances in speed and storage capacity will allow even more sophisticated algorithms to be developed. Perhaps more important, however, is the appearance of new structures and new programming languages specially suited to pattern recognition applications.

Once digital techniques had become an established way of processing speech signals, the virtues of linear prediction analysis became apparent. Originally developed as a technique for transmission bandwidth compression, it soon became a standard tool for speech analysis and has been incorporated into many speech-recognition systems. Although the results obtained with linear-prediction analysis are comparable with those obtained with older methods such as filter-bank analysis, its embodiment in digital systems offers large cost reductions in potential products.

Vector quantisation, a logical extension of linear-prediction analysis embodied in digital systems, was also developed as a technique for bandwidth compression. The effectiveness of vector quantisation as a pattern-recognition technique is in some ways surprising, except that it is similar in many ways to statistical modelling applied to pattern recognition. Developments in this area are still active.

Undoubtedly the single most important development which improved the performance of speech-recognition machines sufficiently for them to be used in practical applications was the introduction of dynamic programming. Dynamic programming was originally proposed as an optimisation technique in process control, but its application to determine the time-registration path in speech recognition solved one of the significant problems. The introduction of statistical modelliing techniques, such as hidden Markov modelling, has proved a powerful means of dealing with the variability of speech. This also constituted a significant advance.

The use of syntax has enabled many speech-recognition algorithms to be used in practical applications. Although the use of syntax cannot be described as a theoretical advance, it has in fact made a significant contribution in constraining the branching factor within limits which enabled recognition performance to reach an acceptable level.

The achievements outlined above apply to discrete utterance recognition. However, advances have also been made in algorithms for the recognition of continuous speech. Perhaps the most significant advance was the realisation that many sources of knowledge, not just acoustic data, contribute to the understanding of a spoken sentence. Although these sources are recognised, our knowledge of many of them is far from complete. No doubt the necessary analyses will be made and the data formalised in the years to come. What is also required is the development of optimum ways of combining these sources of knowledge. Advances in computer technology should enable more sophisticated algorithms to be developed and tested.

9.2 Current problems

Now that speech-recognition systems are being tested in practical situations the significance of their shortcomings can be assessed. Undoubtedly one of the annoying aspects of isolated-word recognisers is the necessity to pause between words. Speaking words in isolation is a most unnatural way of communicating. Connected word recognisers have an obvious advantage, provided their recognition rates are sufficiently high.

One obvious problem which needs to be overcome is that of the effect of noise. In a recent study Wilpon (1985) showed that, with data recorded under laboratory conditions over a private telephone line, a speech-recognition system yielded a recognition accuracy of 98·4% on a digit-recognition task, whilst using the same recogniser a recognition accuracy of only 84·4% was obtained with data collected over the public telephone system. Some of this difference might be due to variations in pronunciation, but as separate templates were formed for each set of data, extraneous noise on the line must have accounted for much of the difference.

For many tasks the limitation of small vocabularies creates a problem. This is particularly so for the voice-operated-typewriter type of application. It is claimed that one of the best current systems (Bahl *et al.*, 1984), which is designed to be used for typing business letters, can operate with a vocabulary of 5000 words, but an artificial syntax is imposed. The problem is that for this type of application an increase of two orders of magnitude (from 50 to 5000 words) in the size of the vocabulary is required above that of a typical digit recogniser.

With large vocabularies the training problem can become acute. It is therefore advisable to adopt a speaker-independent philosophy so that training does not need to be carried out by each individual user. The combination of speaker independence and large vocabulary creates problems which are only beginning to be addressed.

Finally there is the problem of sentence recognition. People only use isolated words in special circumstances (although it can be argued that talking to a computer is very special!). They normally speak sentences with natural syntax. Speech-recognition devices will be much more acceptable to users when the problem of machine understanding of speech has been solved.

9.3 Lines of research

Although the way to solve all of these problems is not clear at the moment there are several lines of research which appear promising. There are two main approaches. One is to develop the pattern-matching techniques which have proved so successful in isolated-word recognisers, and to extend these so that they may be applied to more complex linguistic structures. The other is to collect more data about the way speech is used in real situations, and then to apply artificial-intelligence techniques to use this knowledge to solve the continuous speech recognition problem.

9.3.1 Speech signal-processing research

No matter which of these approaches is adopted the problem of separating speech from noise needs to be addressed. The main reason for hoping that a solution to this problem can be found is that humans are much better than machines at recognising speech in noise. Spoken digits can be recognised with almost complete accuracy with a signal/noise ratio of $-6\,dB$ (Miller *et al.*, 1951), yet a typical speech recogniser (Bridle *et al.*, 1984) had a digit recognition rate of only 48% at $+3\,dB$ (although this was increased to 86% by noise compensation). As environmental noise levels range from 30 to 100 dB, speech signal/noise levels in places where speech recognisers might need to be used are often 0 dB or less.

The way in which the human auditory system copes with small (or negative) signal/noise levels is not known. One way to study this situation is to simulate the processing of the lower levels of the auditory system by means of a computer model incorporating knowledge of the physiological mechanisms involved (for a review see Evans, 1982). Computational models of the peripheral auditory system have been investigated by Lyon (1984) and Seneff (1984). It is known that there are several effects such as neural adaptation and lateral suppression (Section 2.4.1) which may well enhance the speech signals relative to the noise. There is some evidence that a recogniser based on auditory processing performs better in noise than one based on linear-prediction analysis (Dologlou, 1984) or a filter bank (Hunt and Lefebvre, 1986).

An alternative approach is to study auditory streaming or grouping (Section 2.4.6). Certain sound fragments, such as those having a common fundamental, appear perceptually to have originated from the same source and so are grouped together. If the rules employed by the auditory system to form these groups can be elucidated, then these rules could be incorporated into recognition algorithms to separate the speech signals from the noise.

Another problem with artificial speech-recognisers is that they tend to perform worse with female voices than males. On the other hand Doddington (1980) found no difference in the performance of human listeners with male and female speech. Some insight into this problem might be gained by investigating speech processing in physiological or psychological models of the human hearing system.

If such models do offer a solution to either the noise or the sex-difference problems, then special hardware will need to be developed so that this type of signal processing can be incorporated into real-time recognition systems.

9.3.2 Speech-pattern-processing research

Despite the success of dynamic time warping, such techniques are computationally intensive during the recognition process so that special hardware is being developed for real-time operation (Section 6.2). Statistical modelling is also computationally intensive, but more so during the training than during the recognition phase. Fast recognition systems using hidden Markov modelling based on conventional microcomputers have been built.

The application of adaptive constraint satisfaction networks to speech recognition should continue. This research is in its infancy, but appears to be of great promise. The structure of such systems is thought by some to resemble the networks of neurones in the human brain; so there is the possibility of being able to develop more human-like recognition capabilities.

With large-vocabulary systems the development of sub-word pattern-matching techniques seems to be the way forward, though it is not yet clear what units should be employed. The use of demisyllables looks promising, but more research is required to examine and systematise context effects. Unlike whole-word pattern-matching techniques, it should be possible to develop approaches using sub-word units which can be applied to very large vocabularies.

When dealing with large vocabularies, speaker-dependent techniques are more difficult to apply because of the amount of training involved. If speaker-independent systems are to be developed, more attention will need to be given to regional dialects. There are two possible approaches. If clustering techniques are employed, the databases used for training the systems will need to have sufficient speakers from each dialect group to match all of the dialects in the user population. If a more analytic approach is adopted, exhaustive analyses of all the dialects will be required together with an investigation of the use of phonetic features in each dialect.

One of the neglected areas is the use of intonation data in speech recognisers. This is understandable with isolated-word systems as the only use of intonation is to enable nouns to be distinguished from verbs in such words as 'subject' and 'object'. In practical isolated-word systems these are almost never viable alternatives.

Intonation is also used to indicate the degree of uncertainty of a reply. The word 'yes', for example, spoken with a rise–fall intonation contour suggests that the listener definitely agrees, whereas spoken with a fall–rise it suggests some degree of reservation. Presumably an expert system incorporating a speech recogniser could use this information to modify the conditional probabilities in its inference system.

In discrete-utterance recognisers in which words are spoken in isolation, the end of a phrase or sentence is currently indicated by a special word such as 'enter'. In normal pronunciation, strings of digits are spoken with a fall on the last digit. This intonation could be used to determine the end of the string, making the special word unnecessary.

In linguistic structures larger than a word, intonation plays a more central role. It is used to indicate the important words in a sentence, and can be used to signal syllable boundaries (Ainsworth, 1986).

9.3.3 Speech-knowledge-processing research

One ultimate aim of speech-recognition research is to enable people to interact with machines as easily as they do with other human beings. It is not surprising, therefore, that several lines of automatic speech-recognition research are converging with studies of brain mechanisms. It is believed that better speech processors could be built by simulating the processing of the peripheral auditory system. The behaviour of networks of adaptive processing elements is being studied as a means of providing recognition devices. The hope is that speech knowledge can become embodied in such networks. The structure of these networks bears more than a passing resemblance to certain areas of the brain. These lines of research offer exciting possibilities as advances in computer technology have provided the facilities for large simulations to be performed in manageable periods of time.

It must be remembered, however, that a child takes a dozen or more years to become fluent in its native language (Section 2.5.1). Of course, many other skills and behaviour patterns are learned in this time, but during the waking hours auditory stimulation, much of it vocal, will be present most of the time and internal processing probably continues during sleep. Training an adaptive network with a 100 000 word vocabulary might, therefore, take a considerable amount of time. Fortunately electronic devices are somewhat faster than neural ones and structured stimulation might produce more efficient adaptation.

It remains an open question as to whether this approach to representing speech knowledge in a machine is superior to the more traditional approach of building on conventional linguistic analysis.

Human beings show considerable variation in their linguistic abilities. Adaptive machines with statistical structures might exhibit similar variations. However, once a machine has been created which shows signs of linguistic genius, it should be easy to reproduce it.

References

ABERCROMBIE, D. (1965): 'Studies in phonetics and linguistics' (Oxford University Press, Oxford)

ACKENHUSEN, J. G., and RABINER, L. R. (1981): 'Microprocessor implementation of an LPC-based isolated word recogniser'. IEEE ICASSP, 746–749

ACKROYD, M. H. (1974): 'Commercial applications of speech recognition'. IEE Digest No. 1974/9, 7

ADDIS, T. R. (1972): 'Human behaviour in an interactive environment using a simple spoken word recogniser', Int. J. Machine Studies, 4, pp. 255–284

AINSWORTH, W. A. (1968a): 'First formant transitions and the perception of semivowels', J. Acoust. Soc. Am., 44, pp. 689–694

AINSWORTH, W. A. (1968b): 'Perception of stop consonants in synthetic CV syllables', Language & Speech, 11, pp. 139–155

AINSWORTH, W. A. (1970): 'Estimation of speech synthesiser parameters from acoustic waveforms', Int. J. Man-Machine Studies, 2, pp. 291–302

AINSWORTH, W. A. (1972): 'Duration as a cue in the recognition of synthetic vowels', J. Acoust. Soc. Am., 51, pp. 648–651

AINSWORTH, W. A. (1973): 'A system for converting English text into speech', IEEE Trans., AU-21, pp. 288–290

AINSWORTH, W. A. (1974): 'Influence of precursive sequences on the perception of synthesised vowels', Language & Speech, 17, pp. 103–109

AINSWORTH, W. A. (1975): 'Intrinsic and extrinsic factors in vowel judgments' in 'Auditory analysis and perception of speech' (Academic Press) pp. 103–113

AINSWORTH, W. A. (1976): 'Influence of fundamental frequency on perceived vowel boundaries'. Speech Communication Seminar, Vol. 3, pp. 123–129

AINSWORTH, W. A. (1985): 'Noise and communication' in TEMPEST, W. (Ed.): 'The noise handbook' (Academic Press, London) pp. 69–86

AINSWORTH, W. A. (1986): 'Pitch change as a cue to syllabification', J. Phonetics, 14, 257–264

AINSWORTH, W. A., and LINDSAY, D. (1984): 'Identification and discrimination of Halliday's primary tones', Proc. Inst. Acoust., 6, pp. 301–306

AINSWORTH, W. A., and LINDSAY, D. (1986): 'Perception of pitch movements on tonic syllables in British English', J. Acoust. Soc. Am., 79, pp. 472–480

AINSWORTH, W. A., PALIWAL, K. K., and FOSTER, H. M. (1984): 'Problems with dynamic frequency warping as a technique for speaker-independent vowel classification', Proc. Inst. Acoust., 6, pp. 301–306

ALLEN, J. B. (1974): 'Synthesis of pure speech from a reverberant signal'. US Patent No. 3 786 188

ALLEN, J. B., BERKLEY, D. A., and BAUERT, A. (1977): 'Multimicrophone signal-processing technique to remove room reverberation from speech signals, J. Acoust. Soc. Am., 62, pp. 912–915

ASHER, J. J. (1972): 'Childrens' first language as a model for second language learning', *Modern Language J.*, **56**, pp. 133–139

ASHTON, R. (1985): 'Voice input of warehouse inventory'. Proc. Speech Tech '85 (Media Dimensions Inc. NY) pp. 266–267

BAHL, L. R. (1984): 'Some experiments with large vocabulary isolated-word sentence recognition'. Proc. IEEE ICASSP

BAHL, L. R., and JELINEK, F. (1976): 'Decoding for channels with insertions, deletions and substitutions with applications to speech recognition', *IEEE Trans.*, **IT-21**, pp. 404–411

BAKER, J. K. (1975): 'The DRAGON system – an overview', *IEEE Trans.*, **ASSP-23**, pp. 24–29

BAKER, J. M., PALLETT, D. S., and BRIDLE, J. S. (1983): 'Speech recognition performance assessment and available databases'. Proc. IEEE ICASSP, pp. 527–530

BAKIS, R. (1976): 'Continuous-speech recognition via centisecond acoustic states'. 91st. ASA Meeting, Washington

BANATRE, J. P., FRISON, P., and QUINTON, P. (1982): 'A systolic algorithm for connected word recognition'. Proc. ICASSP

BARNETT, J. (1973): 'A vocal data management system', *IEEE Trans.*, **AU-21**, pp. 185–188

BATCHELOR, B. G., and WILKINS, B. R. (1969): 'Method for location of clusters of patterns to initialise a learning machine', *Electron. Lett.*, **5**, pp. 481

BAUM, L. E. (1972): 'An inequality and associated maximization technique in statistical estimation for probabilistic functions of a Markov process', *Inequalities*, **3**, pp. 1–8

BAUM, L. E., and Sell, G. R. (1968): 'Growth transformations for functions on manifolds', *Pac. J. Math.*, **27**, pp. 211–227

BELLMAN, R. (1957): 'Dynamic programming' (Princeton University Press)

BENNETT, D. C. (1968): 'Spectral form and duration cues in the recognition of English and German vowels', *Language & Speech*, **11**, pp. 65–85

BERGLAND, G. D., and DOLAN, M. T. (1979): 'Fast Fourier transform algorithms' *in* WEINSTEIN, C. J., *et al.* (Eds.): 'Programs for digital signal processing' (IEEE Press, New York) pp. 1.2.1–1.2.18

BERMAN, J. V. F. (1984): 'Speech technology in a high workload environment'. Proc. 1st Int. Conf. Speech Technology, Brighton, pp. 69–76

BISIANI, R. (1985): 'Computer systems for high performance speech recognition' *in* 'New systems and architectures for automatic speech recognition and synthesis' (Springer Verlag, Berlin) pp. 169–190

BLADON, A. (1983): 'Two formant models of vowel perception: shortcomings and enhancements', *Speech Communication*, **2**, pp. 305–313

BLADON, R. A. W., and FANT, G. (1978): 'A two-formant model and the cardinal vowel'. STL-QPSR, pp. 1–8

BLOOM, P. J. (1980): 'Evaluation of a dereverberation process by normal and impaired listeners'. Proc. IEEE ICASSP, pp. 500–503

BREGMAN, A. S. (1978): 'The formation of auditory streams' *in* 'Attention and performance Vol. III' (Lawrence Erlbaum Associated, Hillsdale NJ)

BRIDLE, J. S. (1973): 'An efficient elastic method for detecting given words in running speech', Proc. Brit. Acoust. Soc. Spring Meeting, paper 73HC3

BRIDLE, J. S. (1983): 'Connected word recognition for military systems'. Final Report of the NATO AC/43 (Panel III RSG10) Project, pp. 1–43

BRIDLE, J. S., and BROWN, M. D. (1979): 'Connected word recognition using whole word templates'. Proc. Inst. Acoust. Autumn Conf., pp. 25–28

BRIDLE, J. S., BROWN, M. D., and CHAMBERLAIN, R. M. (1982): 'An algorithm for connected word recognition'. Proc. ICASSP 1982

BRIDLE, J. S., and MOORE, R. K. (1984): 'Boltzmann machines for speech pattern processing', *Proc. Inst. Acoust.*, **6**, pp. 315–322

BRIDLE, J. S., PONTING, K. M., BROWN, M. D., and BORRETT, A. W. (1984): 'A noise compensating spectrum distance measure applied to automatic speech recognition'. *Proc. Inst. Acoust.*, **6**, pp. 307–314

BRIDLE, J. S., and RALLS, M. P. (1985): 'An approach to speech recognition using synthesis-by-rule' *in* FALLSIDE, F., and WOODS, W. A. (Eds.): 'Computer speech processing' (Prentice Hall, Englewood Cliffs, NJ) pp. 277–292

BROADBENT, D. E. (1971): 'Decision and stress' (Academic Press, London)

BROADBENT, D. E. and LADEFOGED, P. (1960): Vowel judgements and adaptation level, *Proc. Roy. Soc. B*, **151**, pp. 384–399

BROWN, M. K., and RABINER, L. R. (1982): 'An adaptive ordered graph search technique for dynamic time warping for isolated word recognition', *IEEE Trans.*, **ASSP-30**, pp. 535–544

BRUNDAGE, W. J. (1985): 'Consumer applications of speech recognitions'. Proc. Speech Tech '85 (Media Dimensions Inc., NY) pp. 150–154

BUISON, L., MERCIER, G., GRESSER, J. Y.,. QUERRE, M., and VIVES, R. (1974): 'Phonetic decoding for automatic speech recognition of words'. Speech Communication Seminar, Stockholm, pp. 189–196

BURR, D. J., ACKLAND, B. D., and WESTE, N. (1984): 'Array configurations for dynamic time warping', *IEEE Trans.*, **ASSP-32**, pp. 119–128

BURTON, D. K., SHORE, J. E., and BUCK, J. T. (1985): 'Isolated word speech recognition using multisection vector quantization codebooks'. *IEEE Trans.*, **ASSP-33**, pp. 837–849

BUZO, A., GRAY, A. H., GRAY, R. M., and MARKEL, J. D. (1980): 'Speech coding based upon vector quantization', *IEEE Trans.*, **ASSP-28**, pp. 562–574

CARHART, R., JOHNSON, C., and GOODMAN, J. (1975): 'Perceptual masking of spondees by a combination of talkers', *J. Acoust. Soc. Am.*, **58**, p. 535(A)

CARLSON, R., FANT, G., and GRANSTROM, B. (1975): 'Two-formant models, pitch, and vowel perception' *in* 'Auditory analysis and perception of speech' (Academic Press) pp. 55–82

CARLSON, R., GRANSTROM, B., and HUNNICUTT, S. (1982): 'A multi-language text-to-speech module'. STL-QPSR/1981, pp. 18-28

CHANG, S. H. (1956): 'Two schemes of speech compressing system', *J. Acoust. Soc. Am.*, **28.**, pp. 565–572

CHAPANIS, A. (1975): 'Interactive human communication', *Sci. Am.*, **232**, pp. 36–42

CHERRY, E. C. (1953): 'Some experiments on the recognition of speech with one and two ears', *J. Acoust. Soc. Am*, **25**, pp. 975–979

CHIBA, T., and KAJIYAMA, M. (1941): 'The vowel, its nature and structure'. Phonetic Society of Japan 1958

CHOLLET, G., and GAGNOULET, B. P. (1982): On the evaluation of speech recognizers using a reference system. Proc. IEEE ICASSP, pp. 2026–2029

CHOMSKY, N., and HALLE, M. (1968): 'The sound pattern of English' (Harper & Row, New York)

CLASSE, A. (1939): 'The rhythm of English Prose' (Blackwell, Oxford)

COHEN, A., SLIS, I. H., and 'T HART, J. (1967): 'On tolerance and intolerance in vowel perception' *Phonetica*, **16**, pp. 65–78

COLE, R. A., RUDNICKY, A. I., ZUE, V. W., and REDDY, D. R. (1980): 'Speech as patterns on paper' *in* 'Perception and production of fluent speech' (Erlbaum) pp. 3–50

COOK, C. (1976): 'Word verification in a speech understanding system'. Proc. ICASSP 1976, pp. 553–556

COOKE, N. (1984); 'The flight testing and system integration of direct voice input devices in the civil flight deck'. Colloquium on Speech Input/Speech Output, IERE, London

COOLEY, J. W., and TUKEY, J. W. (1965): 'An algorithm for the machine calculation of complex Fourier series', *Math. Comput.*, **19**, p. 297

COVER, T. M., and HART, P. E. (1967): 'Nearest neighbor pattern classification', *IEEE Trans.*, **IT-13**, pp. 21–27

CRYSTAL, D. (1969): 'Intonation and prosodic systems in English' (Cambridge University Press, Cambridge)

DARWIN, C. J. (1981): 'Perceptual grouping of speech components differing in fundamental frequency and onset-time', *Q. J. Exptl. Psychol.*, **33A**, pp. 185–207

DARWIN, C. J., and BETHELL-FOX, C. E. (1977): 'Pitch continuity and speech source attribution', *J. Exptl. Psychol.*, **2** pp. 23–29

DARWIN, C. J., and DONOVAN, A. (1980): 'Perceptual studies of speech rhythm: isochrony and intonation' *in* 'Spoken language generation and understanding' (D. Reidel), pp. 77–85

DAS, S. K. (1982): 'Some experiments in discrete utterance recognition', *IEEE Trans.*, **ASSP-30**, pp. 766–770

DAVIS, K. H., BIDDULPH, R., and BALASHEK, S. (1952): 'Automatic recognition of spoken digits', *J. Acoust. Soc. Am.*, **24**, pp. 637–642

DAVIS, R., and KING, J. (1977): 'An overview of production systems', *Machine Intelligence*, **8**, pp. 300–332

DE MORI, R., and LAFACE, P. (1980): 'Use of fuzzy algorithms for phonetic and phonemic labelling of continuous speech', *IEEE Trans.*, **PAMI-2**, pp. 136–148

DE MORI, R., and LAFACE, P. (1985): 'On the use of phonetic knowledge for automatic speech recognition' *in* DE MORI, R., and SUEN, C. Y. (Eds.): 'New systems and architectures for automatic speech recognition and synthesis' (Springer, Berlin), pp. 569–591

DEACON, J., MOORE, R. K., PRATT, R. L., RUSSELL, M. J., and TOMLINSON, M. J. (1983): 'RSRE speech data base recordings (1985). Part I: Specification of vocabulary and recording procedure'. RSRE Report No. 83010, pp. 1–3

DELATTRE, P. C., LIBERMAN, A. M., COOPER, F. S., and GERSTMAN, L. J. (1952): 'An experimental study of the acoustical determinants of vowel colour', *Word*, **8**, pp. 195–210

DENES, P., and MATHEWS, M. V. (1960): Spoken digit recognition using time-frequency pattern-matching', *J. Acoust. Soc. Am.*, **32**, pp. 1450–1455

DENNIS, J. B. (1962): 'Computer control of an analog vocal tract'. Speech Communication Seminar Stockholm.

DETTWEILER, H., and HESS, W. (1985): 'Concatenation rules for demisyllable speech synthesis' *in* DE MORI, and SUEN (Eds.): 'New systems and architectures for speech recognition and synthesis' (Springer Verlag) pp. 537–567

DIXON, N. R., and MAXEY, H. D. (1968): 'Terminal analog synthesis of continuous speech using the diphone method of segment assembly' *IEEE Trans.*, **AU-16**, pp. 40–50

DODDINGTON, G. (1980): 'Whither speech recognition?' *in* LEA, W. A. (Ed.): 'Trends in speech recognition' (Prentice-Hall, Englewood Cliffs, NJ) pp. 556–561

DODDINGTON, G. R., and SCHALK, T. B. (1981): 'Speech recognition: turning theory into practice', *IEEE Spectrum*, Sept., pp. 26–32

DOLOGLOU, Y. (1984): 'Evaluation des performances d'un modele du systeme auditif en reconnaisance de la parole (comparison avec la prediction lineaire)'. These DI Grenoble

DRENNEN, T. G. (1980): 'Voice technology in attack/fighter aircraft' *in* HARRIS, S. G. (Ed.): Proc. Symp. on Voice Interactive Systems Applications and Payoffs (Dallas), pp. 199–211

DUDLEY, H. (1939): 'Remaking speech', *J. Acoust. Soc. Am.*, **11**, pp. 169–177

DUDLEY, H., and BALASHEK, S. (1958): 'Automatic recognition of phonetic patterns in speech', *J. Acoust. Soc. Am.*, **30**, pp. 721–732

EVANS, E. F. (1982): 'Representation of complex sounds at cochlear nerve and cochlear nucleus levels' *in* CARLSON, R., GRANSTROM, B., and LINDBLOM, B. (Eds.): 'Representation of speech in the peripheral auditory system' (Elsevier Biomedical Press, Amsterdam) pp. 27–42

FALLSIDE, F., and YOUNG, S. J. (1978): Speech output from a computer-controlled water-supply network. *Proc. IEEE.*, **125**, pp. 157–161

FANT, G. (1960): 'Acoustic theory of speech production' (Mouton s'Gravenhage)

FANT, G. (1975): 'Non-uniform vowel normalisation'. STL-QPSR 2–3, pp. 1–19

FANT, G. (1979): 'Glottal source and excitation analysis'. STL-QPSR 1979, pp. 85–107

FANT, G., and MARTONY, J. (1962): 'Instrumentation for parametric synthesis (OVE II)'. STL-QSPR 1962, p. 18

FENNEL, R. D., and LESSER, V. R. (1975): 'Parallelism in AI problem solving: a case study of Hearsay II'. Tech. Rep. CMU, 1–49

FISHER, M. (1986): 'Voice control for the disabled' *in* BRISTOW, G. (Ed.): 'Electronic speech recognition' (Collins, London) pp. 309–321

FLANAGAN, J. L. (1955): 'A difference limen for vowel formant frequency', *J. Acoust. Soc. Am.*, **27**, pp. 613–617

FLANAGAN, J. L. (1956): 'Automatic extraction of formant frequencies from continuous speech'. *J. Acoust. Soc. Am.*, **28**, pp. 110–118

FLANAGAN, J. L. (1957): 'Difference limen for formant amplitude', *J. Speech Hearing Disorders*, **22**, pp. 205–212

FLANAGAN, J. L. (1965): 'Speech analysis, synthesis and perception' (Springer Verlag, New York)

FLANAGAN, J. L., and LUMMIS, R. C. (1970): 'Signal processing to reduce multipath distortion in a small room', *J. Acoust. Soc. Am* ., **47**, pp. 1475–1481

FLANAGAN. J. L., and SASLOW, M. G. (1958): 'Pitch discriminaiton for synthetic vowels', *J. Acoust. Soc. Am.*, **30**, pp. 435–442

FLETCHER, H. (1953): 'Speech and hearing in communication' (Van Nostrand, New York)

FLETCHER, H., and MUNSON, W. A. (1937): 'Relationship between loudness and masking', *J. Acoust. Soc. Am.*, **9**, pp. 1–10

FORGIE, J. W., and FORGIE, C. D. (1959): 'Results obtained from a vowel recognition computer program', *J. Acoust. Soc. Am.*, **31**, pp. 1480–1489

FOURCIN, A. J., *et al.* (1977): 'Speech processing by man and machine'. Recognition of Complex Acoustic Signals Dahlem Konferenzen, pp. 307–351

FOURCIN, A. J. (1975): 'Speech perception in the absence of speech productive ability' *in* 'Language and cognitive deficits and retardation' (Butterworths)

FOURCIN, A. J., and LENNENBERG, E. (1973): 'Language development in the absence of expressive speech'. IBRO UNESCO

FRAZIER, R. H., SAMSON, S., BRAIDA, L. D., and OPPENHEIM, A. V. (1976): 'Enhancement of speech by adaptive filtering'. Proc. IEEE ICASSP, pp. 251–253

FRISON, P., and QUINTON, P. (1985): 'An integrated systolic machine for speech recognition' *in* 'New systems and architectures for automatic speech recognition and synthesis' (Springer Verlag, Berlin) pp. 145–168

FRY, D. B. (1955): 'Duration and intensity as physical correlates of linguistic stress', *J. Acoust. Soc. Am.*, **27**, pp. 765–768

FRY, D. B. (1958): 'Experiments in the perception of stress', *Language & Speech*, **1**, pp. 126–152

FRY, D. B., ABRAMSON, A. S., EIMAS, P. D., and LIBERMAN, A. M. (1962): 'The identification and discrimination of synthetic vowels', *Language & Speech*, **5**, pp. 171–189

FRY, D. B., and DENES, P. (1958): 'The solution of some fundamental problems in mechanical speech recognition', *Language & Speech*, **1**, pp. 35–58

FU, K. S. (1982): 'Syntactic pattern recognition and its applications (Prentice-Hall, Englewood Cliffs, NJ)

FUJIMURA, O. (1976): 'Syllables as concatenated demisyllables and affixes', *J. Acoust. Soc. Am.*, **59**, p. 55

FUJIMURA, O., MACCHI, M. J., and LOVINS, J. B. (1977): 'Demisyllables and affixes for speech synthesis'. Proc. 9th. Int. Congr. Acoust., pp. 51–53

FUJISAKI, H., and KAWASHIMA, T. (1968): 'The roles of pitch and higher formants in the perception of vowels', *IEEE Trans.*, **AU-16**, pp. 73–77

FUJISAKI, H., and KAWASHIMA, T. (1971): 'A model for speech perception – quantitative analysis of categorical effects in speech discrimination'.Annual report of the Engineering Research Institute University of Tokyo 30, pp. 59–68

FUKUNAGA, K. (1972): 'An introduction to statistical pattern recognition' (Academic Press, New York)

GARY, J. O. (1975): 'Delayed oral practice in the initial stages of second language learning' *in* 'New Directions in Second Language Teaching' (Tesol, Washington)

GELB, I. J. (1963): 'A study of writing' (University of Chicago Press)

GERSTMAN, L. J. (1968): 'Classificaiton of self-normalised vowels', *IEEE Trans.*, **AU-21**, pp. 78–80

190   References

GILL, G. S., *et al.* (1978) 'A recursive segmentation procedure for continuous speech'. Tech. Report Comp. Sci. Dept., Carnegie-Mellon Univ.

GILLMAN, R. (1975): ' A fast frequency domain pitch algorithm', *J. Acoust. Soc. Am.*, **58**, p. S62

GOLD, B. (1966): 'Word-recognition computer program.' MIT Tech. Report No. 452, pp. 1–21

GOLD, B., and RABINER, L. R. (1969): 'Parallel processing techniques for estimating pitch periods of speech in the time domain', *J. Acouct. Soc. Am.*, **46**, pp. 442–448

GRAY, A. H., and MARKEL, J. D. (1979): 'Linear prediction analysis programs (AUTO-COVAR)' *in* WEINSTEIN, C. J., *et al.* (Eds.): 'Programs for digital signal processing' (IEEE Press, New York) pp. 4.1.1–4.1.7

GREEN, P. D., and AINSWORTH, W. A. (1972): 'Towards the automatic recognition of spoken Basic English' *in* 'Machine perception of patterns and pictures'. Inst. Phys., Conf. Ser. No. 13, pp. 161–168

GREEN, P. D., and WOOD, A. R. (1984): 'Reasoning about the acoustic realisation of semivowels, using an intermediate representation – the speech sketch', *Proc. Inst. Acoust.*,, **6**, pp. 343–350

GREENBLATT, R., KNIGHT, T., and HOLLOWAY, J. (1980): 'A LISP machine'. Fifth Workshop on Architectures for Non-numeric Processing, Asilomar

GRUENZ, O., and SCOTT, L. O., (1949): 'Extraction and portrayal of pitch of speech sounds', *J. Acoust. Soc. Am.*, **21**, pp. 487–495

HAGGARD, M., AMBLER, S., and CALLOW, M. (1970): 'Pitch as a voicing cue', *J. Acoust. Soc. Am.*, **47**, pp. 613–617

HALLIDAY, M. A. K. (1963): 'The tones of English'. *Archivum Linguisticum*, **15**, pp. 1–28

HARMAN, H. H. (1967): 'Modern Factor Analysis' (University of Chicago Press)

HARRIS, K. S. (1958): 'Cues for the discrimination of American English fricatives in spoken syllables', *Language & Speech*, **1**, pp. 1–7

HARRIS, K. S., HOFFMAN, H. S., LIBERMAN, A. M., DELATTRE, P. C., and COOPER, F. S. (1958): 'Effects of third formant transitions on the perception of voiced stop consonants', *J. Acoust. Soc. Am.*, **30**, pp. 122–126

HARRISON, W. A., LIM, J. S., and SINGER, E. (1986): 'A new application of adaptive noise cancellation', *IEEE Trans.*, **ASSP-34**, pp. 21–27

HAYES-ROTH, F., MOSTOW, D. J., and FOX, M. (1978): 'Understanding speech in the Hearsay II system' *in* 'Natural communication with computers' (Springer Verlag, Berlin)

HECKER, M. L. H. (1962): 'Studies of nasal consonants with an articulatory speech synthesiser', *J. Acoust. Soc. Am.*, **34**, pp. 179–188

HEINZ, J. M., and STEVENS, K. N. (1961): 'On the properties of voiceless fricative consonants', *J. Acoust. Soc. Am.*, **33**, pp. 589–596

HENDERSON, G. K., DIXON, A. T., and ELLENDER, J. H. (1984): 'Use of speech recognition in the structural analysis of offshore platforms'. Proc. 1st Int. Conf. Speech Technology, Brighton, pp. 203–215

HERSCHER, M. (1979): 'Voice control wheelchair product: analysis of cerebral palsy candidates'. Tech. Report, Threshold Technology Inc.

HESS, W. J. (1983): 'Pitch determination of speech signals' (Springer Verlag, Berlin)

HINTON, G. E., SEJNOWSKI, T. J., and ACKLEY, D. H. (1984): 'Boltzmann machines: constraint satisfaction networks that learn'. Tech. Report CMU-CS-84-119, pp. 1–42

HOBBS, G. R. (1984): 'The application of speech input/output to training simulators'. Proc. 1st Int. Conf. Speech Technology, Brighton, pp. 121–134

HOFFMAN, H. S. (1958): 'Study of some cues in the perception of voiced stop consonants', *J. Acoust. Soc. Am.*, **30**, pp. 1035–1041

HOLMES, J. N. (1980): 'The JSRU channel vocoder', *Proc. IEEE* , **127F1**, pp. 53–60

HOLMES, J. N. (1982): 'Formant synthesisers: cascade or parallel'. JSRU Research Report No. 1017

HOLMES, J. N., and KELLY, L. C . (1960): 'Apparatus for segmenting the formant frequency regions of a speech signal'. Brit. P.O. Res. Report 20566

HOLMES, J. N., MATTINGLY, I. G., and SHEARME, J. N. (1964): 'Speech synthesis by rule', *Language & Speech*, **7**, pp. 127–143

HOWIE, J. H. (1986): 'Speech technology applied to automotive assembly inspection'. Speech Tech '86 (Media Dimensions Inc., NY) pp. 115–117

HUGHES, G. W. (1961): 'The recognition of speech by machine'. MIT Tech. Report No. 395, pp. 1–62

HUGHES, G. W., and HALLE, M. (1956): 'Spectral properties of fricative consontants', *J. Acoust. Soc. Am.*, **28**, pp. 303–310

HUNT, M. J. (1981): 'Speaker adaptation for word-based speech recognition systems', *J. Acoust. Soc. Am.*, **69**, p. S41

HUNT, M. J., and LEFEBVRE, C. (1986): 'Speech recognition using a cochlear model'. Proc. IEEE ICASSP, pp. 1979–1982

ITAKURA, F. (1975): 'Minimum prediction residual principle applied to speech recognition', *IEEE Trans.*, **ASSP-23**, pp. 67–72

ITAKURA, F., and SAITO, S. (1972): 'On the optimum quantization of feature parameters in the PARCOR speech synthesizer'. Proc. IEEE Conf. Speech Comm. Processing, NY, pp. 434–437

JACOBSON, R., FANT, G. C. M., and HALLE, M. (1952): 'Preliminaries to speech analysis'. MIT Tech. Report No. 13

JELINEK, F. (1976): 'Continuous speech recognition by statistical methods'. *Proc. IEEE*, **64**, pp. 532–556

JELINEK, F., MERCER, R. L., BAHL, L. R., and BAKER, J. K. (1977): 'Perplexity – a measure of the difficulty of speech recognition tasks', *J. Acoust. Soc. Am.*, **62**, Suppl. 1, p. S63

JORDAN, W. T. (1985): 'Voice contolled closed circuit television for space shuttle orbiter'. Proc. Speech Tech '85 (Media Dimensions Inc, NY) pp. 311–312

JUANG, B.-H., WONG, D. Y., and GRAY, A. H. (1982): 'Distortion performance of vector quantization for LPC voice coding', *IEEE trans.*, **ASSP-30**, pp. 294–304

KAHN, D. (1980): 'Syllable-based generalizations in English phonology' (Garland, New York)

KAHNEMAN, D. (1973): 'Attention and effort' (Prentice-Hall, Englewood Cliffs, NJ)

KELLY, J. L., and GERSTMAN, J. L. (1961): 'An artificial talker driven from a phonetic input', *J. Acoust. Soc. Am.*, **33**, pp. 835-(A)

KLATT, D. H. (1977): 'Review of the ARPA speech understanding project', *J. Acoust. Soc. Am.*, **62**, pp. 1345–1366

KLATT, D. H. (1979): 'Speech perception: a model of acoustic-phonetic analysis and lexical access', *J. Phonetics*, **7**, pp. 279–312

KLATT, D. H., and STEVENS, K. N. (1973): 'On the automatic recognition of continuous speech: implications of a spectrogram-reading experiment', *IEEE Trans.*, **AU-21**, pp. 210–217

KOBATAKE, H., INARI, J., and KAKUTU, S. (1978): 'Linear predictive coding of speech signals in a high ambient noise environment'. Proc. IEEE ICASSP, pp. 472–475

KOPEC, G. E., and BUSH, M. A. (1985): 'Network-based isolated word digit recognition using vector quantization', *IEEE Trans.*, **ASSP-33**, pp. 850–876

KRUSKAL, J. B. (1964): 'Multidimensional scaling by optimising goodness of fit to a nonmetric basis', *Psychometrica*, **29**, pp. 1–27

KUHN, M. H., and TOMASCHEWSKI, H. H. (1983): 'Improvements in isolated word recognition', *IEEE Trans.*, **ASSP-31**, pp. 157–167

KURZWEIL, R. (1985): 'The Kurzweil voicewriter: a large vocabulary voice activated word processor'. Proc. Speech Tech '85 (Media Dimensions Inc.) pp. 33–38

LADEFOGED, P., and BROADBENT, D. (1957): 'Information conveyed by vowels', *J. Acoust. Soc. Am.*, **29**, pp. 98–104

LADEFOGED, P., HARSHMAN, R., GOLDSTEIN, L., and RICE, L. (1978): 'Generating vocal tract shapes from formant frequencies', *J Acoust. Soc. Am.*, **64**, pp. 1027–1035

LAMEL, L. F., RABINER, L. R., ROSENBERG, A. E., and WILPON, J. G. (1981): 'An improved endpoint detector for isolated word recognition', *IEEE Trans.*, **ASSP-29**, pp. 777–785

LAWRENCE, W. (1953): 'The synthesis of speech from signals which have a low information rate' in 'Communication theory' (Butterworth, London)

LEA, W. A. (1973): 'An approach to syntactic recognition without phonemics', *IEEE Trans.*, **AU-21**, p. 249

LEA, W. A. (1979): 'Critical issues in airborne applications of speech recognisers'. SCRL Final Report NADC Contract, N62269-78-M-3770

LEA, W. A. (1980): 'Prosodic aids to speech recognition' in 'Trends in speech recognition' (Prentice-Hall) pp. 166–205

LENNENBERG, E. H. (1967): 'Biological foundations of language' (Wiley, New York)

LEONARD, R. G. (1984): 'A database for speaker-independent digit recognition'. Proc. IEEE ICASSP, pp. 42.11.1–42.11.4

LEVINSON, N. (1947): 'The Wiener RMS (root mean square) error criterion in filter design and prediction', J. Math. Physics, 25, pp. 261–278

LEVINSON, S. E. (1985): 'A unified theory of composite pattern analysis for automatic speech recognition' in FALLSIDE, F., and WOODS, W. A. (Eds.): 'Computer speech processing' (Prentice-Hall, Englewood Cliffs, NJ) pp. 243–276

LEVINSON, S. E., RABINER, L. R., and SONDHI, M. M. (1983): 'Speaker-independent digit recognition using hidden Markov models. Proc. ICASSP, 1983, pp. 1049–1052

LEVINSON, S. E., RABINER, L. R., and SONDHI, M. M. (1983): 'An introduction to the application of the theory of probabilistic functions of a Markov process to automatic speech recognition', Bell Syst. Tech. J., 62, pp. 1035–1074

LIBERMAN, A. M., COOPER, F. S., SHANKWEILER, D. P., and STUDDERT-KENNEDY, M. (1967): 'Perception of the speech code', Psych. Rev., 74, pp. 431–461

LIBERMAN, A. M., DELATTRE, P., and COOPER, F. S. (1952): 'The role of selected stimulus-variables in the perception of unvoiced stop consonants', Am. J. Psychol., 65, pp. 497–516

LIBERMAN, A. M., DELATTRE, P. C., and COOPER, F. S. (1958): 'Cues for the distinction between voiced and voiceless stops in initial position', Language & Speech, 1, pp. 153–167

LIBERMAN, A. M., DELATTRE, P. C., COOPER, F. S., and GERSTMAN, L. J. (1954): 'The role of consonant-vowel transitions in the perception of stop and nasal consonants', Psych. Monographs, 68, pp. 1–13

LIBERMAN, A. M., DELATTRE, P. C., GERSTMAN, J. L., and COOPER, F. S. (1956): 'Tempo of frequency change as a cue for distinguishing classes of speech sounds', J. Exptl. Psychol., 52, pp. 127–137

LIBERMAN, A. M., HARRIS, K. S., HOFFMAN, H. S., and GRIFFITHS, B. C. (1957): 'The discrimination of speech sounds within and across phoneme boundaries', J. Exptl. Psychol., 54, pp. 358–368

LIM, J. S. (1978): 'Evaluation of a correlation subtraction method for enhancing speech degraded by additive white noise', IEEE Trans., ASSP-26, pp. 471–472

LIM, J. S. (1983): 'Speech enhancement' (Prentice-Hall, Englewood Cliffs, NJ)

LIM, J. S., and OPPENHEIM, A. V. (1978): 'All-pole modelling of degraded speech', IEEE Trans., ASSP-26, pp. 197–210

LIM, J. S., OPPENHEIM, A. V., and BRAIDA, L. D. (1978): 'Evaluation of an adaptive comb filtering method for enhancing speech degraded by white noise addition', IEEE Trans., ASSP-26, pp. 354–358

LINDBLOM, B. (1963): 'Spectrograph study of vowel reduction', J. Acoust. Soc. Am., 35, pp. 1773–1781

LINDBLOM, B., and STUDDERT-KENNEDY, M. (1967): 'On the role of formant transitions in vowel recognition', J. Acoust. Soc. Am., 42, pp. 830–843

LINDSAY, D. (1984): 'The analysis and classification of FO contours', Proc. Inst. Acoust., 6, pp. 337–342

LINGGARD, R. (1985): 'Electronic synthesis of speech' (Cambridge University Press)

LISKER, L. (1957a) 'Closure duration and the intervocalic voiced-voiceless distinction in English', Language, 33, pp. 41–49

LISKER, L. (1957b): 'Minimal cues for separating /l,r,w,y/ in intervocalic position', Word, 13, pp. 256–267

LOWERRE, B. T. (1976): 'The Harpy speech recognition system.' Ph. D. Thesis, Carnegie-Mellon University

LOWERRE, B. T., and REDDY, R. (1980): 'The Harpy speech understanding system' *in* 'Trends in speech recognition' (Prentice-Hall) pp. 340–360

LYON, R. (1984): 'Computational models of neural auditory processing'. Proc. IEEE ICASSP, pp. 36.1.1–4

MAGOR, S., HESTER, R., and SIMPSON, R. (1982): 'Signal-processing microcomputer builds FFT-based spectrum analyser' *in* 'Signal processing with the TMS320' (Texas Instruments) pp. 21–36

MAKHOUL, J. (1975): 'Linear prediction of speech: a tutorial review', *Proc. IEEE*, **63**, pp. 561–580

MARKEL, J. D. (1972): 'Digital inverse filtering: a new tool for formant trajectory estimation', *IEEE Trans.*, **AU-20**, pp. 129–137

MARKEL, J. D., and GRAY, A. H. (1976): 'Linear prediction of speech' (Springer Verlag, Berlin)

MARR, D. (1982): 'Vision' (W.H. FREEMAN)

MARTIN, T.B. (1976): 'Practical applications of voice input to machines,' *Proc. IEEE*, **64**, pp. 487–501

MATSUMOTO, H., and WAKITA, H. (1979): 'Frequency warping for nonuniform talker normalization.' *Proc. IEEE ICASSP*, pp. 566–573

McCANDLESS, S. S. (1974): 'An algorithm for automatic formant extraction using linear prediction spectra,' *IEEE Trans.*, **ASSP-22**, pp. 135–141

McCLOUD, P. (1977): 'A dual-task response modality effect: suport for multiprocessor models of attention,' *Q. J. Exp. Physchol.*, **29**, pp. 651–667

MEISEL, W. S. (1984): 'Speech-to-text systems — the users' needs.' Proc. 1st Int. Conf. Speech Technology, Brighton, pp. 161–168

MEISEL, W. S. (1986): 'Towards the "talkwriter"' *in* BRISTOW, G. Electronic speech recognition (Collins, London) pp. 338–348

MELOCCO, J.M. (1984): 'Voice command in combat aircraft.' Military Technology, MILTECH 6/84, pp. 44–46

MERCIER, G., NOUHEN, A., QUINTON, P., and SIROUX, J. (1980): 'The KEAL speech understanding system,' in 'Spoken language generation and understanding' (D. REIDEL) pp. 525–543

MILLER, G. A., HEISE, G. A., and LICHTEN, W. (1951): 'The intelligibility of speech as a function of the context of speech materials,' *J. Exp. Physch.*, **41**, pp. 329–335

MILLER, G. A., and LICKLIDER, L. C. R. (1950): 'The intelligibility of interrupted speech,' *J. Acoust. Soc. Am.*, **22**, pp. 167–173

MILLER, G. A., and NICELY, P. E. (1955): 'An analysis of some perceptual confusions among some English consonants,' *J. Acoust. Soc. Am.*, **27**, pp. 338–352

MILLER, R. L. (1953): 'Auditory tests with synthetic vowels,' *J. Acoust. Soc. Am.*, **25**, pp. 114–121

MITCHELL, O. M., and BERKLEY, D. A. (1970): 'Reduction of long-time reverberation by a centre-clipping process,' *J. Acoust. Soc. Am.*, **47**, pp. 84(A)

MINSKY, M. (1975): 'A framework for representing knowledge,' *in* 'The physology of computer vision' (McGraw Hill, New York)

MONAHAN, B., JOOST, M. G., and FISHER, E. L. (1985): 'Multi-modal command strategies for expert CAD systems.' Proc. Speech Tech'85 (Media Dimensions Inc., NY) pp. 62–64

MOORE, C. A., MOORE, R. D., and RUTH, J. C. (1984): 'Applications of voice interactive systems — military flight test and the future.' Proc. AIAA/IEEE 6th Digital Avionics Systems Conference Baltimore, 301–308

MOORE, R. K. (1977): 'Evaluating speech recognizers,' *IEEE Trans.*, **ASSP-25**, pp. 178–183

MOORE, R. K. (1981): 'Dynamic programming variations in automatic speech recognition.' Proc. Inst. Acoust. Spring Conf., pp. 269–272

MOORE, R. K. (1986): 'Computational techniques' *in* BRISTOW, G. (Ed): Electronic speech recognition' (Collins London) pp. 130–157

MOORE, R. K., RUSSELL, M. J., and TOMLINSON, M. J. (1982): 'Locally constrained dynamic programming in automatic speech recognition.' Proc. IEEE ICASSP, pp. 1270–1273

MOSER, H. M. (1969): 'One-syllable words' (Merrill, Columbus OH)

MUCCIARDI, A. N., and GROSE, E. E. (1972): 'An automatic clustering algorithm and its properties in high dimensional spaces,' *IEEE Trans.*, **SM-2**, pp. 247

MUNSON, W. A., and MONTGOMERY, H. C. (1950): 'A speech analyser and synthesizer,' *J. Acoust. Soc. Am.*, **22**, pp. 678 (A)

MYERS, C., RABINER, L. R., and ROSENBERG, A. E. (1980). 'Performance tradeoffs in dynamic time warping algorithms for isolated word recognition,' *IEEE Trans.*, **ASSP-28**, pp. 623–635

MYERS, C. S., and RABINER, L. R. (1981): 'A level buiding dynamic time warping algorithm for connected word recognition,' *IEEE Trans.*, **ASSP-29**, pp. 284–296

NEELY, S. T., and ALLEN, J. B. (1979): 'Invertibility of a room impulse response,' *J. Acoust. Soc. Am.*, **66**, pp. 165–169

NELSON, A. L., HERSCHER, M. B., MARTIN, T. B., ZADELL, H. J., and FALTER, J. W. (1967): 'Acoustic recognition by analog feature-abstraction techniques' *in* 'Models for the perception of speech and visual form' (MIT Press) pp. 428

NELSON, D. L. (1985): 'Use of voice recognition to support the collection of product data.' Proc. Speech Tech'85 (Media Dimensoins Inc., NY) pp. 268–272

NEY, H. (1984): 'The use of a one-stage dynamic programming algorithm for connected work recognition,' *IEEE Trans.*, **ASSP-32**, pp. 263–271

NIEMAN, H. (1982): 'The Erlagen system for the recognition and understanding of continuous German speech,' *Informatik Fachberichte*, **57**, pp. 330–348

NILSSON, N. J. (1965): 'Learning machines' (McGraw-Hill, New York)

NILSSON, N. J. (1971): 'Problem-solving methods in artificial intelligence' (McGraw-Hill New York)

NILSSON, N. J. (1980): 'Principles of artificial intelligence' (Tioga Press New York)

NOLL, A. M. (1964): 'Short-time spectrum and "cepstrum" techniques for vowel pitch detection,' *J. Acoust. Soc. Am.*, **36**, pp. 296–302

NOLL, A. M. (1967): 'Cepstrum pitch determination,' *J. Acoust. Soc. Am.*, **41**, pp. 293–309

NORDMARK, J. O. (1968): 'Mechanisms of frequency discrimination,' *J. Acoust. Soc. Am.*, **44**, pp. 1533–1540

NORTH, R. A., and ADIST, D. J. (1983): 'Applications of interactive voice technology for the advanced attack helicopter.' Honeywell Systems & Research Center Minneapolis, Final Report-83SRC36

NORTH, R. A., and LEA, W. A. (1982): 'Application of advanced speech technology in manned penetration bombers.' Honeywell Systems & Research Center Report AFWAL, TR-82-3004.

O'CONNOR, J. D., GERSTMAN, L. J., LIBERMAN, A. M., DELATTRE, P. C., and COOPER, F. S. (1957): 'Acoustic cues for the perception of /w, j, r, l/ in English,' *Word*, **13**, pp. 24–43

OGDEN, C. K. (1930): 'Basic English. An introduction with rules and grammar.' Psyche Miniatures No. 29 (Kegan Paul, London)

OLSON, H. F., and BELAR, H. (1956): 'Phonetic typewriter,' *J. Acoust. Soc. Am.*, **28**, pp. 1072–1081

OLSON, H. F., BELAR, H., and SOBRINO, R. (1962): 'Demonstration of speech processing system consisting of a speech analyser, translation typer and synthesizer,' *J. Acoust. Soc. Am.*, **34**, pp. 1535–1538

OPPENHEIM, A. V., and SCHAFER, R. W. (1975): 'Digital signal processing.' (Prentice-Hall, Englewood Cliffs, NJ)

OSHIKA, B. T., ZUE, V. W., WEEKS, R. V., NEU, H., and AURBACH, J. (1974): 'The role of phonological rules in speech understanding research.' IEEE Symp. Speech Recognition, pp. 204–207

PALIWAL, K. KI.., AGARWAL, A., and SINHA, S. S. (1982): 'A modification over Sakoe and Chiba's dynamic time warping algorithm for isolated word recognition, *Signal Processing*, **4**, pp. 1–5

PALIWAL, K. K., and AINSWORTH, W. A. (1985): 'Dynamic frequency warping for speaker adaptation in automatic speech recognition,' *J. Phonetics*, **13**, pp. 123–134

PALIWAL, K. K., and RAO, P. V. S. (1982): 'Synthesis based recognition of continuous speech,' *J. Acoust. Soc. Am.*, **71**, pp. 1016–1024

PALIWAL, K. K., AINSWORTH, W. A., and LINDSAY, D. (1983): 'A study of two-formant models for vowel identification,' *Speech Communication*, **2**, pp. 295–303

PALLETT, D. S. (1985): 'Performance assessment of speech recognizers,' *J. Res. Nat. Bur. Standards*, **90**, pp. 1–17

PARSONS, T. W. (1976): 'Separation of speech from interfering speech by means of harmonic selection,' *J. Acoust. Soc. Am.*, **60**, pp. 911–918

PATRICK, E. A. (1972): 'Fundamentals of pattern recognition' (Prentice-Hall, Englewood Cliffs, NJ)

PECKHAM, J. (1982): 'Automatic speech recognition,' *New Electronics*, Sept., **21**, pp. 24–25

PECKHAM, J. B. (1984): 'Speech recognition — what is it worth?' Proc. First Int. Conf. Speech Technology, Brighton, 39–47

PECKHAM, J. (1986): 'Human factors in speech recognition,' *in* BRISTOW G. (Ed.): 'Electronic speech recognition' (Collins London) pp. 172–187

PECKHAM, J., GREEN, J., CANNING, J., and STEPHENS, P. (1982): 'Logos — a real time hardware speech recognition system.' Proc. IEEE ICASSP, pp. 863–866

PEELING, S. M., MOORE, R.K., and TOMLINSON, M. J. (1986): 'The multi-layer perceptron as a tool for speech pattern processing research.' *Proc. Inst. Acoust.*, **8**, pp. 307–314

PETERSON, G., and LEHISTE, I. (1960): 'Duration of syllable nuclei in English,' *J. Acoust. Soc. Am.*, **32**, pp. 693–703

PETERSON, G. E., and BARNEY, H. L. (1952): 'Control methods used in a study of the vowels' *J. Acoust. Soc. Am.*, **24**, pp. 175–184

PICKETT, J. M. (1957): 'Perception of vowels heard in noises of various spectra,' *J. Acoust. Soc. Am.*, **29**, pp. 613–620

PISONI, D. B. (1973): 'Auditory and phonetic memory codes in the discrimination of consonants and vowels,' *Perception & Psychophysics*, **13**, pp. 253–260

PISONI, D. B., LUCE, P. A., and NUSBAUM, H. C. (1986): 'The role of the lexicon in speech perception' *in* SCHOUTEN, M. E. H. (Ed.): 'The psycophysics of speech perception.' NATO ASI, UTRECHT (Martinus Nijhoff)

POLS, L. C. W., Van der KAMP, L. J., and PLOMP, R. (1969): 'Perceptual and physical space for vowel sounds,' *J. Acoust. Soc. Am.*, **46**, pp. 458–467

POSTOVSKY, V. A. (1974): 'Effects of delay in oral practice at the beginning of second language learning,' *Modern Language J.*, **58**, pp. 229–239

POTTER, R. K., KOPP, G. A., and GREEN, H. C. (1947): 'Visible speech' (Van Nostrand New York)

QUARMBY, D. (1986): 'Silicon devices in speech recognition' in BRISTOW, G. (Ed.): 'Electronic speech recognition' (Collins, London) pp. 200–215

RABINER, L. R. (1977): 'On the use of autocorrelation analysis for pitch detection,' *IEEE Trans.*, **ASSP-25**, pp. 24–33

RABINER, L. R., and GOLD, B. (1975): 'Theory and application of digital signal processing' (Prentice-Hall, Englewood Cliffs, NJ)

RABINER, L. R., LEVINSON, S. E., ROSENBERG, A. E., and WILPON, J. G. (1979): 'Speaker-independent recognition of isolated words using clustering techniques,' *IEEE Trans.*, **ASSP-27**, pp. 336–349

RABINER, L. R., LEVINSON, S. E., and SONDHI, M. M. (1983): 'On the application of vector quantization and hidden Markov models to speaker-independent isolated-word recognition,' *Bell Syst. Tech. J.*, **62**, pp. 1075–1105

RABINER, L. R., ROSENBERG, A. E., and LEVINSON, S. E. (1978): 'Considerations in dynamic time warping algorithms for discrete word recognition,' *IEEE Trans.*, **ASSP-26**, pp. 575–582

RABINER, L. R., and SAMBUR, M. R. (1975): 'Analgorithm for determining the endpoints of isolated utterances,' *Bell Syst. Tech. J.*, **54**, pp. 297–315

RABINER, L. R., SCHAFER, R. W., and DLUGOS, D. (1979): 'Periodogram method for power spectrum estimation' in WEINSTEIN, C. J., et al. (Eds.): 'Progams for digital signal processing' (IEEE Press, New York) 2.1.1–2.1.10

REDDY, D. R., ERMAN, L. D., and NEELY, R. B. (1973): 'A model and a system for machine recognition of speech,' IEEE Trans., AU-21, pp. 229–238

REHSOFT, C. (1984): 'Voice recognition at the Ford warehouse in Cologne.' Proc. 1st Int. Conf. Speech Technology, Brighton, pp. 103–112

RIESZ, R. R. (1928): 'Differential intensity sensitivity of the ear for pure tones,' Phys. Rev., 31, pp. 867–875

RIGOLL, G. (1984): 'Experiences in interfacing voice input/output devices to host computers, NC-machines and robots.' Proc. First Int. Conf. Speech Technology, Brighton, pp. 93–101

RODMAN, R. D., MOODY, T. S., and PRICE, J. A. (1985). 'Speech recogniser performance with dysarthric speakers: a comparison of two training procedures.' Proc. Speech Tech'85 (Media Dimensions Inc., NY) pp. 65–71

ROSEN, G. (1958): 'Dynamic analog speech synthesier,' J. Acoust. Soc. Am., 30, pp. 201–209

ROSENBERG, A. E. (1971): 'Effect of glottal pulse shape on the quality of natural vowels,' J. Acoust. Soc. Am., 49, pp. 483–490

ROSENBURG, A. E., RABINER, L. R., and WILPON, J. G. (1980): 'Recognition of spoken spelled names for directory assistance using speaker-independent templates,' Bell Syst. Tech. J., 59, pp. 571–592

ROSENBERG, A. E., RABINER, L. R., WILPON, J. G., and KHAN, D. (1983): 'Demisyllable-based isoalted word recognition system,' IEEE Trans., ASSP-31, pp. 713–725

ROSENBURG, A. E., and SCHMIDT, C. E. (1979): 'Automatic recognition of spoken spelled names for obtaining directory listings,' Bell Syst. Tech. J., 58, pp. 1797–1823

ROSENBLATT, F. (1961): 'Principles of neurodynamics: Perceptrons and a theory of brain mechanisms' (Spartan Books, Washington DC)

ROSS, M. J., SCHAFFER, H. L., COHEN, A., FREUBERG, R., and MANLEY, H. J. (1984): 'Average magnitude difference function pitch extractor,' IEEE Trans., ASSP-22, pp. 353–361

RUMELHART, D. E., HINTON, G. E. and WILLIAMS, R. J. (1986): 'Learning internal re-presentations by error propogation' in RUMELHART, D. E., and McCLELLAND, J. L. (Eds.): 'Parallel distributed processing: Explorations in the microstructure of cognition: Vol. I. Foundations' (MIT Press)

RUSSELL, M. J. and MOORE, R. K. (1985): 'Explicit modelling of state occupancy in hidden Markov models for automatic speech recognition.' Proc. IEEE ICASSP, pp. 5–8

SAKAI, T., and DOSHITA, S. (1963): 'The automatic recognition system for conversational sound,' IEEE Trans., EC-12, pp. 836–846

SAKOE, H. (1979): 'Two-level DP-matching — A dynamic programming-based pattern matching algorithm for connected word recognition,' IEEE Trans., ASSP-27, pp. 588–595

SAKOE, H., and CHIBA, S. (1970): 'A similarity evaluation of speech patterns by dynamic programming (in Japanese),' Inst. Electron. Comm. Eng., Japan, pp. 136

SAKOE, H., and CHIBA, S. (1971): 'A dynamic programming approach to continuous speech recognition.' Proc. 17th Int. Congr. Acoust., Paper 2OC13

SAKOE, H., and CHIBA, S. (1978): 'Dynamic programming algorithms optimization for spoken word recognition,' IEEE Trans., ASSP-26, pp. 43–49

SAMBUR, M. R., and JAYANT, N. S. (1976): 'LPC analysis/synthesis from speech inputs containing quantizing noise or additive white noise,' IEEE Trans., ASSP-24, pp. 448–494

SAMBUR, M. R., and RABINER, L. R. (1975): 'A speaker-independent digit-recognition system,' Bell Syst. Tech. J., 54, pp. 81–102

SAMBUR, M. R., and RABINER, L. R. (1976): 'A statistical decision approach to the recognition of connected digits,' IEEE Trans., ASSP-24, pp. 550–558

SCHARTZ, R. M. (1976): 'Acoustic phonetic experiment facility for the study of continuous speech.' Proc. IEEE ICASSP, pp. 1–4

SCHARTZ, R. M., and ZUE, V. W. (1976): 'Acoustic phonetic recognition in BBN SPEECHLIS.' Proc. IEEE ICASSP, pp. 21–24

SCHNEIDER, W., and SHIFFRIN, R. M. (1977): 'Controlled and automatic human information processing: I. Detection, search and attention,' *Psych. Rev.*, **84**, pp. 1–66

SCHROEDER, M. R. (1968): 'Period histogram and product spectrum: new methods for fundamental frequency measurement,' *J. Acoust. Soc. Am.*, **43**, pp. 829–834

SCULLY, C., and CLARK, G. C. F. (1986): 'Analysis of speech signal variation by articulatory synthesis,' Speech Input/Output IEE Conf. Pub. 258, pp. 83–87

SEBESTYEN, G. S. (1962): 'Pattern recognition by an adaptive process of sample set construction,' *IRE Trans.*, **IT-8**, pp. 582–591

SEBESTYEN, G., and EDIE, J. (1966): 'An algorithm for non-parametric pattern recognition,' *IEEE Trans.*, **EC-15**, pp. 908–915

SELIGER, H. W. (1978): 'Implications of a multiple critical periods hypothesis for second language learning' *in* 'Second language acquisition' (Research Academic Press) pp. 11–20

SENEFF, S. (1984): 'Pitch and spectral estimation of speech based on auditory synchrony model.' Proc. IEEE ICASSP, p. 36.2.1–4

SHANNON, C. E. (1960): 'Coding theorems for a discrete source with a fidelity criterion' *in* MACHOL, R. E. (Ed.): 'Information and decision processes' (McGraw-Hill NY) pp. 93–126

SHEARME, J. N. (1959): 'A simple maximum selecting circuit,' *Electronic Eng.*, **31**, pp. 353–354

SHIFFRIN, R. M., and SCHEIDER, W. (1977): 'Controlled and automatic human information processing: II. Perceptual learning, automatic attending and a general theory,' *Psych. Rev.*, **84**, pp. 127–190

SHIPMAN, D., and ZUE, V. (1982): 'Properties of large lexicons: implications for advanced word recognition system.' Proc. IEEE ICASSP, pp. 546–549

SHORE, J. E., and BURTON, D. V. (1983): 'Discrete utterance speech recognition without time alignment,' *IEEE Trans.*, **IT-29**, pp. 473–490

SHOUP, J. E. (1980): 'Phonological aspects of speech recognition' *in* 'Trends in speech recognition' (Prentice-Hall) pp. 125–138

SHOWER, E. G., and BIDDULPH, R. (1931): 'Differential pitch sensitivity of the ear,' *J. Acoust. Soc. Am.*, **3**, pp. 275–287

SIMON, C., and FOURCIN, A. J. (1978): 'A cross-language study of speech pattern learning,' *J. Acoust. Soc. Am.*, **63**, pp. 925–935

SINGLETON, R. C. (1979): 'Mixed radix fast Fourier transforms' *in* WEINSTEIN, C. J., *et al.* (Eds.): 'Progams for digital signal processing' (IEEE Press, New York) pp. 1.1.4–1.1.18

SMITH, D. C., RUSSELL, M. J., and TOMLINSON, M. J. (1986): 'Rank-ordering of subjects involved in the evaluation of automatic speech recognisers.' RSRE Memo No. 3926

STEAD, L. G., and JONES, E. T. (1961): 'The SRDE speech bandwidth compression project.' SRDE Project Report 1133

STEVENS, K. N. (1959): 'Effect of duration on identification,' *J. Acoust. Soc. Am.*, **31**, pp. 109

STEVENS, K. N. (1968): 'On the relations between speech movements and speech perception,' *Zeit. Phon. Sprach. Komm.*, **21**, pp. 102–106

STEVENS, K. N., and HOUSE, A. S. (1961): 'An acoustical theory of vowel production and some of its implications,' *J. Speech Hear. Res.*, **4**, pp. 303

STEVENS, S. S., and DAVIS, H. (1938): 'Hearing' (Wiley New York)

STOLFO, S., MIRANKER, D., and SHAW, D. F. (1983): 'Architecture and applications of DADO: A large scale parallel computer for artificial intelligence' Int. Joint Cont. on AI

STREVENS, P. (1960): 'Spectra of fricative noise in human speech,' *Language & Speech*, **3**, pp. 32–48

SUOMI, K. (1984): 'On talker and phoneme information conveyed by vowels: A whole spectrum approach to the normalization problem.' *Speech Communication*, **3**, pp. 199–209

TAGGART, J. L., and WOLFE, C. D. (1981): 'Voice recognition as an input modality for the Tacco preflight data insertion task in the P-3C aircraft.' Masters Thesis Naval Postgraduate School Montery, NTIC Access-A105568

TALBERT, J. L., *et al.* (1963): 'A real-time adaptive speech recognition system.' Stanford Electronic Labs. Tech. Doc. Report No. ASD-TDR-63-660, pp. 1–18

TAPPERT, C. C. (1974): 'Experiments with a tree search method for converting noisy phonetic representation into standard orthography.' IEEE Symp. Speech Recognition, pp. 261–266

TAPPERT, C. C., and DAS, S. K. (1978): 'Memory and time improvements in dynamic programming algorithms for matching speech patterns,' *IEEE Trans.* **ASSP-26**, pp. 583–586

TAPPERT, C. C., DIXON, N. R., and RABINOWITZ, A. S. (1973): 'Application of sequential decoding for converting phonetic to graphemic representation (ARCS)', *IEEE Trans.*, **AU-21**, pp. 255

TAYLOR, M. (1986): 'Voice input applications in aerospace' in BRISTOW, G. (Ed.): 'Electronic speech recognition' (Collins, London) pp. 322–337

TRIBOLET, J. M., and QUATIERI, T. F. (1979): 'Computation of the complex cepstrum' in WEINSTEIN, C. J., *et al.* (Eds.): Programs for digital signal processing' IEEE Press, New York, 7.1.1–7.1.11

TUCKER, W. H., and BATES, R. H. T. (1978): 'A pitch estimation algorithm for speech and music,' *IEEE Trans.*, **ASSP-26**, pp. 597–604

ULDALL, E. T. (1971): 'Isochronous stresses in RP' in 'Form and Substance' (Akademisk Forlag, Copenhagen) p. 205

UNDERWOOD, M. J. (1984): 'Human factors aspects of speech technology.' Proc. 1st Int. Conf. Speech Technology, Brighton, pp. 233–228

VELICHKO, V. M., and ZAGORUYKO, N. G. (1970): 'Automatic recognition of 200 words,' *Int. J. Man-Machine Studies*, **2**, pp. 223–234

VINTSYUK, T. K. (1971): 'Element-wise recognition of continuous speech composed of words from a specified dictionary,' *Kibernetica*, **7**, pp. 133–143

VITERBI, A. J. (1967): 'Error bounds for convolution codes and an asymtopically optimal decoding algorithm', *IEEE Trans.*, **IT-13**, pp. 260–269

VYSOTSKY, G. J. (1984): 'A speaker-independent discrete utterance recognition system combining deterministic and probabilistic strategies', *IEEE Trans.*, **ASSP-32**, pp. 489–499

VOIERS, V. D. (1977): 'Diagnostic evaluation of speech intelligibility' in HAWLEY, M. (Ed.): 'Benchmark papers in acoustics: Vol. II. Speech intelligibility and speaker recognition' (DOWDEN, HUTCHINSON and ROSS, STROUDSBURG) pp. 374–387

WAKITA, H. (1977): 'Normalization of vowels by vocal-tract length and its application to vowel identification,' *IEEE Trans.*, **ASSP-25**, pp. 185–192

WANG, W. S. Y. (1959): 'Transition and release as perceptual cues for final plosives,' *J. Speech Hear. Res.*, **2**, pp. 66–73

WARREN, D. H. D. (1982): 'A view of the fifth generation and its impact,' *The AI Magazine*

WEBSTER, A. G. (1919): 'Acoustical impedance and the theory of horns and the phonograph,' *Proc. Nat. Acad. Sci.*, **5**, pp. 275–282

WEINSTEIN, C. J., *et al.* (1979): 'Programs for digital signal processing' (IEEE Press, New York)

WHITE, R. W., PARKS, D. L., and SMITH, W. D. (1984): 'Potential flight applications for some voice recognition and synthesis systems.' AIAA/IEEE 6th Digital Avionics Systems Conference, Baltimore, pp. 1–5

WIDROW, B., *et al.*, (1975): 'Adaptive noise cancelling: Principles and applications,' *Proc. IEEE*, **63**, pp. 1692–1716

WILPON, J. G. (1985): 'A study of the ability to automatically recognise telephone quality speech from large customer populations,' *AT & T Tech. J.*, **64**, pp. 423–451

WILPON, J. G., and RABINER, L. R. (1983): 'On the recognition of isolated digits from a large telephone customer population,' *Bell Syst. Tech. J.*, **62**, pp. 1977–2000

WIREN, J., and STUBBS, H. L. (1956): 'Electronic binary selection system for phoneme classification,' *J. Acoust. Soc. Am.*, **28**, pp. 1082–11091

WISE, J. D., CAPRIO, J. R., and PARKS, T. W. (1976): 'Maximum likelihood pitch estimation,' *IEEE Trans.*, **ASSP-24**, pp. 418–423

WITTEN, I. H. (1982): 'Principles of computer speech' (Academic Press, London)

WOHLFORD, R. E., SMITH, A. R., and SAMBUR, M. R. (1980): 'The enhancement of word-spotting techniques.' Proc IEEE ICASSP, pp. 209–21.

WOOD, D. (1985): 'A survey of algorithms and architectures for connected speech recognition' *in* 'New systems and architectures for automatic speech recognition and synthesis' (Springer, Berlin) pp. 233–28

WOOD, D., and URQUHART, R. B. (1984): 'An architecture for a connected speech recognition algorithm.' Proc. 7th. Conf. on Pattern Recognition

WOODS, W. A. (1974): 'Motivation and overview of SPEECHLIS: an experimental prototype for speech understanding research,' *IEEE Trans.*, **ASSP-23**, pp. 2–10

ZWICKER, E., and FASTL, H. (1972): 'On the development of the critical band,' *J. Acoust. Soc. Am.*, **52**, pp. 699–702

ZWICKER, E., TERHARDT, E., and PAULUS, E. (1979): 'Automatic speech recognition using psychoacoustic models,' *J. Acoust. Soc. Am.*, **65**, pp. 487–498

Subject Index

Author Index

04